FINDING SATISFACTION IN CHRIST

A Devotional Study of Colossians

DUSTIN CROWE

Finding Satisfaction in Christ: A Devotional Study of Colossians
© 2020 by Dustin Crowe

All rights reserved. This book or parts thereof may not be reproduced in any form, stored in any retrieval system, or transmitted in any form by any means—electronic, mechanical, photocopy, recording, or otherwise—without prior written permission of the publisher, except as provided by United States of America copyright law.

Printed in the United States of America

Unless otherwise indicated, Scripture quotations are from the ESV® Bible (The Holy Bible, English Standard Version®), copyright © 2001 by Crossway, a publishing ministry of Good News Publishers. Used by permission. All rights reserved.

Scripture references marked NIV are taken from The Holy Bible, New International Version®, NIV®, copyright © 1973, 1978, 1984, 2011 by Biblica, Inc.™

ISBN: 978-0-578-54347-5

Cover image and design: Megan Bitting

Visit www.indycrowe.com for additional resources on Colossians, including small group discussion guides, and for information about contacting the author

To Lily Mae,
may you find deep satisfaction
in the fullness of Jesus.

TABLE OF CONTENTS

INTRODUCTION

Is this a Devotional, Commentary, or Christian Living Book? Yes!

The church needs more books bridging the continental divide between in-depth, academic commentaries and shallow, emotionally driven devotionals. The typical commentary provides profound insights into God's Word, but it's up to the pastor to translate that on Sunday to their congregants. Those same congregants often rely upon devotionals, but many devotionals skim over the Bible and focus solely on our experience.

This book aims to help people see Jesus in Colossians and take the beautiful truths they read with them for the day once they close the book. Scripture has the power both to teach our minds and grip our hearts. Jesus not only saves us but He satisfies us. Discipleship includes growing in knowledge and seeking Him through our practices and obedience, but it's also about a daily journey to find your fulfillment in Jesus above anything else in this world.

Most of us need introduced to Christ's glorious person and work in such a way that there's a clear connection to how Jesus changes every arena of our lives. My hope is to help inch us in that direction by planting our feet in Scripture and pointing us to Christ.

If your Christian life often feels empty or like it's missing something, the answer isn't to look beyond Jesus but to go deeper with Jesus. The fullness of God and every longing of our hearts is found in Him. We will not be satisfied apart from Him, but Scripture promises we can be fulfilled by Him. You need to be in God's Word to do that, and Colossians provides a great starting point.

This book is primarily about Jesus as Colossians reveals Him to us. Getting to know Jesus and seeing His glory and goodness is why Colossians exists, which means it's why *this* book exists. Right knowledge drips down to our heart and we begin to *feel* differently about the God we're getting to know.

Then sure enough the drip seeps a little further and we *behave* differently. It won't happen all at once or perfectly. Our minds are weak and our hearts leak, but we keep going back to the well and bringing up more palate-pleasing and soul-satisfying water.

Finding Satisfaction in Christ walks through the four chapters of Colossians in ten sections. Each section includes an introduction and six devotionals on a verse or two. To encourage readers to go deeper, each devotional includes additional resources to guide reflection and response.

Less of Me, More of Him

Maybe you're approaching this study because you sense the need to get into God's Word beyond an casual and occasional manner. Whatever your motives and desires, the purpose of this study extends beyond simply gaining info on the Bible, getting your act together in your spiritual disciplines, or whipping you into shape morally. All those might be needed, but what we need most is seeing and knowing Jesus Christ. All the information, context, and studying are of no use if they don't direct your heart towards Jesus in worship.

I pray this study of Colossians encourages you in the lifelong process of discovering more of Jesus. He is the supreme and sufficient Savior. He is and has everything we need and desire. That means we don't need a new game-plan for our life or a few strategies to fix what's wrong; we just need to look to Jesus and let our weary souls rest in Him. He will satisfy and sustain us. The fullness of who He is will overflow into us so our fulfillment is found in Him.

Many Christians become frustrated with how slowly and how little they grow. Sin gets deep into the fibers of the heart and it's not easily washed out. This will be a lifelong struggle so take a long-view and strap yourself in for the trip. Part of why our effort seems so futile is because we focus on ourselves and lose sight of Christ. The Christian life becomes about what we need to do (feeling overwhelmed?) or what we're not doing (feeling crushed?).

We spend hours in front of the mirror of self and we don't like what we see. Our time would be better spent looking at Jesus, and then thinking about what we look like in Him.

If we are *in Christ*, then the truest and most important things about us are inseparable from our new identity in Him. *Who we are* is now answered by *whose we are* (God's) and *who we're united to* (Jesus). God doesn't see what we see in the mirror but He sees us through the lens of His perfect Son. This is why we call the gospel good news. Paul wrote to the church at Colossians to remind them about Christ's glory and how God remakes us through Christ, in Christ, and for Christ.

I'm convinced we settle for far too little of Jesus in our life. We assume we know all there is to know about Him because we've been a Christian for many years and sat through our fair share of church services. But none of us have plumbed the depths of understanding Jesus. If it's easy to marginalize Jesus to Sundays and the occasional prayer when you need help, then you're not seeing Jesus as He's revealed to us in the Scriptures. The only way to warm up affections for Jesus and attention given to Jesus is being awed by Jesus. Colossians holds up Jesus so our hearts are gripped by Him.

Don't settle for little sips of Jesus but drink big gulp after big gulp of His grace and truth. We see and savor Him and then we reflect Him.[1] We look like Jesus by looking at Jesus.

Colossians is all about Jesus, who He is and what He's done as the all-sufficient Savior, and how He changes us as we walk in Him. This letter continually holds up Jesus Christ to us so we would look at Him, and by looking at Him we would look like Him. My prayer is for you to see Christ in a way that leads to *finding satisfaction in Christ.*

---

[1] My thinking has been shaped by John Piper's "Christian Hedonism," and like-minded pastors and theologians. This book's focus on looking at Jesus assumes we'll like what we see and that joy in him fuels obedience.

A PRIMER ON COLOSSIANS: CONTEXT AND BACKGROUND

The apostle Paul penned Colossians as a letter to real people he cared about. It's personal, contextual, pastoral, and theological. Colossians isn't an impersonal book presenting data, theories, or opinions on a subject. It's personal because Paul saw himself as a shepherd working hard for the maturity (1:29) of beloved brothers and sisters in Christ.

Colossians is a contextual letter. It's set in a historical and cultural context with specific people in mind to address the issues in their church. If we can adjust our lenses from our contemporary situation to the original context, we may see with clearer vision.

Paul's theology in Colossians isn't written as an academic treatment. He writes as a pastor caring for the sheep. He doesn't explain all the nuts and bolts of the hypostatic union (Jesus has two natures in one person). Instead, he encourages them with news of how Christ being raised from the dead frees them from fear of the evil they encounter. Theology, for Paul, isn't something to theorize on for a good debate, but his message aims to propel their joy in Christ and faithfulness to Him.

The purpose behind this introductory material isn't to have a few points to impress our church friends but to better know the story behind the letter. Let's consider the five basic arenas of research: who, when, where, what, and why. Then let's get into the actual letter of Colossians!

Who, When, and Where?

Paul identifies himself as the author of Colossians (1:1; 4:18). For three years he ministered in the important coastal city of Ephesus (Acts 19:10). While there, Jews and Gentiles from all over the map came and heard Paul's message. Epaphras, a native of Colossae (4:12), was likely converted under Paul's ministry while in Ephesus. Upon returning home Epaphras shared the gospel and helped birth the church at Colossae. Paul writes from a Roman prison around 60–62 AD (4:16) and sends this letter with Tychicus (4:7) and Onesimus (4:9).[2]

Since Colossae probably wasn't covered in your world history class, here are a couple of details. It was a smaller city that remained diverse. It was part of the Roman province of Asia, located in modern day Turkey. Although further inland than the more important cities like Ephesus and Laodicea, it resided on an important highway when the Roman Empire proved quite mobile.

The diversity of Colossae likely led to its blending of religious beliefs (syncretism). Paul's recipients were primarily Gentile, but a small Jewish presence existed. The city's dominant worldview would have been polytheistic, highly syncretic, and heavily infused with the ideology of the Roman Empire's greatness. They were immersed in an environment of pluralism where people borrowed from the religious and philosophical ideas of the day. If you're thinking this sounds similar to today, then you're tracking with me. "Nothing new under the sun."

Why and What?

It's clear some false teaching has crept into the church, either from inside or outside. What the "Colossian heresy" is exactly we don't know. We only hear Paul's side of the conversation and he's more interested in talking about what's true than what's false. Despite this ambiguity of the source or the ideas spreading, we know they were being tempted to find something outside of or beyond Christ. At its core, the false teaching was "not according to Christ" (2:8). Word of these erroneous ideas and the danger they brought with them reached Paul in prison—probably from Epaphras.

---

[2] See Appendix "Key Characters in Colossians" for more information on these individuals.

Because Paul connects our beliefs (theology) to how we live (practice) he writes to convince them of the complete sufficiency of Christ alone and to root them in their identity as saints in Him. It is a letter steeped in the person and work of Jesus Christ and demonstrates His Lordship over all of creation as the crucified and risen Savior. Calvin writes, "this Epistle…to express it in one word, distinguishes the true Christ from a fictitious one."[3] Paul richly defends and describes a theology of Jesus Christ where beliefs inform ethics. Colossians springs from Paul's love and concern for the local church. In it he warns and teaches for the purpose of seeing believers grow to full maturity in Christ.

As we see more clearly the beauty and glory[4] of Jesus—the image of God—the Spirit transforms us into Christ's likeness. In our old man (in Adam), the image of God was scuffed and marred nearly beyond recognition. But, as a new person (in Jesus), we're being cleaned, refashioned, and remade so we reflect the image of God—which was our original purpose (Genesis 1:26–28). Here again we see doctrine and application intertwined as Paul holds up a robust theology of Jesus so we might see and savor Him in all His beauty and glory, supremacy and sufficiency. By looking *at* Christ we look *like* Christ.

> The reason Christians do not glorify and enjoy God more is that they do not look beyond themselves. They look into themselves, finding either demoralizing failure or (far worse) an illusion of success. They live in either self-hatred or self-admiration. But either way, they are bound up within themselves, with far too little certainty and joy. But the gospel

---

3 John Calvin, *Commentaries on the Epistles to the Philippians, Colossians, and Thessalonians*, trans. Henry Beveridge, vol. 21 of *Calvin's Commentaries* (Grand Rapids: Baker, 2003), 134.

4 Here's how I'm using the important word "glory." Glory (noun): the wonderful and weighty fullness of all God is and possesses as God. Glorify (verb): to exalt, honor, lift up, make much of, or magnify.

emphasizes what God does—God in all the fullness of his being for all the need that you have. That is encouraging.[5]

The Focus of Colossians

When we study a book of the Bible, we need a reminder it's *part* of the Bible but not the whole. We let other passages help us interpret Colossians and we bring all the biblical data together to form conclusions. I mention this because Colossians doesn't address everything there is to know. Some themes might be more important overall in the Bible but they play less of a role in Colossians. Because I'm trying to let Colossians do the talking, there are significant Scriptural truths for our growth missing from this book.

Some truths mentioned less in Colossians are the role of the Holy Spirit, justification by faith alone through grace alone, Jew and Gentile relationships, the return of Christ, suffering, the local church, or how conversion takes place. Because it's written primarily to a Gentile audience, there's less about the Old Testament system with its sacrifices, priests, temple, and so forth.

Some themes highlighted in Paul's letter are the sole sufficiency and supremacy of Jesus Christ, the need for perseverance in the faith, the cross and atonement, resurrection, union with Christ, Christ's ascension and reign over all, spiritual warfare, the source of knowledge, prayer and thanksgiving, reflecting the image of Christ, walking worthy of Christ, living out our identity in Christ, and bearing fruit that shows God is accomplishing His plan from Eden to spread His glory throughout the whole earth.

---

[5] Ray Ortlund, *Supernatural Living for Natural People* (Scotland: Christian Focus Publications, 2013), Chapter 2, page 362 of Kindle version.

GRIPPED BY THE GOSPEL (1:1–8)

Many people skim the greetings and goodbyes of New Testament letters. You might think it's just the niceties that don't add much. Despite the temptation, don't skip over this opening section (1:1–8) to get to "the real stuff." Most books, including Paul's letters, set a tone right out of the gate. The first words hint at ideas coming later. The introductions are the trailers that give us a sneak-peek of what's ahead.

Right away we'll see three clusters of three. At the heart of the letter is the God we serve: Father (1:3), Son (1:3), and Holy Spirit (1:8). Second, the opening focuses on the gospel's importance. The gospel isn't something we do but a message of truth that's heard (1:6), understood (1:6), and learned (1:7). And third, the trio of Christian virtues exhibiting fruit are faith (1:4), love (1:4), and hope (1:5).

Paul praises God for birthing churches around the Gentile world through the gospel. God spelled out the original purpose of humanity in the garden. He created mankind in His image (Genesis 1:26–27) and then gave the mission: "Be *fruitful* and *multiply* and *fill* the earth and *subdue* it" (Genesis 1:28). This physical command served a higher purpose as humans would spread the image of God and the glory of God as they filled up the earth (Habakkuk 2:14). However, sin quickly entered the picture and seemingly thwarted the purposes of God (Genesis 3).

In Colossians 1 we see God accomplishing this original plan through those in Christ. By the Spirit, they have put on the new self "which is being renewed in knowledge after the *image* of its creator" (3:10). The gospel is in the entire world "*bearing fruit and growing*" (2:6). Through the kingdom of God all of creation is being brought under Christ's *dominion* again (1:14, 20).

Just like the serpent tempted Adam and Eve to find something else— something he claimed God withheld from them—so now false teachers had slithered into the church and whispered that there's something to add to Jesus to arrive at spiritual knowledge.

The church participates in the new creation and Paul writes to hold up the supremacy and sufficiency of Jesus Christ. He admonishes them to look nowhere else for the fullness of salvation, for knowledge, and for life. Paul writes Colossians out of his desire to bring us into maturity in Christ by redirecting our eyes to His matchless glory. Our first section (1:1–8) sets the stage for this by thanking God for the good work He started in them. All they need to do is stay rooted in Jesus and they will continue to thrive.

WHO ARE YOU?

"Paul, an apostle of Christ Jesus by the will of God, and Timothy our brother, to the saints and faithful brothers in Christ at Colossae: Grace to you and peace from God our Father" (Colossians 1:1–2).

Imagine you meet someone tomorrow and they ask you to describe yourself. What would you say? Who are you? Try summarizing who you are in ten words or fewer (really, try it).

Paul introduces himself as "an apostle of Christ" (1:1). He writes not on his own authority but on behalf of Christ. In Colossians, Paul acts as a tour-guide pointing out the can't-miss sites of Jesus and explaining what's being seen in Him. Every paragraph radiates with the grandeur and supremacy of Jesus, His Lordship over all, and the sufficiency of Christ's work for us.

Jesus Christ is everywhere in Colossians. There are no rabbit trails taking us away from Jesus but only hidden passages leading us to discover new things about Him.

Paul quickly shifts from himself to the believers at Colossae. He defines his readers in relation to Jesus. The saints—faithful brothers and sisters—are those *in Christ* (1:2). Paul furnishes us with three identity markers in one verse.

Family

He first uses household terminology, "faithful brothers and sisters," to express our family unity as Christians. (Sing Sister Sledge's famous tune, slightly modified: We are family, my faithful brothers and my sisters and me.) We have the same Father.

The same Spirit remakes us into Christ's image so we share similar family characteristics. We belong to one another because we belong to Jesus. The church, "the household of God" (2 Timothy 3:15), should offer all in the family a warm place of welcome. God's people aren't simply those who get together weekly in the same room but they're those joined to one another as brothers and sisters.

Saints

We not only get a new family, we're given a new identity. Some think the word "saints" refers to a special group of VIP Christians, an elite class of miracle workers who earned their way into the stained-glass hall of fame. For others, it's hard to imagine how regular ole' believers could be crowned with as noble a term as "saints." The Bible never uses "saints" for a special group of believers or for those who've attained a higher level of holiness. It refers to all believers in Jesus.

If you are in Christ, you're a saint. Put that on your resume. Christ sets us apart from the world and claimed us as His own. We are holy[6] (or saints) because we are in Christ and we belong to Him. Paul reminds us *who we are* depends on *whose we are*.

In Christ

It's only two words and eight letters but if there's no "in Christ' in the New Testament then we lose everything. Because we're united to Jesus by faith[7] we receive Him and everything that belongs to Him. Everything.

---

[6] Holiness: Belonging to God and being set apart to Him, and therefore separate from sin and the fallen world. It's both a transformational and relational term.

[7] Faith: Trust in Jesus as the Savior who takes our sins and gives new life. Faith includes knowledge, belief, and trust.

We receive through grace[8] what is Jesus's by right: sonship, righteousness, eternal life, an inheritance, the embrace of the Father, and all other spiritual blessings (Ephesians 1:3–14). When God the Father now looks on us he sees us through the lens of His perfect Son Jesus Christ. "Our union with Christ may be summed up in these words: because the Father has immeasurable love for the Son, he has immeasurable love for us."[9]

Competing Identities

Paul's inaugural words remind us who we are. He plants our identity in Jesus. Because we act, think, and speak out of our identity, Paul wants us from the outset to define ourselves by whose we are. We're in Christ. We belong to Him. Because we belong to Him, we're devoted to Him in worship and obedience. Because we are His, we live with the security, joy, and blessing of being loved by Him.

The temptation to define ourselves by something other than Jesus assaults us daily. It's a quiet and subtle temptation. It doesn't knock loudly on the front door but it slips in through the back.

We find our identity in the wrong places. This includes attaching our identity to good things, since even those don't define us. When we find our identity in our career, looks, possessions, spiritual gifts, ministry, what others think of us, successes, how good of a spouse or parent we are, our sexuality, or anything else, we misunderstand the core marker of who we are.

Every day Christ seeks to transform us into *His* image while the world seeks to conform us to *its* image. The image we reflect depends on what identity we live from.

---

[8] Grace: A free and undeserved gift given at the cost of someone else for the joy of the recipient.

[9] Elyse M. Fitzpatrick, *Found in Him* (Wheaton: Crossway, 2013), 144.

The world, your peers, loved ones, friends, and even your own thoughts will fill your head with ideas about who you are or who you should be. They might try to confine you to your personality, skills, your failures or weaknesses, background, or your friend groups.

While some of these details describe you, only Christ defines you.

- You are who God says you are. The Bible alone possesses the authority and objectivity to rightly label you. You are made in God's image. You are in Christ. You belong to God (saints) and His family (brothers and sisters).

- You are not what others think of you (good or bad) or what you think of yourself (positive or negative). You are what God thinks of you.

- You are not chained by what you've done or what's been done to you. You are freed because of what Jesus has done for you.

- Your identity isn't based on the parents you have, the place you're from, your history, or the possessions you own. Your identity is based on your position in Christ. You are God's son or daughter.

I Am Who I Am in Christ

Colossians grabs us by our cheeks, looks us in the eyes, and tells us our identity is *in Christ*. I need that memo engrained on my heart so I can fulfill my responsibilities without turning them into idols.

I also need it when I fall into sin. I'm not in Christ on my good days but on my own on the bad days. The good news of the gospel is we live by grace. Grace means God treats us not according to *our* performance but according to *Christ's* performance. When I sin or when I fail, I need the reminder I'm still in

Christ. I am loved, forgiven, adopted, justified, and I'm promised the hope of one day being glorified. Christ defines me, so I step out of my guilt and into His grace.

Paul identifies us as a faithful family adopted by one Father, holy ones separated to Him, and those now in Christ. Is that how you're thinking about and defining yourself today? Is that the truth by which you approach and relate to God?

As we walk through Colossians, we'll grow in seeing ourselves and our lives through our identity *in Christ*. The more we see Jesus and define ourselves by our identity in Him, the more we'll live as if our life *is* Christ's and not our own. Jesus defines us and Jesus directs us.

Applying Colossians

Questions
1) Which identity-marker most resonates with you? Why?
2) Where are you tempted to find your identity apart from Christ?
3) Since you belong to others in the church, how are you living that out in your commitment to care for those in your church?

Next Steps
- Make a list of ways you think about yourself (some might be positive and some negative). Reflect on how being in Christ changes all of that.
- Keep a list of all the places you find "in Christ" in the Bible. Star or highlight all of the times that the phrase speaks to your identity

For Further Study
- **In Christ**: Colossians 1:28; Ephesians 1:3–14; 2 Corinthians 5:17; Romans 5:12–6:14.
- **Church as household**: 1 Timothy 3:15; 1 Corinthians 4:1; Galatians 6:10; Ephesians 4:19: 1 Peter 4:17.

THANK GOD WHEN YOU THINK OF US

"We always thank God, the Father of our Lord Jesus Christ, when we pray for you" (Colossians 1:3).

When you open an email or an old-fashioned letter (I think those still exist), you know right away if it's good or bad news. The first few words set the tone for what follows.

Since Paul had never visited the city of Colossae, this opening sentence acted as a first impression for his readers. He sets the tone not with a rebuke for their failures—like Galatians—but by affirming God's good work in them. This casts a shadow of encouragement and pastoral love over the entire letter. If New Testament letters had emojis, Paul would have included a big smile or high five.

Paul starts several of his letters with a similar thanksgiving to God (see 1 Corinthians 1:4; 1 Thessalonians 1:2; Ephesians 1:3). He's not casually saying, like so many do, "thank God" when they like the turn of events. Nor does he offer it out of some customary obligation. He knows the Colossians would still be in darkness if God had not intervened. The light and life in them is a supernatural act of God.

If you can recall a time when God powerfully worked in your life or the life of someone close to you, you can likely recall the experience of gratefulness.

True Thankfulness

Thanksgiving goes beyond recognizing acts of kindness. It gets to the character of God and our role as worshippers of Jesus Christ. "Thanksgiving in Paul is an act of worship. It is not focused primarily on the benefits received or the blessed condition of a person; instead, God is the centre of thanksgiving."[10] This explains the overlap in the Bible between words like bless, praise, rejoice, and thank. God's works draw out words of gratitude.

Paul didn't relegate thanksgiving to one month a year but promoted it to a daily rhythm. He glimpsed God's fingerprints everywhere he looked. A Christian with eyes open to the *work* of God possesses a heart primed for the *praise* of God. Thanksgiving then becomes a personal act as we better know God through seeing and responding to who He is and how He's at work.

In verses 3–8, Paul makes one primary assertion: *we give thanks to God because of what He's done among the Colossians.* Yes, later he warns them to avoid false teaching. Yes, they have a long way to go in their walk. And yet, Paul creates an atmosphere of hope, affirmation, and even biblical confidence by recognizing God is at work in them.

More reasons exist to give thanks for God's work than there are reasons to grumble about their failings.

Don't you want to be more like Paul? I'd love to be more inclined to give affirmation and reassurance than criticism.

Saying Thanks

And yet, there's balance; there's speaking the truth in love. Paul doesn't turn a blind eye to the shortcomings and concerns within this church. This isn't a false optimism. He addresses these things head on as he warns and teaches, but he comes out of the gates thanking God. However small our growth might feel, there's an immeasurable distance between where we *were* apart from Jesus and where we *are* now in Him. This gospel-growth in us and among us is God's working for us. For that, Paul gives thanks.

---

10 David Pao, *Thanksgiving* (Downers Grove: Inter Varsity Press, 2002), 28–29.

Light has conquered darkness. Thank you, God.

The dead are alive. Thank you, God.

The broken are made whole. Thank you, God.

Strangers far from God become sons and daughters. Thank you, God.

Sins are washed away. Completely. Permanently. Thank you, God.

Giving thanks leads to many byproducts. God receives praise and believers benefit. Paul commends the Colossians for their faith and love (1:4–8) while rooting such affirmation in God's work (1:3).

Let's be careful not to discourage fellow Christians or diminish God's glory by failing to give thanks. Shortcomings will always be present, and with it the opportunity for discouragement. Sin nips at our heels, haunts our thoughts, and pulls at our hearts. But that's not the only story or even the main story for a believer. As we learned in verses 1–2, our identity is in Christ.

Despite the reasons for disappointment when I look down—or around—there's even more reason to rejoice when I look up. I am in Christ and He is in me. He defines me, directs me, and will ultimately deliver me from the sin and suffering that hangs on like a nasty cold.

Grumpy or Grateful?

Every day presents opportunities to complain and murmur, including when we're frustrated by what we think God hasn't done. Paul exemplifies a heart trusting and in tune with God. He chooses not to grumble but to rest in God and be grateful. Grumbling says I know better than God. Gratitude says God not only knows what's best, but He always gives what's best … at the best time.

Joy and thankfulness don't happen by accident. With eyes wide open, choose to see what God is doing and give thanks for it. Gratitude's foe, grumbling, will try to keep you from walking down this path. The two butt heads, battling atop your heart like two boys in a King of the Hill contest.

Whichever side we give sway to in our thoughts, feelings, and words will have the upper hand. This means we crowd out complaining, criticism, and discouragement by giving thanks, praising God, and appreciating God's gifts and plans. Growing in gratitude requires both an intentional cultivation of thanksgiving and a decision to fight grumbling.

Where have you seen God at work in the lives of His people around you? Even though their faith is imperfect and maturity might be slow, who can you affirm and encourage today by specifying how you see God working in them? Or, to make it personal, what trial, frustration, or pain gnaws at your heart right now and makes thankfulness hard to imagine?

Even in this valley, God's grace for you has not run dry. Give thanks for God's good plan and for His seen and unseen blessings.

Applying Colossians

Questions
1) Why do we grumble more than give thanks and criticize more than we affirm?
2) What are some of the things in verses 3–8 Paul is thankful for?
3) What's one circumstance in your life you find difficult, frustrating, or painful? Not to ignore or minimize the struggle or sorrow, but in the midst of this scenario what can you give thanks for?

Next Steps

- Begin a list (on scrap paper, journal, or phone) of things you are thankful to God for, including spiritual blessings. Start by writing out three specific blessings now.
- Tell someone today what God has done recently so He receives praise. Consider writing an encouraging card to someone, letting them know you are thankful to God for His work in them.

For Further Study

- **Thanksgiving and evangelism**: Psalm 35:18; 100:4; 109:30; Luke 8:39; John 4:39.
- **Giving thanks**: Colossians 2:7; 3:15, 17; 4:2; Ephesians 1:16; 5:20; 2 Thessalonians 2:13–14.

FAITH, HOPE, AND LOVE: MORE THAN CUTE HOME DÉCOR

"since we heard of your faith in Christ Jesus and of the love that you have for all the saints, 5because of the hope laid up for you in heaven" (Colossians 1:4–5).

In the New Testament, faith, hope, and love are the PB and J of the Christian life. They're wonderful and inseparable. One makes the other better. They belong together. As Paul shows us, not only should a Christian possess faith, hope, and love, but each is enhanced by the other.

Verses 4 and 5 state the cause or reason for giving thanks. It's because ("since") Paul has heard of their faith, love, and hope. The Holy Spirit plants the gospel in people's hearts and then cultivates the fruits of faith, hope, and love. This famous trio adorns many Christian homes and coffee mugs, but what does Paul mean by them?

With these words, he celebrates the Spirit-created characteristics of Christians. The Sprit who gave eyes to believe in the gospel is the same Spirit who gives legs to walk in it.

Faith

The Colossian's story began with faith. The church originated out of Ephesus, another city in Paul's ministry. Someone heard the gospel and believed, likely Epaphras (1:7), and then shared this gospel message with others. The next few verses explain this "good news" in multiple ways: the word of truth, the gospel, and the grace of God in truth. Paul gives thanks because they believed what they heard. It is not faith in general but it is faith in something specific, the gospel of Jesus Christ. As people placed their faith in Jesus, a church community was born.

Love

Paul praises God because of their love for one another. Faith in Christ always leads to works of love. Like a paint brush or sponge, the more of God's love we soak up the more we can spread around. We can only express what we experience.

Later in Colossians, Paul condemns theoretical speculations and worldly wisdom in part because they are fruitless. True knowledge leads to works consistent with the gospel message. John tells us this in no uncertain terms: "Let us love one another, for love is from God, and whoever loves has been born of God and knows God. Anyone who does not love does know God, because God is love" (1 John 4:7–8).

As the Colossians cared for God's people, the report of their love circulated until it reached Paul. He knows we do not naturally love others. It's a supernatural work of the Holy Spirit in us. The gospel of grace tells us we don't get what we deserve, but instead God showers us with mercy and grace. This motivates and enables us to show such grace to others in acts of love.

Hope

The New Testament writers usually describe faith as the source of love and hope but in this passage Paul makes hope the fountainhead. The NIV captures this well: "the faith and love that spring from the hope." Paul realizes the faith and love of the church in Colossians springs from their hope laid up in heaven, not from any worldly factor.

This future hope sustains us and drives us into continued faith and love because we live with an eternal perspective in mind. Living in light of the long-view should mark Christians. When we have a large and lasting hope, we will be full of faith and love. When we possess a small and short-lived hope it produces selfishness and self-reliance.

This mindset of maturity means we don't give up when things are hard or results aren't immediate. We don't live based on feelings or how situations appear to be going in this life. Neither internal emotions nor external appearances are ultimate.

God's work over the long-haul provides a lens to correct our nearsightedness when it comes to temporary circumstances. If our hope is set on being healthy, successful, amassing possessions, or being admired by the world, faith will land on the back-burner. If our hope is walking with Christ in this life and then living with Him forever on a restored earth, that hope will produce faith and love in ever-increasing measures.

Paul rejoiced in seeing the gospel spreading and flourishing; and it should be so for us today. Any fruit in the church reminds us to thank God for the planting, watering, and growing of gospel seeds.

Beliefs Matter

One thing learned from this early paragraph is beliefs affect behavior. Beliefs bleed onto all the pages of our life. They show up in our thoughts, desires, emotions, words, and actions.

If you believe mankind is an accident or autonomous, that will govern how you live. If you believe God became a man to die for the very people responsible for His death, and that He rose from the dead and even now offers victory, then you will behave differently. No question, beliefs affect behavior.

Beliefs are deeply planted seeds. In Colossae, their beliefs and hopes sprouted into a remarkable faith in God and love for God's people.

We will see this to be true throughout Colossians and it should guide the way we read the Bible (and this book). Don't simply learn more facts. Let what you learn be a matter of belief that affects behavior. Whether "faith, hope, and love" are inscribed on your morning mug or bathroom art is much less important than whether they're characteristic of your life.

Each day and lesson should teach us true theology that changes us and guides us into new desires, decisions, thoughts, and activities. God's Word prompts prayer as we ask for knowledge to settle into the soil of our heart so it might bear fruit.

Applying Colossians

Questions
   1) What's the relationship between vertical faith in Christ and horizontal love to others?
   2) Can you think of any examples of how you've been able to love someone after coming to Christ in a way you maybe wouldn't have been able to do prior to your faith in Christ?
   3) Which of the three fruits are you stronger and weaker in? How so?

Next Steps
   - Come up with one person to sacrificially love somehow this week. It might be someone you know is going through a struggle or suffering.
   - Think and pray about how you can take steps in serving others in your church and in your life (neighbors, family, co-workers).

For Further Study
   - **Faith, hope, and love**: Romans 5:1–5; 1 Corinthians 13:13; Galatians 5:5–6; Ephesians 4:2–5; 1 Thessalonians 1:3; 5:8; Hebrews 6:10–12; 1 Peter 1:21–22.
   - **Saints**: Colossians 1:2; Ephesians 1:1, 15, 18; 2:19; 3:8; 4:12; 6:18.

NON-REFUNDABLE RESERVATIONS

"since we heard of your faith in Christ Jesus and of the love that you have for all the saints, 5because of the hope laid up for you in heaven" (Colossians 1:4–5).

Have you ever made a dinner reservation over the phone or online? If so, as you drove there you might have become increasingly anxious about whether your reservation went through or was kept. You mentally cross your fingers and try to remain optimistic, hoping a table awaits you. Maybe you search your email looking for the confirmation. Is this what Paul envisioned when he mentions we're "hoping" for something reserved in heaven?

Our culture has reduced the word "hope" to wishful thinking which may or may not occur. "I hope it rains tomorrow" or "I hope I get the present I want." As we read the Bible, "hope" conveys something much more certain than wishing.

New Testament authors employ the word "hope" primarily in two ways. "It can define either the *object* of hope, namely Christ and all that His final coming implies, or the *attitude* of hoping."[11] In Colossians 1, Paul refers to the future, objective hope not the action or attitude of hoping. What is the hope laid up for us in heaven? How you would answer that question.

The Object of Our Hope

It's difficult to delineate one specific thing as the anticipated object of hope because it likely includes all the redemptive benefits wrapped up in Christ. In Ephesians 1:12–14 Paul states our future hope is the inheritance we will acquire. In a similar passage, Peter says through the resurrection of Jesus

---

[11] S. H. Travis, "Hope" in *New Dictionary of Theology*, ed. by Sinclair B. Ferguson, David. F. Wright, and J. I. Packer (Downers Grove: Inter Varsity Press, 1988), 321.

Christ we have the hope of "an inheritance that is imperishable, undefiled, and unfading, kept in heaven for you, who by God's power are being guarded through faith for a salvation ready to be revealed in the last time" (1 Peter 1:3–5).

Our hope is nothing less than all God's plans and promises coming true for us. The happily ever after our hearts long for isn't too good to be true. It's our future. It awaits us.

When sin is removed, when our bodies are resurrected, and we are glorified, we'll receive all the rich blessings God has waiting for us. And, we'll finally have new hearts, minds, and bodies to enjoy it. Every longing, expectation, need, and right desire will be satisfied. Our souls will feel eternally at rest and fulfilled, much like my stomach does temporarily after the family Thanksgiving meal. We will sigh deep breaths of joyful peace.

A Firm Hope

Paul says this hope is laid up for us "in heaven," which conveys the idea that it's protected. The words "laid up" put us at ease that it won't be lost on the way to our destination like mishandled travel luggage. This hope is reserved and kept safe. The reference to heaven takes it even further by pointing out it resides in the domain of God. It's guarded and locked away. No safety box or bank provides a level of security like heaven. Our hope is sure, certain, and secured. Your hope will not and cannot be cancelled, lost, delayed, or taken.

The Liar tells us God will leave us, or we've messed up too much this time, or that our salvation in Christ is in jeopardy. Doubt can creep into our minds as we listen to the whispers. Don't play his deadly games anymore. Silence the lies and listen to God's promises.

For those in Christ, we have an unshakeable hope protected and sealed by God. Though in this life we may have trouble, there is laid up for us a future inheritance with a glory beyond comparison (2 Corinthians 4:17). When we look at ourselves, our faith will be shaky. When we look to Christ and the certainty of the promises of God given in Christ, our faith finds a secure, rock-solid hope.

Jesus is firm and faithful when we are flaky. Every time. All the time. Right now.

The people of Colossae had a hope beyond the here-and-now and bigger than the fleeting offerings of this world—of which there are many: possessions, health, wealth, intelligence, the perfect family, personal happiness, the ultimate career, or respect in the eyes of peers. But if those become your hope you have at least two problems.

None of those are safe and secure. They can be ripped away at any moment. This creates fear, anxiety, control issues, clamoring for holding onto them, and idolatry where we turn good things into god things. If you're always pursuing more of these things or living on the edge of worry about losing them, your hope is likely in an earthly, finite object.

A second problem is these earthly hopes promote selfishness and self-reliance rather than love and faith. God-given hopes cause us to depend on God as the provider and sustainer. They also produce sacrificial love because your hope isn't something you earned or can lose. You're freed to give it away. Make Christ the focus rather than self, and seek His glory rather than your momentary gratification.

Aiming Our Hope

Do an honest self-evaluation. What do you hope in? What do you think will give meaning, joy, or rest? What causes you to use people or see them as getting in your way rather than loving them? If this inventory reveals any idols and false hopes replace them with the eternal, glorious, joy-giving, love-producing hope of all the plans and promises God secured for you in Christ.

Perhaps examining yourself and your weak faith robs you of your assurance and hope. Redirect your gaze off of self and onto the Savior. It's not the strength or degree of your faith that guarantees our salvation and inheritance; it's the *object* of your faith. Jesus is the one saving, holding, and keeping you. He won't let you lose the hope He died to secure.

Jesus tells us none who come to Him by faith will be rejected or driven away (John 6:37), and none will be lost (6:39). Jesus never puts up a "Keep Out" sign to those seeking Him, and He never tells us to "get out" once we're with Him. Neither our faith or faithlessness, nor our sin, nor our enemy can take Christ's people away from Him. Nothing can separate us from Him.

When we believe in Jesus, we're united with Him, and it's a union that never leads to divorce. When we are one with Jesus, we get His righteousness. Based on His righteousness credited (imputed) to us, we're declared justified, and this is a verdict God never reverses. In Jesus, we are made new and given an eternal life, and that life is never revoked or taken away.

We will wander and stumble, but in all our weakness and faithlessness Jesus will be strong and faithful. He will hold me fast. He will hold us fast. He will hold you fast.

Paul didn't believe the old adage, "those who are heavenly-minded are of no earthly good." The hope we have in Christ, which includes present realities and future promises, helps us fight sin, love one another, endure suffering, and pursue knowing God.

When we hope in Jesus, it doesn't mean we put off any chances of joy in this life but we're looking for a deeper, lasting joy. The quick fixes of this world don't compare to the eternal, abundant satisfaction found in Christ.

Applying Colossians

Questions

1) How does a future hope in heaven lead to greater faith and love? How might it help you fight worldly temptation, enduring sadness, or suffering?
2) How can the conveniences and pleasures of life lead to minimizing the goodness of our future hope laid up in heaven?
3) What are potential idols for you? What things do you sin to get or sin if you don't get?

Next Steps

- Make a list of things in the new heavens and new earth you are looking forward to.
- Is there a situation right now that seems to steal your hope and leave you crushed? Reflect on what you're hoping in, something on this earth or something in Christ.

For Further Study

- **Hope**: 1 Peter 1:4–5; Colossians 1:23, 27; 3:4; Ephesians 1:14, 18; Titus 1:2; Hebrews 3:6.
- **Security in Christ**: John 6:37–39; 10:28–29; Philippians 1:6; Romans 8:28–29, 38–39; 1 Thessalonians 3:3.

PAUL REVERE AND PAUL THE APOSTLE

"Of this you have heard before in the word of the truth, the gospel, [6]which has come to you, as indeed in the whole world it is bearing fruit and growing—as it also does among you, since the day you heard it and understood the grace of God in truth, [7]just as you learned it from Epaphras" (Colossians 1:5–7).

A personal passion of mine is history. Any history, but especially American history in the 17th and 18th century. One of my favorite cities is Boston. Boston offers a window into our country's beginnings and allows you to walk in the steps of our nation's founding fathers and revolutionary heroes.

One famed hero is Paul Revere. Although it wasn't *good* news when Paul Revere rode his horse out from Boston, he was *announcing* the British were coming. He was *heralding* or *proclaiming a message* to the people of those towns. His mission was spreading the message.

What Paul the apostle did when he entered cities with the gospel parallels Paul Revere's announcements to colonial towns. In Paul's time, a Roman herald would enter a town and *proclaim* important news, such as a military victory or a pronouncement from the emperor.[12] The modern parallel is the newscaster who relays significant information to a watching world.

The Message

"Gospel" means good news. It's important we remember the gospel is news of historical realities. It's not simply a teaching, a thought, or a way of living. It's an announcement. Paul loved to interrupt the regularly scheduled program of our lives and report this breaking news: God sent His Son to save us from

---

12 See N.T. Wright's explanation of the Roman ideological context for "gospel." N.T. Wright, *Paul* (Fortress Press: Minneapolis, 2005), 62–63, 77.

the prison of our sins so we might truly live. The gospel is *news* because it declares the death and resurrection of Jesus. It is *good* news because through it sinners can freely receive salvation.

Notice the words describing the gospel: it's heard (5, 6), it's the word of truth (5, 6), it's understood (7), and it's taught and learned (7). In pockets of Christianity people want to talk only about a relationship or only about behavior. Paul sees a rational, spoken, propositional message of historical news with a real person at the center. It must be heard, understood, and believed. The message matters.

One of the most succinct summaries of this message comes from 1 Corinthians 15:3–4: "that Christ died for our sins in accordance with the Scriptures, that he was buried, that he was raised on the third day in accordance with the Scriptures."

We are broken people who sin,[13] not just against our fellow human beings, but against God. Our hearts rebel against Him and we choose our own way as opposed to God's way. God, like any good judge and just ruler, must both punish wrongdoing and crush rebellion against Him. Because of this, we all stand condemned and alienated from God.

This is the bad news before the good news. It's essential and you can't skip over it any more than a sane doctor would skip over telling his patient about their cancer before prescribing radiation. But it's also incomplete.

Imagine for a second if all you knew was that a just and righteous God existed. You're aware of the countless wrong thoughts, words, and actions over your lifetime. You know this cannot be good for you. What if that knowledge, or the sense that this must be true, was all the knowledge you had?

---

[13] Sin: rebellion against God that manifests itself in breaking His law, resulting in our condemnation and separation from Him. It combines relational and judicial overtones. We not only reject the Law-Giver but we shun our Father.

It's a heavy, palpable darkness. It's like spiritually living in a room without any windows and no electricity.

But, there is good news. Light shines into our darkness.

God provided a remedy in the person and work of His Son. Jesus, the God-man, lived the perfect life we should have lived and at the cross died a death we deserved. He gave His life as a sacrifice for sins to purchase forgiveness and reconciliation to God.

It is the greatest of exchanges: Christ took our sins and our punishment so that by faith in Him we might receive His righteousness and reward. If we as rebels put down our arms and submit to the rightful authority of God, we can be saved.

That's the gospel at its core. We are sinners. God is holy and this is a big problem. But thankfully, through Jesus we can be forgiven and restored. Don't let familiarity with a message keep it from hitting you with fresh wonder and power.

Ask yourself, have I ever given up the reigns of my life and entrusted Jesus to be Lord? Do I try to pay God back or earn His approval by my performance or do I rest in Christ? If God has redeemed my life, do I live with Him at the center, or, do I give Him a couple of hours on Sunday like I'm doing Him a favor?

The Mission

Having seen the *gospel message*, we should also notice in our passage the *gospel mission*. The mission is getting the message out. When people proclaim God's Word, the Spirit works to create new life in its hearers. Slaves to sin become sons of God. The dead are made alive. The weary are refreshed.

This occurs throughout the book of Acts. The apostles trumpet Jesus as the sole and sufficient savior, and that forgiveness is graciously given when we trust in Him. Through preaching and evangelism God multiplied His church as disciples spread through the Roman world.

The gospel mission happens by sharing the gospel message.

Paul describes the gospel as producing fruit and spreading like a healthy vine (1:6). He rejoices because as Epaphras (1:7) and others embraced the gospel mission, it led to the church "bearing fruit and growing" (1:6).

The mission is to share "the word of truth, the gospel" (1:5). Unleash it so God might work in power. Our confidence is not in ourselves, our wisdom, having all the answers, anything new or exciting, or our ability to change people. Our confidence is in God's gospel.

God saves us through the gospel message and sends us on a gospel mission. Who are you—like Epaphras—investing in by sharing God's Word and pointing them to Jesus?

Applying Colossians

Questions
1) How would you define or explain the gospel in one paragraph?
2) In your family, small group, or local church, how can you regularly rehearse the gospel to one another? How can you comfort one another and motivate one another with God's already completed work?
3) Who are people right now in your life who need to hear or believe in the gospel of Jesus Christ? How can you pray for them? How can you intentionally love them and seek to share the gospel?

Next Steps

- Write out your own testimony, including the words: God, sin, Jesus, grace, and faith.
- Be in prayer about the opportunity to share the gospel with someone this week.

For Further Study

- **Gospel**: Romans 1:16–18; 3:19–26; Galatians 1:9; Ephesians 1:13.
- **Sin**: Genesis 3; Isaiah 59:2; Romans 3:9–18, 23; 5:12–21; 6:23; 1 John 1:9; 3:4.
- **Read the blog:** "Catching God's Vision for Multiplication" by Dustin Crowe at gcdiscipleship.com.

GOSPEL COMMUNITY: A NEW FAMILY IN CHRIST

"Of this you have heard before in the word of the truth, the gospel, 6which has come to you, as indeed in the whole world it is bearing fruit and growing—as it also does among you, since the day you heard it and understood the grace of God in truth, 7just as you learned it from Epaphras our beloved fellow servant. He is a faithful minister of Christ on your behalf 8and has made known to us your love in the Spirit" (Colossians 1:5–8).

Have you ever received a personal letter in the mail? I'm not talking about a bill or a marketing scam but an actual letter. Isn't that a great feeling? I still remember leaving home for college eight hours from everyone I knew. As a homesick student, opening my mailbox to the surprise of an envelope thrilled me. I had not been forgotten. Even today, when I receive a letter in the mail I cast aside the bills and junk mail to read the words written specifically to me.

Paul's concern and love for Christ's church caused him to put pen to paper. He wrote to real people, and the beginning and end of this letter contain the names of those people. Even though some names sound like a *Lord of the Rings* character (Nympha), they were people like you.

They struggled with the allure of sin and not letting the world creep into their faith. Their church needed God's Word to fight false teaching pressing in from the outside. They needed encouragement to endure and not be drawn after things apart from Jesus. Sound familiar? These are the people hungry to hear Paul's words.

Don't read Colossians as if it was a general Christian living book without a specific audience. Read it through the filter of a real person writing to real people to address real concerns.

Paul's Love

In this first section of Colossians, Paul pulls back the curtain and we see what a gospel-created community looked like. The church then and today is a beautiful mess, struggling but glorious.

Paul warns against threats and instructs them in the ways that nurture a healthy church. His concerns aren't the color of the carpet but the condition of their hearts. Whether gently delivering a rebuke or directing their gaze towards Jesus, Paul's aim is always growth in their walk as believers. He labors for this church so they would love Christ more (1:28–29).

The first thing to note is the message of salvation in Christ came to Colossae. These were primarily Gentiles who had never heard the name of Jesus. For three years Paul preached regularly in the nearby city of Ephesus. Many heard Paul there and carried the message to their own towns (Acts 19:10).

The gospel isn't like a souvenir snow globe or post-card you bring back from your trip and put on a mantle. It's a message that needs to be shared. Most likely, Epaphras receives the gospel from Paul in Ephesus and then God uses Epaphras to start the church in Colossae (1:7; 4:12). He then communicates to Paul the exciting news of how the gospel formed their faith, love, and hope (1:4–5).

Their Love

In verses 4–6, Paul notes how belief in the gospel led to fruit in their lives. He mentions love for one another twice (1:4, 8). The church at Colossae had their share of problems but it doesn't appear like a lack of love was one of them. Here we spot a church full of good works, hospitality, kindness, evangelism, and concern for one another. "He has told us about the love for others that the Holy Spirit has given you" (1:8 NLT).[14] These followers of Jesus loved one another in word and in deed.

In this first section of Colossians we see the beauty of the church. It is a family of loving relationships where Jesus followers build one another up through the Word of truth. They're imperfect people clinging to a perfect Savior, together.

You Need the Church

Never underestimate your need for the people and ministry of a local church.

This can be countercultural. Americans fear commitment and approach everything as consumers. The Bible tells us we need other believers, but we brush off this command and hold tight our autonomy. Too often people treat the church as if they can take it or leave it depending on when it's convenient.

Brett McCracken gives the smack upside the head we need. "Christianity doesn't work on the terms of consumerism. . . . Jesus calls us not to individualized, self-styled spirituality but to faith in community, accountable to others. Christianity detached from the church is not really Christianity. It feigns to embrace Jesus while shunning His body (see 1 Corinthians 12, Ephesians 1: 22–23; 5: 23; Colossians 1: 18)."[15]

The church is Jesus's appointed means through which He's known, and by which we're encouraged and directed to Him. It consists of rich and poor, blue-collar and white-collar, light-skinned and dark-skinned and everything in between, male and female, young and old, all united around faith in Jesus Christ. What we *don't* have in common pales when compared to the unity we

---

[14] *Holy Bible: New Living Translation* (Carol Stream, IL: Tyndale House Publishers, 2013).

[15] Brett McCracken, "Church Shopping with Charles Taylor," in *Our Secular Age*, edited by Collin Hansen (Deerfield: The Gospel Coalition, 2017), 80.

do have as brothers and sisters saved by Jesus (1:2), given the Spirit (1:8), and adopted by the Father (1:3).

The church in Colossae holds fast to Jesus Christ. They teach and spread the message of truth and grace and then live out with one another a life of love and grace. God uses this beautiful mess called the church to be His conduit for the increase of His glory and the spread of His gospel. The church is glorious not because it's perfect but because it's Christ's.

Get Messy

Are you going deep with the people of God? Find a local church you can join yourself to and then find a group of people within that church where you can rehearse the gospel to one another. Don't look for "the perfect church," but one that exalts Jesus above all things. Seek a church where the people know themselves to be sinners and know Christ as a friend and savior of sinners.

Roll up your sleeves and get dirty. Cultivate a gospel-community of love, faith, and good works that Paul describes. No matter how imperfect your church is, if it is a doctrinally sound, gospel-teaching, people-loving, and Jesus-following church then stay put. Establish your roots in the soil of a healthy church. [16] Instead of moaning about the things you don't like, humbly serve, love, and care for others to create this special community of gospel-centered friends and family.

Ask how can you be an Epaphras to those around you. Take the things in God's Word you've learned and pass them on to others. As we pour ourselves into others, God pours Himself into us.

---

[16] Though all churches are imperfect, some are healthy and some are unhealthy. Learn more about what makes a healthy church through the printed and online resources of 9marks.org.

Applying Colossians

Questions
1) Why is diversity in the church not only a good thing but a needed thing? How does unity in diversity reflect God?
2) When have you seen the church at its best? What did that look like?
3) How can your family take steps towards serving, loving, caring for, and building up other members in your local church?

Next Steps
- Call or write a thank you note or email to whoever has shared the gospel with you. Do the same to a pastor or leader who has faithfully served you.
- Come up with one specific way to show love to someone at your church this week.

For Further Study
- **Loving one another**: Acts 2:42–47; 4:32–37; 8:1–2; 1 Thessalonians 2:8.
- Research the **"one another" verses** in the Bible. Here are a few places to start: Romans 12:10; 14:19; Galatians 5:13; Ephesians 4:32; Colossians 3:9, 13, 16; 1 Thessalonians 4:18; 5:11; James 5:16.
- Read 1 Corinthians 13 (the love chapter) to see what love looks like.

PRAYING WITH PAUL (1:9–14)

It doesn't take long after Christmas before many of us rethink our Christmas list. What you asked for didn't prove to be quite what you hoped. The realization sets in that there are other goodies out there you want more—and may *need*. The problem isn't that people are bad givers or have horrible taste (certain relatives excluded) but we are bad askers. We don't always know what to ask for or we ask for something that lasts for all of one week.

I see a similar problem in my prayer life. Often, I don't know what to request. Or, I ask for things that aren't bad but I ignore the things most needed. For myself and others, I ask for good health but often neglect praying God would prove Himself to be a helper during bad health. Both prayers are okay, but in the former I'm seeking to avoid discomfort, whereas the latter gets at knowing God in a deeper way.

Paul has much to teach us as he offers a prayer report for the church he loves. His prayers sound different than mine, so I need to listen and learn. He prays for things of the heart leading to maturity in Christ. "In one's practice of prayer, the fundamental distinction is not primarily the one between physical versus spiritual concerns, but between the focus on oneself and the focus on God."[17] Prayer should include a wide range of issues, but its bulls-eye should be matters of the heart.

If I offered you an opportunity to go back in history and peek into Paul's prayer journal, wouldn't you jump at the chance? What would he pray about? What would he ask for other believers? Reading Colossians 1:9–14 provides that occasion to learn about prayer from the apostle Paul.

Over the next six readings (1:9–14), try to make praying for others and praying in line with God's Word a greater focus. God never gets weary of your

---

[17] David Pao, *Colossians & Philemon* (Grand Rapids: Zondervan, 2012), 79.

prayers. He invites us to come to Him and open our hearts to Him. Tim Keller defines prayer as a "personal, communicative response to the knowledge of God."[18] Seeing God in the Word will motivate seeking Him in prayer.

We'll look at a phrase from Colossians 1:9–14 each day and consider how Paul's prayer can guide our praying.[19] Learning about prayer isn't the end goal. It's the starting point to actually praying as a means to experience and know God more deeply.

---

[18] Keller, *Prayer*, 45.

[19] To leave more time for prayer, the "For Further Study" section is removed from this week.

WHO ARE YOU PRAYING FOR?

"And so, from the day we heard, we have not ceased to pray for you" (Colossians 1:9).

Colossians shoots out of the gate with a section on thanksgiving (1:3–8). He simultaneously exalts God and encourages God's people. Paul now transitions into praying for them (1:9–14). Both sections share similar tones of thanksgiving. Both emphasize the knowledge and power of God. Notice the repetition.

"We always thank God" (3)	"giving thanks to the Father" (12)
"Saints" (4)	"saints" (12)
"When we pray for you" (3)	"we have not ceased to pray for you" (9)
"Since we heard of your faith" (4)	"from the day we heard" (9)
"Bearing fruit and growing" (6)	"bearing fruit…increasing" (10)

In his thanksgiving report (1:3–8), Paul affirms God's good work and the initial faith of the Colossians. In his prayer report (9–14), he appeals to God to remain faithful in the work He started and he calls the Colossians to continue in what they began. "The thanksgiving section . . . focuses on the power of the gospel among the believers in Colossae, while the prayer report highlights the need to act in a way consistent with the knowledge that the gospel has imparted."[20] A consistent theme in Colossians surfaces here: the need to press on in the faith.

Praying for Others

Since he first heard the gospel arrived on their doorsteps (vv. 3–8), Paul put the Colossians on his prayer list. He considers them gospel partners, beloved

---

[20] Pao, *Colossians*, 44.

brothers and sisters, so he regularly prays for them. No surprise, the people on our heart make their way into our prayers.

Do you pray for people besides yourself, or your immediate family? What gospel-mission excites you and finds its way into your prayers? Who do you love so much that we can't help but pray for them?

Every Monday morning a godly couple at my church text me. They let me know they're praying for me and what they're praying. It's always a gush of needed wind, filling my sails with encouragement.

Look at the way Paul expresses this in his letter to the Thessalonian church, "But we were gentle among you, like a nursing mother taking care of her own children" (1 Thessalonians 2:8). In the very next verse he says he's eager to share not only the gospel with them but his own life. Praying for others and being prayed over is part of sharing life together. The bond of Christ unites them and both sides lobby for one another in prayer.

Three Ways to Start

Here are three short takeaways. All of us want a radically different prayer life where we go from zero to sixty in a day. Instead of shooting for the moon and lapsing into discouragement because you didn't wake up at 4 a.m. and pray for three hours, start with these small steps. Prayer will never go deep if it doesn't start simple.

First, Paul tells people what he's praying. Although it's good to tell someone you're praying for them, it's even better to verbalize what you're praying. Instead of saying, "I'm praying for you," say, "I'm praying God causes your love for others at your workplace to be strong and clear today."

Don't leave people in the dark about what you're praying. There's a double-barreled encouragement in knowing you're being prayed for and knowing what's being prayed.

Second, Paul doesn't start praying when something goes wrong. He's prayed for them since he first heard of their salvation, and he's never stopped. I must admit I often let people slip out of my prayers until I hear bad news. It would be much better to pray for them in all seasons.

Pre-emptive strikes in prayer are just as necessary as sending in support after an enemy attack. Prayer should be proactive and reactive.

Third, Paul links encouragements to grow in Christ with prayers to God for help. That's liberating news because it means Paul's not putting their walk with Christ entirely on their shoulders and demanding self-produced change. He asks God to help them while he also appeals to them to work out their sanctification. He urges them to persevere while asking God to bring it about.

We work as God works, and we work because God works. Do we ask people to grow without taking them to the throne of God, the one who empowers them? Paul's letters supply a pattern of encouraging other believers to pursue after Christ while praying for God to make it happen.

These three things transfer to our own prayer lives. Pray for others *and* tell them how you're praying. (Please don't tell someone you'll pray for them if you don't intend to follow through.) Pray for people in all seasons of their soul, including the sunny days of summer and the blistering cold of winter. See prayer as real work in helping others grow. Don't wish someone would change but neglect praying for God to change them.

This verse and the subsequent prayer causes us to ask ourselves these questions: Who are we partnering with in the gospel, and who are we praying for? The people God puts in your life are the people to put in your prayers. As you intercede for people you care about, do you only ask for safety, physical health, and material blessing or do you aim for the heart? Do you want God to be big or do you just want life to be easy?

You can't change people and you often can't meet their biggest needs. But you can bring their cause before the One who can. Pray for yourself and pray for one another. Following Christ includes praying for other Christ followers.

Applying Colossians

Questions
1) Who are the people in your life you pray for most often, and why?
2) If you struggle to think of other believers you share life with who you can pray for, are there ways for you to get more involved?
3) Who is someone you can pray for today and encourage them by letting them know what you're praying for them?

Next Steps
- Write down one or two names of people you're ministering too (maybe people in your small group, friends from church, or unbelievers) and pray for them each day this week. Call, email, text, or write a letter to some of those people letting them know how you're praying for them.
- If you have kids, begin helping them to see the value in praying for other gospel partners regularly. Ask them to pray for their Sunday school teachers.

GOD'S WILL: SEEING INTO YOUR FUTURE OR SEEING HIM

"And so, from the day we heard, we have not ceased to pray for you, asking that you may be filled with the knowledge of his will in all spiritual wisdom and understanding" (Colossians 1:9).

The subject of "God's will" has to be at the top of any list of the most controversial and yet most intriguing ideas in the Bible. Many books boldly claim they will help the reader discern God's will or outright state what it is. Countless prayers center on finding out in detailed-fashion what "God's will is for my life." It might be a roadblock keeping you from moving forward because you're waiting for God's will to come with the clarity of a blinking neon sign. This can paralyze people as they wait for a sign God never promised to give, or discourage people as they listen for God to speak in places He never told us to listen.

In the evangelical world, pointing to God's will has also become the "spiritual" way to bail from a dating relationship. Instead of honestly saying, "I don't want to be with you," many young people put the blame on God by saying, "I just sense this isn't God's will for me right now." Surely "God's will" has to be bigger than romance.

Let's try to get at what Paul means when he prays for knowledge of God's will. Of all the things Paul could have asked God to give or do for the Colossians, his first and central request is the knowledge of God's will. With this prayer, is Paul's desire for these believers to gain knowledge from God about something else, or to gain the knowledge of God? Or, to put your own feet to the fire, would you prefer to know answers from God about the uncertainties in your life or know God? Which would give peace? Which would satisfy? Which do you need most?

A Plan or Person

I would guess many people read this verse and assume it refers to God's specific plan for their life. "God's will" has come to be understood as God's direction at a crossroads decision such as whom to marry, what job to take, where to go to school, which fast food restaurant to eat at, and pretty much anything else we can't decide. We make discerning God's will tantamount to peering into the crystal ball of our future.

When Paul refers to the knowledge of God's will he intends to express something else. The knowledge of God's will is the knowledge of God. We cannot know His will—His heart, plan, ways, or what He's revealed—apart from knowing Him.

Paul prays the same way for the church in Ephesus when he asks for God to *"give you a spirit of wisdom and of revelation in the knowledge of him"* (Ephesians 1:17; see also 2 Peter 1:3). The knowledge of God's will is more about a Person than a plan. It's less about downloading our life's blueprint and more about knowing what God has already done through Jesus Christ.

Knowing God's will isn't so much about seeing our future but seeing God. Knowing God is much more important than knowing our next step.

In Christ Alone

The reason Paul prays this for the church at Colossae is because competition existed in the city. False teachers claimed a person doesn't need to give up their ideas of Jesus but they shouldn't limit themselves by following His teachings alone. These "spiritual" teachers whispered into the ears of the Colossians that to be enlightened they should take all sources into account. It's the ongoing temptation to drown out Jesus by making Him one of many voices in the choir instead of letting Him sing solo.

The Bible doesn't give us this option. It firmly holds to the exclusivity of Christ. He is the way, the truth, and the life. Salvation comes through Him alone. Wisdom for life and godliness comes through Him alone. Paul does his best in this letter to convince them in Jesus *"are hidden all the treasures of wisdom and knowledge"* (Colossians 2:3). Whenever we try to *add* to Jesus we end up *taking away* from Jesus. This includes seeking wisdom and truth.

The shouting matches competing for our attention threaten us today. We live in a world where social media and mass communication (e.g., Facebook, Twitter, Instagram, Pinterest, Internet, ebooks, television, ads, checkout line magazines, and on and on) barrage us with competing voices. Even in the realm of spiritual and religious resources, the onslaught of so-called guidance is daunting. The clamoring of opinions and the plethora of options leave us dizzied.

There is even a lot of unchristian garbage cloaked in "Christian" labels. Which books, TV, or radio or radio programs do we listen to and what sources should we trust for knowledge?

In increasing fashion, our culture mirrors the unbelieving culture of Colossae. We must ask God to fill us with the knowledge of His will so the worldly wisdom presented to us cannot take root. We must cram our minds and hearts with the Bible so other things don't have room to creep in.

Paul recognizes what we need isn't a laid-out map of our lives. Often this demand for clarity or knowing what to do next suggests a lack of trust in God. Instead of depending on signs and clear answers for every question of direction, we need the wisdom to know the things that please God, the things that lead us to Him, and what will bring about our maturity in Christ.

Learning to lean on God while on shaky ground is much more valuable to our faith than being comfortable about where we're standing. The most important thing we need today is God.

Focused Prayer

Seeking God for wisdom is a good thing. But, if our prayers turn Him into a divine GPS telling us when and where to turn, then we've missed out on getting to know Him. Miss that and we miss the point of prayer.

As you pray this week, be intentional about seeking God's face and asking for what you need most: Him. As you read His Word, your first priority is seeking and knowing Him, which will help you better know His desires, will, and purposes. Like kids who mimic the desires of their parents, the more we get to know God the more we will have wisdom about His will (1:9), or the things He desires for us and sees as right and good.

God not only changes the focus of our prayer life but its power. "The power of our prayers, then, lies not primarily in our effort and striving, or in any technique, but rather in the knowledge of God."[21]

Small prayers are symptomatic of a small view of God. One antidote is to immerse yourself in the Word so you discover the power and majesty of God and His nearness and love.

But reading the Word without prayer is like having a one-sided conversation. If we only read, whether it be a Christian book or the Bible itself, and don't cement in our heart what we just learned by praying, our meditation might be half-baked.

If we behold the glory, wisdom, supremacy, and goodness of God it will lead us to His throne. Intellectually knowing about God propels us to intimately know God, and this in large part happens in prayer.

---

[21] Keller, *Prayer*, 49.

Applying Colossians

Questions
1) How does Paul's prayer today help you know how to pray better?
2) How do we make sure ideas from the world around us (media, books, leaders, etc.) fit with the wisdom of Scripture?
3) Does your individual and family prayer life include seeking and praising God or is it almost always about your needs? If you have children, are you teaching your kids to pray God-centered prayers?

Next Steps
- Meditate on Scripture this week so God's voice drowns out competing voices.
- Attend your church's prayer time to seek after God's face and not just His hand.
- Spend time praying God-centered prayers of adoration, thanksgiving, and worship. It might help to pray through a passage like Psalm 34 or 100, or Ephesians 1:3–14.

DON'T JUST TALK THE TALK, WALK THE WALK

"so as to walk in a manner worthy of the Lord, fully pleasing to him, bearing fruit in every good work and increasing in the knowledge of God" (Colossians 1:10).

In verse nine, Paul prayed for the knowledge of God. What we see in verse ten is that knowledge leads to fruit. Paul prays for them to be filled with the knowledge of God's will *so they can* walk in a certain way. The former produces the latter.

True theology, true knowledge, isn't information stored in the mind. It must trickle down to our heart, changing our loves, desires, thoughts, and words. As our knowledge of Christ increases so does our understanding of what it means to live a godly life in Him. Since the last three phrases of this verse seem to expand upon and explain the first phrase, we'll focus on what it means "to walk in a manner worthy of the Lord."

Walking

Even though I occasionally walk throughout the day, my car is the primary means by which I get around. In Paul's day, they had yet to discover the automobile, large transit systems, or even bicycles. One could hitch a ride with a camel or donkey on occasion, but largely it was their own two legs doing the work. As they traveled to and from their home to synagogue to the market to their version of Chick-fil-A, walking was their means of making it from point A to B.

Because walking was their life it became a shorthand expression for your everyday behavior. That's passed down to us today in the phrase, "Don't just talk the talk but walk the walk." Live it out.

Paul wants believers to gain the type of knowledge of Jesus that goes past Sunday's lunch and continues throughout the week. Pastor Mark Vroegop often says what makes the Christian life hard is it is so *daily*. "Walking is something nondramatic, rhythmic—it consists of steady, repeated actions you can keep up in a sustained way for a long time. . . . To walk with God is a metaphor that symbolizes slow and steady progress."[22]

The Christian life isn't a quick sprint and there's rarely a crowd on the sideline cheering. There's little glamor and no newscaster waiting to celebrate our efforts. It's a lifetime of steady, faithful steps toward Jesus. Paul gets at this life-encompassing reality by using the term *walk*.

Responsibility or Privilege?

With this understanding of "walk" in mind, we need to wrestle with what it means to walk "in a manner worthy of the Lord." That can be a scary thought when we think about the canyon between His worth and my walk. Does this verse mean I need to earn His approval? If that's the case, I know I'm in trouble because I can't be good enough to be worthy of God's blessing.

Verse 10 can seem like you're being asked to climb Mount Everest. "Walk in a manner worthy of the Lord." "Fully pleasing to him." "Bearing fruit in every good work." Those seem like big asks for someone who is just trying not to mess things up too much today.

Before letting the discouragement settle in, remember that Paul isn't putting this all on their shoulders. He's praying to God on their behalf. His prayer for them to know God (1:9) suggests God is the One doing the heavy lifting. It's a prayer pulling them towards this vision of discipleship, not a prod telling them to make it happen on their own.

---

[22] Tim Keller, *Walking with God through Pain and Suffering* (New York: Dutton, 2013), 236.

"The idea isn't that we are worthy by virtue of how we walk but that we should walk in a way that reflects or displays how much He is worthy of such obedience on our part."[23] Paul's not saying we earn Christ's presence in our life by our worth but that the way we live should reflect the worth of Christ.

Understanding this phrase makes all the difference. If "walk" means *earn* then this verse amounts to a ton of bricks being dropped on my already weak shoulders. What an impossible task! But, if "walk" means my life now gets to reflect the worth of the gospel then it injects a whole new sense of glory and purpose into every single day. What an amazing privilege!

Paul uses the same idea when writing to the Philippians: "Only let your manner of life be worthy of the gospel of Christ" (1:27). He provides a couple examples of how our small lives reflect gigantic realities. First, we endure suffering as one church so it shows an undivided unity that the gospel creates (1:27–30). And second, when we humble ourselves and put others first, we reflect the most glorious of gospel truths: that Jesus humbled Himself by taking on a human nature and by laying down His life for the ultimate good (salvation) of those who didn't deserve it (2:1–11).

As unbelievable as it seems, God created us to be image-bearers. Through the work of the Spirit, we're being remade into the image of Christ so that our lives embody beautiful truths about God and the gospel (Colossians 3:10).

Learning for Living

What Paul prays for is that the Colossians would know God in such a way that He makes them different. We must be on guard against learning for learning's sake. Jen Wilkin writes, "A lot of people think that the reason they are to study the Bible is so that they can know the Bible well. But when we study the Bible, we should always be coming to an increased knowledge of God that

---

[23] Sam Storms, *The Hope of Glory* (Wheaton: Crossway, 2008), 58.

leads to an increased love of God."[24] Genuine love for God motivates grateful obedience to God. Good doctrine should lead to godly living.

God joins truth and love so don't separate them. You won't have Christ-centered deeds without Christ-centered doctrine. You won't become Christ-like apart from the knowing what Christ *is* like.

Because Jesus has changed our lives, we ask Him to change our walk. The more we mature in Christ (1:28) the more our walk will reflect the glory and beauty of Him.

For example, a husband or wife who experience God's grace firsthand can reflect that in the way they give grace to their spouse. This displays the beauty of the gospel. A Christian humbled by their sin and grateful for the inexhaustible patience of God can show patience to the coworker who drives them crazy or the family member who never seems to get it together. This tangibly demonstrates God's goodness to others.

Live your life to show the worth of Christ. Because it's the gracious work of God in us, our growth doesn't promote ourselves but God's power at work in us.

Circling back, all this leads us back to our knees in prayer. The knowledge of God leads us to seek God in prayer, which is the wind in our sails pushing us forward in our walk with Christ. We link verses 9 and 10 to pray: "God, help me to know you so well that you invade every aspect of my daily walk, rhythms, and relationships. Be at work in me and through me. May I walk so closely with you that others could see you in me." Then, like Paul, pray the same things for others around you.

---

[24] Jen Wilkin, "The Best Reason to Read the Bible," *Crossway* July 14, 2017. Accessed on March 27, 2018 https://www.crossway.org/articles/the-best-reason-to-read-the-bible/.

Applying Colossians

Questions
1) How does the knowledge of God (1:9) lead to living a fruitful life pleasing to Him (1:10)?
2) How does knowing your life reflects Jesus cause a healthy fear? Joy? Purpose?
3) If married, where do you see your spouse imaging God, or walking in a manner reflecting His worth, in their life? If you have kids, how are they living out what they're learning about God?
4) How can you encourage those closest to you in the mundane "daily-ness" of the Christian walk?

Next steps
- Reflect upon the major parts of your day (work, school, family time, friend time, recreation, etc.) and consider if each part is lived "in a worthy manner."
- Ask someone (spouse, friend, roommate, small group member) to be praying with you about a couple specific ways you can grow in reflecting Christ.

BE EMPOWERED WITH ALL POWER BY GOD'S POWER

"May you be strengthened with all power, according to his glorious might, for all endurance and patience with joy" (Colossians 1:11).

Can you think of an experience where you needed to do something but knew you needed help? It might be an ongoing challenge. Even thinking about the hurdle sends a shudder of fear or frustration down your spine.

I hate moving. It's so much work and always takes three times longer than planned. Imagine if I packed everything in my house but had to move it out alone in a couple of hours. There's no way. I could try as hard as I wanted but I'm not getting it all moved unless I call in the troops for help. (If you own a pickup truck, you get this call routinely.) It's a job bigger than one person. Help is needed in the form of many hands, or at least a few strong ones.

If your house is on fire you don't fight it on your own. Don't spray your tiny little faucet-head at the flame. Call for help! The fire department has the powerful hoses you don't have. Some things we need to do are too big to handle on our own with our limited power and resources.

The high-bar of yesterday's verse forces us to look for help from someone else. How can we possibly walk worthy of the gospel, bear fruit, and please God (1:10)? Thankfully, God supplies all He seeks from us if we will walk in step with Him. Paul prays that God would strengthen (empower) them with all power according to His glorious might (power).

Insufficient Resources

Just as the world offers so-called "wisdom" it also offers its own forms of power. Some say we get power by tapping into our strength, gaining confidence, building self-esteem, trampling the competition, or an endless supply of FiveHour Energy. As kids, we thought power came from eating spinach, since that's what Popeye did, or that only superheroes had real power. Our culture says power comes from within by tapping into our hidden potential, by speaking things into existence, thinking positively, or even sending out the right vibes.

There are even a number of campaigns tied to the slogan, "I am enough." However, we know from experience—and Scripture—that we're not enough. No one is. We have just enough power and wisdom to get ourselves into a jam, but not enough to get ourselves out. In fact, this messaging appeals because we feel powerless and want to believe we're not. But, be honest, aren't there areas of your life you've wanted to change and never have been able to? Isn't there something you wish you could make happen or "fix" in your life, but you can't?

The truth is we aren't powerful. We're actually pretty weak, vulnerable, and limited. But God isn't chained by our weaknesses and liabilities. The discouragement in admitting our frailty is answered by the hope found in an all-powerful God.

The *world* tells you that you have all the power you need. The *Word* tells you that God has all the power you need but lack. Which do you want to rely on when you don't want to speak evil of those speaking evil of you, when anxiety floods in, or in the valleys of loneliness and despair? What happens when the floor underneath you crumbles or the enemy attacks? We don't have power within to face all these giants. We must be strengthened by God's power.

God's Power

In order to see today's prayer realized in our lives, we need to know two things. We first have to know God's power is at our disposal to help us. Sometimes we don't realize or remember the resources we have in Christ. As we neglect who God is and what He has for us, we fight battles with the most important weapons for spiritual warfare left on the shelf.

Second, we need to know the power given to us is a God-sized power.

> If we underestimate the depths of our sin, we will underestimate the cure. You don't bring a squirt gun to a bazooka fight, as they say, and we don't fight Satan, sin, and death with a Bible study, a worship song, a clean voting record, or a tithe check. Only something so dramatic as a holy God suffering and dying in our place can provide a cure.[25]

The prophet Jeremiah saw the power that delivered Israel. "Ah, Lord GOD! It is you who have made the heavens and the earth by your great power and by your outstretched arm! Nothing is too hard for you" (Jeremiah 32:17). God created everything, and He did so without working up a sweat.

Death seems like the unstoppable and unconquerable force. Paul reminded the church in Ephesus that God flexed His muscles and might when He raised Jesus from the dead. "According to the working of his great might that he [God] worked in Christ when he raised him from the dead" (Ephesians 1:19–20). Even death and sin are puny and powerless foes against God.

This is again why seeking the knowledge of God (Colossians 1:9) in the Word before focusing on our needs is practical. Seeing God's attributes, character, works, and promises bolsters our confidence in Him. We learn He desires to help. He knows how and when to help. And He's powerful in His help. Small views of God lead to trusting in self, but big views of God lead to trusting in Him.

What trial, circumstance, temptation, or problem are you facing today? I'm not saying it's a small issue; it probably isn't. What I am saying is however big of a giant you're battling—and however many times it has knocked you down

---

[25] Daniel Montgomery, *Faithmapping* (Wheaton: Crossway, 2013), 78.

before—if you realize how powerful your God is then nothing in your life will be too big or too tough to face.

Ask God to empower you in your weakness. Just like a good earthly-parent loves to help their kids, our Father loves it when we ask for His help. He loves you and longs to provide for you what you can't do on your own. Your maturity and joy bring joy to Him.

Paul prays for the Colossian church to experience the power of God. It's the same power that created the universe and raised the dead. It's the same power that with a snap of the finger put the stars in their place and with one word calmed the wind and waves. If that God-sized power is available for you then what will you face that God cannot carry you through?

God's power will outmatch any foe you face. You may not be up to the task but God is. Let's pray prayers for ourselves and for others that correspond to God's measure of power instead of our own measure of power.

Applying Colossians

Questions
1) What are some things in creation demonstrating God's power?
2) Can you recall any times or examples where you saw God's power at work in you or in someone around you? What are other examples from Scripture where God's power can be seen?
3) What's something you're walking through right now where you could use God's power? How can you bring your spouse, a friend, or your small group alongside of you in prayer?

Next Steps
- Mail a card, send a letter, or call someone to let them know you're praying for them and the power of God supporting them.
- Have your eyes open today to see in creation the power of God.

GIVE THANKS, AND MEAN IT

"with joy, giving thanks to the Father, who has qualified you to share in the inheritance of the saints in light" (Colossians 1:11–12).

If you were or are a perfectly behaved kid, then the example I'm about to give may not be familiar. But for the rest of us—the honest ones—who occasionally misbehaved, you can likely recall a similar picture.

When I was a kid I loved getting gifts. Who doesn't! Christmas and my birthday were the two most important days of the year. Few things are as exciting as unwrapping a present with your name on it. Unfortunately, there were several times someone gave me a gift and I forgot to say thank you. It could have been because the anticipation and thrill of tearing through the paper only to discover tube socks or a hokey sweater left me bewildered and forgetful. Or, if it was something I really wanted, I might have been so caught up in the pleasure of my new game or toy that I forgot all about the fact that someone gave it to me. Usually my embarrassed mom would remind me in a strong but hushed whisper or firm nudge to the ribs that I needed to say thank you, with an "or else" implied.

Thankfully, parents instill this important principle in kids from a young age. When someone does something for you or gives something to you, the proper response is to tell them "thank you." It's not simply a matter of etiquette but it's a relational exchange of some sort. The focus isn't so much on the formality but on the importance of a heartfelt expression of thanks.

A person has given you something you didn't earn that had a cost to it and was given out of kindness. The more you appreciate the gift or the more needed it was in your life, the more thankful you will be.

In Colossians 1:11–12, Paul prays they would be a people thankful to God for His gracious acts and gifts towards them. Thankfulness permeates

Colossians. Paul puts giving thanks at the heart of following Christ (1:3; 2:7; 3:15, 17; 4:2). This should not surprise us since our relationship with God begins and ends with grace. Everything we have has been given to us by God. None of it is deserved or earned apart from God (1 Corinthians 4:7).

No Thanks

There could be many reasons we don't give thanks to God but here are two. One culprit of our ingratitude is entitlement. We believe we deserve everything (and more) God does for us and gives to us. If you think you've done a pretty good job in life and you're not that bad of a person, then in your mind it makes sense that God would bless you. "Good people" often become ungrateful people because they're angry at God for not rewarding their hard work.

A second reason you might not give thanks would be you don't actually know the gifts God has lavishly poured on you. If this is the case, then a good prayer would be asking God to help you see all the blessings He's showered upon you. Pray for open eyes to be stunned by provision, protection, unmerited blessings, mercy despite your sin, and grace in times of need.

The more you see God's gifts, God's actions for you, and God's help in your life, the more you will spill over with joy and thanksgiving. Ann Voskamp writes, "The art of deep seeing makes gratitude possible. And it is the art of gratitude that makes joy possible."[26] We need eyes to see both what God gifts us and that it is God giving it.

Grace to Overcome Ingratitude

Whereas a life of living by grace leads to gratefulness, a life of living by performance leads to grumbling. When we think we've lived a good life and

---

[26] Ann Voskamp, *One Thousand Gifts* (Grand Rapids: Zondervan, 2010), 118.

have done everything we should, then we expect or even demand that God reward us accordingly. When we don't see God rewarding us (or paying us our dues) like we think we deserve then we grumble against Him and get angry.

It's only when we recognize our sin and God's mercy that we know any good thing in our life is a gift God freely gave us. We live by grace and are thankful with anything above the judgment we deserved.

Living by works turns us into whiners. "They owe me this. God owes me that. No one does all the things I do. I never get anything in return despite all I do for others. I've always tried to be a good person." But the gospel makes us grateful. "I can't believe how good God is to a messy, hard-hearted sinner like myself."

While gratitude and joy typify people living on grace, those caught in the performance treadmill are characterized by grumbling and discontentment. Gary Thomas writes, "I like to think of thankfulness as God's 'spiritual air freshener.' It replaces the stale odor of resentment with clean, fresh-smelling air for the soul to breathe."[27] Which would you rather be in the lives of those around you: a pleasing aroma inviting you in or a sour smell making you want to escape?

If everything you have is of grace (undeserved, unprovoked, and costly) then everything in life is an opportunity to give thanks. The key to joy for Paul is not more stuff in your life but thankfulness over what God has already done for you.

Growth in Gratitude

God's gifts to you open up opportunities to give thanks to Him. If thanksgiving isn't a regular part of your life or you struggle to know what you should be grateful for, then the answer isn't just hearing "be more thankful."

---

[27] Gary Thomas, *The Glorious Pursuit* (Colorado Springs: NavPress, 1998), 139.

Meditate on grace and how God has treated you in Christ. Dwell upon how Jesus loved you by being broken to pieces for you and how he keeps loving you even now as your sympathetic high-priest.

Think about what you deserve because of your sin and stubbornness. Then think about the undeserved mercies and blessings God repeatedly pours on you. How often have you made a disaster out of things and God has redeemed it for your good?

Consider everything you have in Christ, and give thanks.

As you move through your day, look around and consider the countless blessings. Start a list and you'll be pleasantly surprised with how many gifts are dropped in your lap every day. You don't create or earn them, and they don't come from nowhere. God gives them. Each is a chance to give thanks to the Giver of every good and perfect gift (James 1:17).

The antidote to grumbling or a lack of gratitude is more gospel in your life. It's the only medicine you can't overdose on and are always in need of. It reminds us how little we deserve from God and yet how much we've been given from God. And He doesn't hold it over our head or demand us to pay Him back; it's free to us because it was bought by Jesus.

Choose to give thanks instead of grumbling. Let the gospel work its way through your mind and your heart until you feel gratitude for the countless ways God has graciously cared for and loved on you.

Applying Colossians

Questions
1) How do thankfulness, gratitude, contentment, and joy relate to one another?

2) Begin listing some of the blessings in your life. If you're with others, have everyone name at least one good blessing from God.

3) How might gratitude provide a right perspective and endurance during trials?

Next Steps

- Tell a family member or friend something you're thankful they've done for you.
- Keep building on the list of blessings you've started by adding to it all week.
- If you use social media, post something specific about the way God has blessed you.

SET FREE BY THE KING

"He has delivered us from the domain of darkness and transferred us to the kingdom of his beloved Son, in whom we have redemption, the forgiveness of sins" (Colossians 1:13–14).

Paul's prayer leads to a climactic close, flowing from asking things on behalf of the Colossians to celebrating their salvation. Paul ends this prayer by rejoicing in God's work for them through Jesus. Verses 12–14 contrast where we used to stand (outside of Christ) and where we now stand (in Christ). While verses 16–20 will show us what (or who) we've been redeemed *to*, 13–14 keep us from forgetting the prison we're freed *from*.

Imprisoned People

Paul paints a picture of our redemption using metaphors every culture and age can understand. Whether or not we know it, we enter earth as prisoners. There is an insurgent authority; a ruler of this worldly dominion who is evil and malicious. In a parallel passage (Acts 26:18), Paul asserts that Satan is this worldly king and our sin is the chain keeping us in bondage. This domain of darkness is a place of oppression and peril, requiring a rescue or deliverance. Our sin keeps us locked in this prison with no hope of escape and no glimmer of light. The situation is bleak and crushing.

Your mind might go to any number of movies where the people are held captive or are in a dark and seemingly hopeless situation. They're in need of rescue. A deliverer is called for. Stories written in books and movies capture the desperate reality we're trapped in as well as our need for a hero to come along and save us.

The triumphant movie hero who smashes evil and delivers the helpless that we see in our movies points to a true reality. This well-known story doesn't originate with screenwriters in Hollywood but with God's eternal plan. The story our hearts long for is the good news of the gospel, the true tale of a king who comes to save in the most dramatic of forms.

Although the condition and condemnation of our sin is terrible news, there is greater news that must be proclaimed. There is another king. Unlike the evil oppressor this is a good king who rules with justice and mercy.

Light pervades this kingdom. We exchange the chains of slavery for the benefits of citizenship. God treats us as sons and daughters. Satan is a terrible and evil ruler who seeks only the harm of his captives, but Jesus Christ is the beloved Son of God who seeks the good of all the citizens under His rule. It's not only that we're freed from oppression. Just as important, we're brought under the care and direction of our Creator-Redeemer-King who can lead us into the life He envisioned for us.

But how does one imprisoned by their sin and lost in darkness enter such a wonderful kingdom? What can we do to get in? How do we experience it even now?

Freedom

The good news is the King rescues and redeems His citizens. The forgiveness of their sins was bought through His blood (Ephesians 1:7). Redemption points to someone being purchased out of slavery. Jesus gave His life and shed His blood on the cross to redeem a people out of darkness. "In whom we have redemption, the forgiveness of sins" (Colossians 1:14).

Our sins are the only chains Satan has to hold us condemned and imprisoned. When by faith we are united to Jesus we are forgiven and through that forgiveness comes freedom from the chains that once shackled us (see Colossians 2:14–15).

If you've never repented[28] from your sin and turned to Jesus for forgiveness, now's the time. If you're a follower of Christ, we need reminded the Father has forgiven and welcomed us. We stub our spiritual toes daily but we return to the cross and we rest in Christ's righteousness alone.

> We are saved, sanctified, and sustained by what Jesus did for us on the cross and through the power of the resurrection. If you add to or subtract from the cross, even if it is to factor in biblically mandated religious practices like prayer and evangelism, you rob God of his glory and Christ of his sufficiency. Romans 8:1 tells us that there is not condemnation for us, not because of all the great stuff we've done but because Christ has set us free from the law of sin and death. My sin in the past: forgiven. My current struggles: covered. My future failures: paid in full all by the marvelous, infinite, matchless grace found in the atoning work of the cross of Jesus Christ.[29]

Paul will throughout this letter bring up what Jesus Christ has done for us as His people. Every ethical command and encouragement to press on to maturity is rooted in the prior work of Christ. When we consider that our King sacrificed His life to set us free it makes serving Him and following Him a joy, not a duty.

We can wake up knowing the biggest problem of our life is resolved (sin) and the greatest joy available is now ours (God). Jesus doesn't redeem us and then leave us on our own. He redeems us so we might live in His kingdom with Him, which means under His rule and care (Colossians 1:14). Redemption signals both freedom out of bondage and into a place of belonging.

---

[28] Repentance: Despairing over the insufficiency of yourself and in brokenness over sin turning to God for rescue.

[29] Matt Chandler, *The Explicit Gospel* (Wheaton: Crossway, 2012), 15.

Charles Wesley's classic hymn "And Can it Be?" puts this wonderful theology into words we can sing.

> Long my imprisoned spirit lay, Fast bound in sin and nature's night;
> Thine eye diffused a quickening ray, I woke, the dungeon flamed with light;
> My chains fell off, my heart was free, I rose, went forth, and followed Thee.
> Amazing love! How can it be, That Thou, my God shouldst die for me?[30]

If you're a believer in Christ, don't leave the gospel at the door by assuming it was only for your salvation. Jesus died to save us from our sins and He lives to lead us as our Lord. Christ's work for you was meant to free you, give new life daily, and place you under the smile of God's love.

We can boldly approach the throne of God in prayer in the name of Jesus. On our own we'd shrink away from talking to God and seeking to know Him. But through the atoning, redeeming, saving work of Jesus we're invited to enter God's presence with confidence (Hebrews 4:14–16).

How does the good news of freedom from bondage speak to you today as you wrestle with ongoing shame, when you stumble, when sin feels like it has power over you, or when you question whether God could be for you? How does it woo you into prayer, coming to the Father through the name and merits of the Son? Jesus came to set you free, so live in that freedom today by walking in the gospel of a crucified but resurrected Christ.

Applying Colossians

Questions

---

[30] Charles Wesley, "And Can It Be That I Should Gain?" (No. 260) in *Hymns for the Family of God* (Franklin, TN: Brentwood-Benson Music Publishing, 1976).

1) How do you remind yourself of what you've been brought out of, and what it cost?

2) What about the gospel are you thankful for today?

3) As a believer, where might the message of freedom or deliverance through Christ be applicable for you today?

Next Steps

- Pray that God would use any missionaries you support or pray for to see people around the globe rescued and redeemed.
- Read and pray through all of the lyrics to "And Can It Be?" by Charles Wesley.

THE KING OF CREATION AND THE CHURCH
(1:15–20)

Paul began with a double-barreled thanks to God and affirmation to the church for the fruit in Colossae (1:3–8). In the second section, he moved from thanksgiving to praying that God would grow and spread what He started (1:9–14).

The next section of Colossians (1:15–20) is all about the soul-stirring supremacy of Jesus. It's almost as if Paul mentions the work of redemption in 12–14 and now he can't help but go on about Jesus. We shouldn't be surprised. Colossians is all about the glory, supremacy, and preeminence of the exalted Jesus, and the jaw-dropping miracle that we're being remade in His image. Paul never tires of the wonders of Jesus. In this section, we'll see why.

It's helpful to know a little historical context in Colossians. The Colossian church was tempted to say Jesus is a good place to start but there are more ingredients to add. Paul wrote to convince them that Jesus isn't just one important person among many but He's supreme and sufficient all by Himself. There's no Jesus and something else or Jesus and a next step. Jesus is enough. This whole section is the sudden outburst of theological worship that the mere thought of Jesus brought out of Paul. Here we see theology, doxology, and apologetics merging into one rushing river of praise.

It's as if Paul is saying, "Let me fill you in on Jesus just in case you've forgotten." He points to the absolute and unrivaled supremacy of Jesus Christ over creation and the new creation (the church). Some scholars believe this was an early Christian hymn or poem. It's hard to tell for sure but we know Paul puts a right theology of the person and work of Jesus at the center of his faith. The Christian walk involves many things, but none of them are as important as knowing Jesus.

Right knowing about Jesus leads to right worship of Him and right obedience to Him. Theology is never speculative or only rational. It's practical. It works its way through us. Paul knows what truly changes people is setting the heart on seeing and savoring Jesus.

Too often we want to-do lists, but getting lost in delightful worship of Jesus will push you towards righteousness more than any prohibitive boundaries ever will. This is why in Colossians 3:1–2 Paul says to think on these things (i.e., Jesus) as the catalyst for our sanctification. As we wade into this next section, grow in your theology. See the beauty and supremacy of Jesus. Find your heart increasing in love for the King.

JESUS IS GOD ON DISPLAY

"He is the image of the invisible God" (Colossians 1:15a).

For good or bad, many of us have been told we look like one of our parents. In some circumstances, like a six-year-old boy told he's the spitting image of his dad, this might excite the hearer. In other cases, such as a teenage girl who's told she looks increasingly like her mom, the news might not be received with enthusiasm.

Appearance is where it starts but we mirror our parents in other ways. Growing up I was much more likely to catch my dad with a basketball in his hand than a wrench. To this day I can drain a three-pointer with the best of them but my handyman skills go little further than duct-tape and a hammer. Like father, like son.

Jesus is the perfect image of God the Father. Jesus comes to earth so we can see and better know what the Father is like. Paul uses "image" language in Colossians 1:15 to say Jesus shows us in flesh what the non-fleshed God is like. Long before it was cool to "express yourself," God expressed Himself in the person of Jesus.

God in Flesh

In John 1:1 we're taken back as far as the story will go. In the beginning, the second person of the Trinity[31] is called the Word. "Word" implies several things, including the divine self-expression.

---

[31] The doctrine of the Trinity teaches that God is one essence and three persons (tri-unity). We believe in one God—monotheism—who is eternally three distinct persons: Father, Son, and Holy Spirit. The three key affirmations are: 1) there is one God, 2) there are three distinct persons, and 3) each person is equally and fully God.

Words communicate. They allow one person to make other things known, verbally or written, to another. Jesus, the Word, is God's self-revelation. Jesus communicates who God is and what He's like in the clearest and most tangible form: a human person.

In John 1:14 we see the remarkable beauty of the incarnation. God the Son becomes a flesh and blood human being like us as He lives among us. Just in case we haven't gotten the point, John spells it out in the last verse of the prologue by saying Jesus has made God known to us (18).

It's not that God was completely unknowable through Creation around us or even through His relationship with Israel in the Old Testament. But, if Creation is a somewhat scrambled picture and the Old Testament is a black-and-white picture of God, then the incarnation is the IMAX 3D in full surround-sound showing of God.

Every word Jesus speaks, every miracle He performs, every act of love and mercy, every redemptive encounter, these all show us who God is and what He is like.

Jesus tells Phillip, "Have I been with you for so long and you still don't know who I am? Whoever has seen me has seen the Father" (John 14:8–9). Jesus shows us the otherwise unseen God.

Phillip isn't the only one to ask to see God. Every person wrestles with the questions, "Is there a God? If so, what might He be like?" There are many who conclude there must be a Creator God out there somewhere but His purposes and character remain unknown. Even for a Bible-toting Christian, who God is can remain somewhat vague in our minds and we might wonder what God is like.

Jesus comes so there would be no need to speculate about God. He puts flesh (literally) to the character of God.

In the incarnation, where Jesus can be seen, touched, and heard, God gives a full and clear expression of Himself to mankind. When we read about the emotions Jesus felt, or we see how he cared for the hurting, or we see the depth of love in His friendships, or we gaze at any of the other pictures of Jesus in the NT, we see God before our eyes in clear and compelling ways.

Look at Jesus

This is again an area where what we think about God (theology) directly affects our relationship with God. Some people struggle to understand what God is like because their earthly father ruined the term "Father." Others possess false conceptions of God because they project onto Him what they imagine Him to be like based on how others operate. Then there's the crafty serpent who from Eden until today continues to breathe out lies about God.

The Bible must inform our view of God so we *think* of Him rightly and then *relate* to Him rightly.

Jesus stands in the gap not only as a mediator, but as the one who translates the transcendent God to us by becoming a man and living as God with us. He comes as the one who can reveal or express God to us precisely because He is the God-man.

Just like how I reflected my Dad in the opening illustration (thanks for the skills, Dad!), Jesus is the Son who looks like, acts like, and images His Father. If you want to see God just look at Jesus.

As you go throughout your day, let your mind wander to things you've seen about Him in the gospels or even so far in Colossians. The more we think about Jesus—as revealed in the Bible, not as discussed on cable TV or by religious clichés—the more we will think rightly about who God is and what He is like.

Paul tells the Corinthian church that just like a parent rubs off on their child, the more we look at Jesus the more He will rub off on us (2 Corinthians 3:18). This motivates the Colossians to live consistently with being a new person. Since we are in Jesus, who is the perfect image of God, we are being remade into image-bearers of our Creator (3:10).

Applying Colossians

Questions
1) How does our mission of imaging God parallel that of Jesus as the image of God?
2) What are some of the benefits of reading the Gospels and letting Jesus be the lens through which we view God?
3) What are some ways you see Jesus in such a way that it helps you know the Father better?

Next Steps
- Read a Gospel with a focus on how Jesus shows us God. Or read Colossians again and highlight any descriptions of Jesus or actions Jesus performed.
- Ask a friend to help keep you accountable by looking at Christ and becoming like Him instead of looking at idols and becoming like those things (lust, envy, materialism).

For Further Study
- **God's Image**: Genesis 1:26–28; John 1:1–18; 2 Corinthians 4:4; Hebrews 1:3.
- Read a book on the person and work of Jesus, such as *Seeing and Savoring Jesus Christ* by John Piper; *Rejoicing in Christ* by Mike Reeves; *Gospel Deeps* by Jared Wilson; or *Finding the Love of Jesus from Genesis to Revelation* by Elyse Fitzpatrick.

EVERYONE LOVES THE FIRSTBORN

"He is the image of the invisible God, the firstborn of all creation. 16 For by him all things were created, in heaven and on earth, visible and invisible, whether thrones or dominions or rulers or authorities—all things were created through him and for him. 17 And he is before all things . . ." (Colossians 1:15–17a).

In every culture and generation, you can imagine people sitting underneath the vast starry night, dazzling and yet daunting. Gazing up, aware we are but the tiniest speck of dust on an unimaginably expansive universe we ask, "Where did all of this come from? And why is it here? Is there something, someone beyond the night's sky?"

It's no surprise that people everywhere are pulled into transcendence and arrive at the same thoughts. Creation prompts us to ask who made this majestic place. We're manufactured with a built-in longing to know that answer.

> Back, back, back and we peer into endless ages, yet there never was nothing. Someone has the honor of being there first and always. He never became or developed. He simply was. To whom belongs this singular, absolute glory? The answer is Christ, the person whom the world knows as Jesus of Nazareth.32

These verses proclaim Jesus is not only the Lord of the church but He's the Lord of creation. He made it. He rules it. He sustains it. He cares for it. It exists for Him and it all points to His glory.

---

32 John Piper, *Seeing and Savoring Jesus Christ* (Wheaton: Crossway, 2004), 21– 22.

Allow the force of these phrases in Colossians 1:15–17 to stretch your mind and stir your hearts for Jesus. Find rest and strength in the knowledge of who Jesus is and knowing He's at work for you.

Firstborn of all creation

The concept of the firstborn is a loaded theological word. In the Bible, it often doesn't mean the first to be born in time, and in Colossians it clearly cannot mean the first created being.[33] The passage itself clarifies Jesus is not a created being and a notch below God. He is the one who creates *all* things because He is God. "For by him all things were created…And he is before all things, and in him all things hold together" (1:16–17).

Further into the letter Paul again speaks without hesitation or qualification to Jesus being fully and truly God. "For in him all the fullness of God was pleased to dwell" (1:19; cf. 2:9). Paul never doubts the divinity of Jesus, nor does he demote Him to a junior varsity level of God. What then does Paul mean by calling Him the firstborn, both here in verse 15 and later in verses 18?

This rich term of firstborn often means first in rank, authority, and honor. God called Israel His firstborn because of their favored status (Exodus 4:22). The Psalms pick up this language for the firstborn as the Messiah over all. "And I will make him the firstborn, the highest of the kings of the earth" (Psalm 89:27).

The author of Hebrews follows suit by connecting the firstborn (Hebrews 1:6) with the maker (1:10). The one who created *all* at the beginning and now rules *all* is the exalted Messiah (1:1–14). "So when Paul called Christ the

---

[33] See theological appendix "Jesus: Created or Creator" for a more in–depth explanation of "firstborn of all creation" and supporting scriptural evidence for the divinity of Jesus.

'firstborn of all creation,' he meant that highest honor belongs to him. Christ is completely supreme in creation!"[34]

Paul takes this powerful theology of Jesus and shocks the hearts of the Colossians back to life. He reminds them they don't just follow the highest spiritual hero or the greatest teacher. They follow the King of Creation. Their Messiah is the Maker. Jesus is above all because He was before all.

Creator of all things

Everything in existence—everything—shares one grand and glorious creator: Jesus. The buck stops with Jesus and there's no one to pull rank on the one who existed before all things (1:17), the one who created all things (1:16), and the one who sustains His handiwork (1:17).

Just in case we're unclear about what might fall under the umbrella of "all things" Paul says, "For by him all things were created, in heaven and on earth, visible and invisible, whether thrones or dominions or rulers or authorities" (1:16).

The things we can't even see, whether life-threatening diseases or spiritual beings, are no match for the Creator. Whatever might cause us to fear is under the mighty hand of God. If Christ is the maker and ruler of all things, then nothing is outside of His control. We have hope that He can accomplish His plans even through natural disasters, unjust rulers, physical diseases, and anything else that fits in the categories of visible and invisible.

This also means that the astounding creation surrounding us is a pale shadow compared to its maker. The magnanimity, beauty, and breadth of creation should be a daily reminder of how big God is and that He's more than capable of handling the mess in our life.

---

[34] R. Kent Hughes, *Philippians, Colossians, and Philemon* (Wheaton: Crossway, 2013), 231.

This same God looks on us with love, concern, and compassion. Jesus is transcendent over everything and yet present with us. He is above us and yet with us. Amazingly, Christians not only get to know *about* the God who made everything but He draws near to us. We can know Him and be known by Him. Our understanding of Jesus is supported by the unshakeable ballasts of His transcendent glory and His nearness as our Redeemer. He is simultaneously far beyond us and intimately close to us.

What are you going through today that's too big for the Creator and Sustainer of all things to handle? What are you trying to control and fix that needs handed over to Jesus? When we shrink our views of Jesus, our problems look even larger. But if Jesus is before all and above all, then you can trust Him with it all.

Not only that, but if God designed the world around us then it should point us back to Him. What did you (or will you) see, smell, hear, taste, or touch today that reminds you God is a creative, joy-giving, generous God who delights in His handiwork? What blessings and provision do you receive from Him that can lead you to give thanks? How are His attributes and activity displayed in the visible and invisible world we inhabit? What good gifts in this world can help you better love and worship the one who designed and gave them?

If Jesus rules, reigns over, and outranks anything in the universe, then just imagine His power and glory. The bigness or beauty or breath-taking characteristics of creation give just an inkling to the wonder and worth of its Creator.

Applying Colossians

Questions
1) What is the relationship between all things coming from Jesus (source) and all things being for Jesus (goal)?
2) How does Jesus's authority, rank, and power over all things help you face the circumstances of today and this week?
3) How does a big view of Jesus help us trust and lean on Him?
4) What in creation causes wonder in you? How can you delight in and worship Jesus who designed and made all things?

Next Steps
- Observe the bigness of creation today. Take a few minutes outdoors, or capitalize on your drive home by opening your eyes to see God's glory in creation.
- Listen to or read "All Creatures of our God and King" or "Fairest Lord Jesus."
- Write out one thing that prompts worship to Jesus because of His transcendence over all, and one thing prompting worship because of His humility in drawing near.

For Further Study
- **Christ above all**: Hebrews 1:4–14; 2:8; Romans 11:33–36; Colossians 1:13, 16, 18; 2:10, 15; 3:1.
- **God cares for us**: Psalms 8:3–9; 65:9; 103:13–19; 144:3–4; Hebrews 2:6–8.

KEEP IT TOGETHER!

"And he is before all things, and in him all things hold together" (Colossians 1:17).

The opposite of all things holding together is all things falling apart. Simple enough, right? We need verses like Colossians 1:17 because there will be days and seasons where it feels like everything is crumbling. Amid pain or hard circumstances, our life collapses before us. With weary minds, tired bodies, worn-out spirits, and emotions that feel like they've been tumbling in the dryer for way too long, nothing makes sense. In the furnace of these trials, answers escape us. All we know is, *this feels so hard.*[35]

We're always aware of the potential for life to bring a tidal wave at us, but that awareness doesn't prevent the wave's force from taking us under. After exhausting our energy to get above the water, another wave smacks us and the disorientation sets in as we scramble to collect ourselves.

Hardships, pain, and trials leave us staggering with the same sentiments. How did this happen? What should I do? Will this ever get better? Why can't I catch a break? Why isn't God stopping this? The questions never stop but life goes on.

Who Over Why

In times like this we may ask *the why question*, but in reality, our hearts really long for an answer to *the who question*. What matters most when things in our world appear to fall apart is that God would stay with us. Above all, we crave His nearness.

---

[35] One way we respond is lament. For an excellent introduction to lament, see *Dark Clouds, Deep Mercy* by Mark Vroegop. For stories of believers finding hope during trials, see *Storm Clouds of Blessing* by Janice M. Cappucci.

For Christians who've walked through the valleys they know the lowest low can be survived if God is near. But, if God is absent (or seems absent), there is no getting through. Puritan Richard Sibbes understood this truth well. "If we cannot rejoice in the world, yet we may rejoice in the Lord. His presence makes any condition comfortable."[36]

There's nothing more comforting than to know: "When you pass through the waters, I will be with you; and through the rivers, they shall not overwhelm you" (Isaiah 43:2). Just two chapters before this, God comforts His people with these words: "Fear not, for I am with you; be not dismayed, for I am your God; I will strengthen you, I will help you, I will uphold you with my righteous right hand" (Isaiah 41:10).

If you're crawling through a valley right now, read those verses again, slowly. He is with you. He's with you in the valley or the darkness or the raging waters. He's with you when you don't see or sense it.

In suffering and pain, most of us don't need all our questions answered. We need the precious reminder God is with us and won't leave us.

Too often when we go through pain or when those close to us are suffering we only pray for them to get past the suffering. Our gut reaction is to plead "get me out." That might be a good prayer—and it's understandable—but don't miss the chance to experience the nearness of God as He draws near to the weak. Don't just help people get through life's struggles. Help them see God as a very-present help in the middle of those struggles.

When the news you've dreaded hearing comes or the doctors still don't have an answer, fall into the arms of God. When you're disappointed with how life has turned out or when your marriage is shaky, draw near to God and He will draw near to you. When your prayers go unanswered and you're

---

[36] Richard Sibbes, *The Bruised Reed* (Carlisle: Banner of Truth, reprinted 2008), 9.

tempted to stop talking to God, keep trusting and holding on to Him. When you lose a job or when a person you love is ripped from you, don't turn away from the One who holds all things together but turn to Him. He is with you and He is for you, even when it seems like He's against you.

Faith Over Feelings

We also need perspective beyond our limited vantage point. We *feel* like everything around us is falling apart. It *appears* like someone must not have been at the helm. But, feelings and appearance, though real, are not always true and are never ultimate. God is still in control.

The Bible reminds us that God providentially cares for and sovereignly[37] orchestrates our life. There is no moment where control escapes Him. At no point does He walk away from His throne. Jesus holds all things together (1:17).

Plant that theological flag firmly into your heart now so when life does fall apart, Christ's good and wise sovereignty is an established fact and not a question. Lean into it and learn it in small trials so when trust is stretched in bigger trials, it might bend but not break. Things around us are falling apart, but even in this, Jesus is holding all things together.

Our Powerful King

We've considered how this section points to Jesus as King. In verse 15, Paul says Jesus is the image of God. He is the rightful heir to His father's throne and he rules in line with the will of His father. In verse 16, Paul emphasizes

---

[37] Providence refers to God's governance of His people and all that happens in our world. The guiding force in our universe isn't fate, luck, or an impersonal force but the good, absolutely wise, and intimately relational God. Sovereignty refers to God's absolute *authority* over all things and His *ability* to control all things. We might differentiate Sovereignty as God's right to rule all and Providence as God's actual exercise of that right.

the unrivaled authority and rank of the king. Here in verse 17, he identifies Jesus as the king who rules, sustains, and ensures the well-being of all in His kingdom. He cares for and oversees everything happening in His domain.

Jesus not only creates, but He sustains what He creates. "[Jesus] upholds the universe by the word of his power." (Hebrews 1:3) He completes what He begins. He is faithful to finish anything He starts.

He doesn't give up on people, projects, or plans and move to something else. He never drops the ball. That's not only true in creation, but it's true for you. Even when life feels like it's falling apart, Jesus holds everything together.

His *power* declares nothing keeps Him from accomplishing His plans.

His *wisdom* signifies that He knows how to use his power to best order all things for our good and His glory.

His *goodness* and *love* assure us that everything that comes from His hand springs from the fountainhead of goodness.

When life unravels, we should find comfort knowing Jesus is holding all things together in his power, wisdom, goodness, and love.

> Ye fearful saints, fresh courage take; The clouds ye so much
> dread
> Are big with mercy and shall break, In blessings on your head.
> Judge not the Lord by feeble sense, But trust Him for His
> grace;
> Behind a frowning providence, He hides a smiling face.[38]

---

[38] William Cowper, "God Moves in a Mysterious Way" (No. 603) in *Hymns for the Family of God* (Franklin: Brentwood– Benson Music Publishing, 1976).

Applying Colossians

Questions
1) Is there something in your world right now that feels like it's falling apart? How does this verse help you live by God's Word and not your senses and feelings?
2) What are the things you need to know in the midst of suffering and pain?
3) How does growing in our theology of God's sovereignty, goodness, wisdom, and grace before going through the suffering help us endure?

Next Steps
- As you read the Bible this week take note of any mentions of God's Sovereignty or His good purposes in suffering.
- Send an encouraging letter, email, text, or call a friend in the midst of suffering. Just be there to listen, to pray for them, and to remind them that God is still with them.
- Read or listen to the songs "God Moves in a Mysterious Way," "Be Near," or "It is Well."

For Further Study
- **God's Sovereignty in suffering**: Genesis 50:20; Matthew 10:29; Romans 8:28.
- Read a book on suffering such as *Walking with God through Pain and Suffering* by Tim Keller, *When God Weeps* by Joni Eareckson Tada. Or, read a fiction novel like *The Horse and His Boy* by C.S. Lewis to learn about God's providence in the form of a story.
- Learn to lament by reading *Dark Clouds, Deep Mercy* by Mark Vroegop.

MATURITY: A TOP-DOWN APPROACH

"And he is the head of the body, the church" (Colossians 1:18).

An organization reflects the person at the top. The leader provides vision, direction, and decision-making. The rise or fall of the business depends on the company's head. Some examples where this has worked well might be the meteoric rise of Apple under Steve Jobs or Chick-fil-A under Truett Cathy.

The same relationship applies to the church and its leader. This is great news for the church since Jesus, the "Head" of the body, is the authority over creation (1:15), worldly rulers (1:16), and evil spiritual forces (1:16).

The first half of verse 18 conveys at least three ideas related to Christ's headship over the church: his authority, his oneness and care for the body, and the strength for the body found in its head. Jesus is over this church, with his church, and for his church.

Authority

This verse continues the emphasis begun in verse 15: the sole sufficiency and supremacy of Jesus above all things. Verse 18 transitions from Christ's rule over the world to his rule over his people: creation to new creation.

The church is the universal people of God and the community that will be resurrected from the dead (1:18b). In the Bible, "head" signifies sole authority. There should be no doubt about who the church belongs to (Jesus). It does not belong to a pope, synod, bishops, pastor(s), staff, or elders. The church as a whole, and each gospel-believing church, belongs to Jesus.

How does Christ's position as head of the church affect the way we think and feel about Jesus? Or, to ask it differently, why would Paul want the Colossians to know Jesus is the head of the church?

We entrust ourselves to the leadership of one clothed in the fullness of wisdom, power, and love. We submit ourselves to the one in authority, and submitting is much easier when we know He's full of grace and looking out for our good. He is no tyrannical dictator to be feared but a King to be loved.

The false teaching in Colossae was "not according to Christ" (2:8) and its proponents were "not holding fast to the Head" (2:18). Paul argues that there's no other authority to be put on par with Him. Anything undermining the supremacy and sufficiency of Jesus attacks the very head of the body.

No spiritual leaders from other religions, no other leaders within Christendom, no other figure in the Bible is co-leader of the church. Jesus alone is Head of his church. He's the authority.

Oneness

The second thing taught in this verse is the oneness between Jesus and his church. The metaphor of "head" and "body" signifies unity. Jesus not only has authority *over* the church but He's one *with* the church.

There seems to be a reciprocal relationship here. His health is our health and our hurt is his hurt. The head is not indifferent to a wound to the foot or to the stomach. The head registers the pain in the body. This is staggering. Think about the empathy, love, compassion, and concern Jesus feels and expresses toward us as his people.

To look at just one example, Acts 7–9 retells the honest but horrible picture of Paul (Saul) murdering Christians and ravaging the church. When Paul is stopped in his tracks on the way to Damascus, Jesus reveals Himself and accuses Paul of persecuting Him. He doesn't say you've persecuted my people—which is true—but He says you (Paul) have persecuted *me*.

This is mind-blowing in the best of ways. Jesus is so united to and one with his body that their pain in persecution is his pain. This empathy isn't simply that of an onlooker, as if Jesus sees it from afar and has compassion toward us. It's the empathy of oneness. Jesus feels the persecutions, suffering, sorrows, and pains of the church. He isn't just watching; he feels the weight of what's crushing you. He's with you and you are not alone. What a unity of love between the head and the body, Christ and his people.

Strength

We're also given great hope because Jesus is the Head of the church. It gives hope because our strength, our victory, our place, and our future are wrapped up in Jesus. He is our source of power when we are weak (Colossians 1:11). He is our victory when we cannot defeat the enemies on our own. We have in Jesus the strength we lack in ourselves.

Though we often feel like dead weight, Jesus picks us up, tosses us onto his shoulders, and carries us forward. This is what it means for Him to be the Head of the church.

At an individual or church level, any hope of strength and success isn't on us but it rests on Him. A little piece of advice: let it stay there. Don't try to take it on yourself, and in doing so, take his place. Be content to let Jesus lead and you follow. Let Him be the head; you be the body.

For the Colossians, this meant they didn't have to fear any evil spiritual-forces because Jesus had authority over them (1:16). It means the resurrection of Jesus was the first-fruits of the resurrection of Christians (1:18).

Paul gets into this in 3:1–4, but since Jesus is now our Head in heaven, it changes our citizenship and behavior in this life. It gives hope because during life's struggles and woes we have an Ascended High-Priest interceding for and loving on His people.

Just as the high priest in Israel (Exodus 28) carried the names of the tribes on his breastplate, so now Jesus carries our names on His heart. Our union and oneness with Jesus includes Him bringing us into the presence of the Father (Hebrews 4:14–16). Matthew Henry gave us great encouragement when he wrote:

> How near should Christ's name be to our hearts, since he is pleased to lay our names so near his! and what a comfort it is to us, in all our addresses to God, that the great high priest of our profession has the names of all his [people] upon his breast before the Lord *for a memorial*, presenting them to God.... Let not any good Christians fear that God has forgotten them, nor question his being mindful of them upon all occasions, when they are not only engraven upon the *palms of his hands* (Isa. 49:16), but engraven upon the heart of the great intercessor.[39]

Jesus persevered in victory and now stands for us in heaven as the Sovereign Ruler of all and the Redeemer of his people. Our hope is not in ourselves or better circumstances in this world. Our power is not from within or from something around us. Our hope and power are in Jesus. "Jesus, our head, is already in heaven; and if the head be above water, the body cannot drown."[40]

Jesus reigns so we can rest.

---

[39] Matthew Henry, *Matthew Henry's commentary on the whole Bible: complete and unabridged in one volume* (Peabody: Hendrickson, 1994), 134.

[40] John Flavel, *The Fountain of Life* from *The Works of John Flavel*, 6 vols. (Carlisle: Banner of Truth Trust, reprinted 1968), 176.

Applying Colossians

Questions

1) Which one of the three focuses mentioned is most applicable to you today? Why?
2) How does the passage from Acts and thinking about Jesus's oneness with us change your thoughts about and affections for Him?
3) Are there any ways you usurp Jesus's authority by trying to take control or by asking Him to keep out?
4) If Jesus is the Head ruling his body, what role does the Word (the Bible) play?

Next Steps

- Spend time thinking through how Jesus's authority over the church, unity with the church, and hope given for the church helps the hard situation you're in today.
- Meditate today on the Supremacy of Jesus and how that helps in suffering and trials.
- Work on memorizing Colossians 1:15–20 this week.

For Further Study

- **Church as the body metaphor**: Romans 12:4–8; 1 Corinthians 12:12–31; Ephesians 1:23; 4:12–16; Colossians 2:19.
- **Jesus as the Head**: Colossians 1:18; 2:10, 19; Ephesians 1:22; 4:15; 1 Corinthians 11:3.
- **Jesus suffering *with* us**: Romans 8:17; Acts 9:4; 2 Corinthians 1:5; Philippians 3:10; 1 Peter 4:13.

THE GRATEFUL DEAD

"And he is the head of the body, the church. He is the beginning, the firstborn from the dead, that in everything he might be preeminent" (Colossians 1:18).

The phrase "firstborn from the dead" sounds a little dark; almost like it should be a zombie movie title. The current influx of zombie and vampire movies and the steady drop in church attendance shows us what our culture finds more interesting. And yet, the Bible tells us a story with even more drama. The sci-fi imagination of the walking dead isn't as exciting as God becoming a man, being put to death by the men and women he came for, and then outdoing death as he's resurrected to an indestructible and unending life. And all this to rescue the living dead (spiritually) who killed Him.

The story is so captivating that comics, movies, and novels often borrow from the gospel. Think about how many storylines move from humanity getting itself in a desperate predicament to some superhero coming from beyond to rescue us, often at the cost of their life. Sound familiar? That's because the story of Jesus becoming one of us, dying to save us, rising to conquer death's power, and winning the victory over evil is the greatest of stories. And while many stories are made up in the minds of men, this Story began in the mind of God and was lived out in human history. Men recorded it and retold it so it would be passed down from generation to generation and from nation to nation.

Creation to New Creation

We observed in 1:15 that the theological metaphor "firstborn of all creation" signified the highest ranking and greatest among a group. Paul sets up a wordplay by mentioning "firstborn of all *creation*" and "firstborn from the *dead*."

Jesus is the head over all creation He made and He's also head over the new creation He redeemed. Paul shifts the focus from creation (1:15–17) to the church in verse 18. Not only is He the highest authority over both realms but both point back to His glory. "All things were created through him and *for him*" (1:16). "He is the beginning, the firstborn from the dead, that in everything *he might be preeminent*" (1:18).

Further support for this idea comes from "he is the beginning." By "beginning" in verse 18, it doesn't refer to the beginning in terms of time but as the *source* of the church.[41] The new creation (the church) finds its origins in Jesus just as creation finds its origin in Him (1:15–17). "The redemption achieved in Christ is indeed the new Genesis: the church really is the new humanity (3:10–11)."[42]

The one who spoke creation into existence by his breath births the church into being by his blood.

With Christ's resurrection, the new creation dawns. Because I'm united with Jesus and my future follows Him, *His* resurrection assures *my* resurrection. "The resurrection of Christ initiates this end-time resurrection; his resurrection guarantees and, indeed, stimulates the resurrection of all who follow (1 Corinthians 15:20; cf. Acts 26:23; Matthew 27:52–53). In this sense, he is not only the first one to experience resurrection; he is the 'founder' of the new order of resurrection."[43] Jesus is the firstborn from the dead and this gives us the rock-solid hope of a future resurrection from the dead.

At the Fall (Genesis 3), God's good creation was corrupted in Adam and the process of de-creation began. Chaos, distortion, and ruin wrapped their

---

[41] Pao provides several verses in the Septuagint—Greek translation of the Old Testament—where it refers to origins (Genesis 1:1) or head of a group (Genesis 40:20; Exodus 6:25). David Pao, *Colossians & Philemon* (Grand Rapids: Zondervan, 2012), 100.

[42] N.T. Wright, *Colossians & Philemon* (Grand Rapids: Eerdmans, 1986), 69.

[43] Douglas Moo, *The Letters to the Colossians and to Philemon* (Grand Rapids: Eerdmans, 2008), 129.

cold fingers around the universe, including human beings. But through Jesus's resurrection we see the reversal of that process beginning (regeneration[44] and sanctification) and the outcome of that process guaranteed (glorification).

It is the resurrection and ascension of Jesus that brought about the in-breaking of the new creation. In his resurrection, Jesus kicked open and stepped through the doors of the new creation. As those united to Him, we participate in this new creation kingdom now in part and await its full consummation on a new earth. Jesus is the trail-blazer who not only clears a path through death and into resurrection but He puts us on His back and carries us there.

Peace in Pain

Christians can have peace amid pain, suffering, disappointment, and trials, because we know what awaits us. We can endure temporary hardships because God has promised an eternity where things will finally be as they should. We set our eyes down the road and the prize keeps us going.

One day we will have uninterrupted peace and joy upon joy without a second of letdowns. One day we will have new, properly working bodies. Tears will be a thing of the past. One day our hearts will finally love righteousness and we'll be mesmerized by the unveiled glory of God as Jesus dwells with us.

All of that is ours now by right because of Jesus, although we still await possession of it. We've been given the title and we're just awaiting what's ours to be delivered to our doorsteps.

The new creation isn't entirely postponed until the future. Even today, it's breaking into our lives. New levels of peace, joy, rest, and wholeness through

---

[44] Regeneration: the new spiritual life given to believers at conversion as the Holy Spirit makes dead sinners into living, reborn people.

Christ whet our spiritual taste-buds. One day I will be resurrected but today I experience a piece of that when God gives new life to me (John 3:3).

As those who have risen with Christ even now (Colossians 2:12; Romans 6:1–14) we can fight against sin with the power of the resurrected King. Although we do it dimly, believers reflect the new creation they are in Christ (2 Corinthians 5:17). We hold out to the world a vision of the way life was meant to be and the way it one day will be again.

Jesus is the hope and the source of the church for new life today and an eternal life that will be here in no time. He reigns over both creation and the church. He changes our past, redefines our present, and gives us a future beyond our best dreams and deepest longings. This is life-changing truth for your present and eternity-shaping truth for your future.

Applying Colossians

Questions
1) How do Creation and Redemption point to the supremacy of Jesus?
2) How might we reflect Christ's new creation kingdom in our lives?
3) What are areas that Christ's return and consummation of all things will restore and make right again in our world and in our own lives?

Next Steps
- Jot down something you're sacrificing now (vacation, money, time, acceptance, health). Write next to it how God will more than reward you in the future kingdom.

For Further Study
- **Resurrection**: 1 Corinthians 15:20–28, 42–49; Ephesians 1:20–21; Acts 3:15; 4:10; 13:30–34; Romans 6:1–4.
- **Jesus is the firstborn from the dead**: Acts 26:23; 1 Corinthians 15:20–26, 42–49; Revelation 1:5.

RECLAIMING WHAT WAS LOST

"For in him all the fullness of God was pleased to dwell, and through him to reconcile to himself all things, whether on earth or in heaven, making peace by the blood of his cross" (Colossians 1:19–20).

Every year, as the weather warms I look forward to growing a vegetable garden. Fresh vegetables and fruits grown in a garden taste almost completely different—in a good way—from what you purchase in a store. A home-grown tomato and a store-bought tomato couldn't be further apart.

I also find gardening helpful for illustrating little lessons in life. A sprouted seedling's desperate pursuit of the sun's light shows me how I should live. Another lesson might be that even though sometimes growth is slow or stunted, there's still life in there and the plant is growing. Some days, when discouraged about my own spiritual walk, this little reminder gives me needed encouragement.

I also enjoy gardening because there's something relaxing and rewarding about seeing a garden I've tended move from an empty space of dirt to a thriving, healthy plot full of fresh vegetables. A visual sore spot becomes a vibrant source of food.

When I garden there's a great commitment to care for *my* garden. I invest the time to till up the ground, plant seeds, water and weed, fight off bugs, watch it blossom, and then wait as the red tomato gets to just the right size and freshness. If weeds overtake it, I work even harder to ensure its health. If birds or bunnies try to destroy it, I find some way of scaring them off or keeping them out. I care for the garden because it's mine.

Because creation comes from Jesus's creative mind and is his handiwork, He doesn't give up on it. All of creation—spiritual and physical—is Christ's, and He faithfully pursues its restoration. Adam plunged mankind and the universe into the brokenness of sin. Jesus (the second Adam) rescues it out of chaos, reconciles it back to God, and restores it in peace to its design.

Lord of All

The scope of what Christ redeemed matches the scope of what He created. "*All things* were created through him and for him" (1:16) and He reconciles "to himself *all things*" (1:20). We tend to think of Christ's work primarily, if not solely, as it relates to the salvation of human beings. That's understandable because it's the focus of Christ's death in the Bible. But, there's also a bigger, overarching story involving the whole universe. The death of Jesus not only pays for our sin but it brings God's creation back into order and alignment with Him.

Paul has made it clear in 1:15–18 that Jesus is Lord over creation and the church (new creation). He's entitled to this Lordship because both come from Him and because both have been reconciled by Him. "Through the work of Christ on the cross God has brought his entire rebellious creation back under the rule of his sovereign power. Of course, this 'peace' is not yet fully established. The 'already/not yet' pattern of New Testament eschatology must be applied to Colossians 1:20."[45]

This not only shows us how the world, which was lost, can be made new again, but it also shows us the heart of a relentless God. God does not give up on what He starts. His work is His, from its beginning until completion.

God rescues the hopelessly lost, restores the broken and disregarded, and brings peace out of chaos. For the Christian who sees themselves rightly, this should provide great hope. Our sin, our mess, the junk drawer of our lives, the chaos we live in, our hurts, and our own repetitive failings are not intimidating or too daunting for God.

---

[45] Pao, *Colossians*, 136–37.

He pursues what's lost and carries to completion what He begins. If He can bring reconciliation to the fallen universe, He can restore me or that person in my life who seems completely lost. My salvation depends not on my strength but on God's unwavering commitment to complete the work He began (Philippians 1:6).

Jesus keeps and cares for what is his (John 6:37). He finishes what He starts.

Made to be Mirrors

Another application from this is seen in Paul's emphasis that we're being remade and restored into the image of God (3:10). We reflect Him to the world around us as his image-bearers and we represent his Lordship by caring for that same world.

This is at once an amazing privilege and an intimidating responsibility. Christians reflect God by being peacemakers and reconcilers. We mirror God by not giving up on hopeless situations, disorderly environments, and messy people. We say something true about our God by finishing what we start and following through with our commitments. We fulfill our role as image-bearers by caring for our work, the things we create, what we cultivate, the earth we inhabit, and our possessions.

Nothing in this life is therefore meaningless. Everything is under the Lordship of Jesus and all we do *reflects* Christ and is *for* Christ. We are stewards in every area of life.

Caretakers of Creation

This also forces us to consider implications of Christ's redemption extending to all of creation. If Genesis 1 doesn't do it, this should convince us of creation's value.[46] There is no physical versus spiritual dichotomy. God cares about people but He also cares about all creation.

This affects our attitude towards creation today and how we think of Christ's return to complete redemption. When Jesus returns, He will restore the physical earth for us. "God's great future purpose was not to rescue people out of the world, but to rescue the world itself, people included, from its present state of corruption and decay."[47]

This encourages us to enjoy the physical creation and to see it as good. We can enjoy Jesus through creation since it is from Him, belongs to Him, and points to His glory. In 2:16–23, Paul argues against an ascetic view of life that sees the physical world as dangerous or unimportant. He offers in its place a way of life where all creation and whatever we do might be enjoyed through and in Jesus.

Colossians helps us see that Christ's Lordship and his glory are greater than we ever imagined. When Isaac Watts wrote the great hymn "Joy to the World", he included how redemption lets "heaven and nature sing." "No more let sins and sorrows grow, nor thorns infest the ground; He comes to make His blessings flow Far as the curse is found."[48]

Which of these do you need to remember today? Is it the promise that our relentless God finishes the work He starts? Is it that nothing is too far out of His reach to be reconciled back to Him? Is it that creation includes God's good gifts to be both enjoyed and cared for? Or is it that we who are in Christ

---

[46] See *Creation Care* by Douglas Moo and Jonathan Moo for a helpful treatment on creation's value, our role as image- bearers placed within creation to care for and keep it, and creation's destination or resurrection when Christ returns. See also *Remember Creation* by Scott Hoezee; *Consider the Lilies* by T.M. Moore; *The Bible and Ecology* by Richard Bauckham.

[47] N.T. Wright, *How God Became King* (New York: Harper Collins, 2011), 45.

[48] Isaac Watts, "Joy to the World!" (No. 171) in *Hymns for the Family of God* (Franklin: Brentwood- Benson Music Publishing, 1976).

get the chance to image our creative, caring, pursuing, reconciling, and patient God?

God reclaims, pursues, keeps, and cares for what is His, even when it's lost, messy, or seemingly ruined. This gives us hope and it also helps us know how to live. We see who God is to the world and we mirror Him in the world.

Applying Colossians

Questions
1) How can you reflect the character and actions of God as displayed in verse 20 (peacemaker, restorer, finisher, pursuer, etc.)?
2) Are there any people or situations you've given up on you need to keep asking God to work in?
3) What are ways you can better enjoy creation or steward creation in light of God's design of it and plans to restore it?

Next Steps
- Think through some people or situations you've given up on as hopeless. Commit to praying again and ask God to help you be a peacemaker and restorer.
- Think about how to view creation and the physical in light of Genesis 1 and Colossians 1.

For Further Study
- **Cosmic scope of redemption**: Colossians 2:14–15; Romans 8:19–22; 2 Peter 3:13; Revelation 21–22.
- Read *Things of the Earth* by Joe Rigney; *Enjoy* by Trillia Newbell; or *Eyes Wide Open* by Steve DeWitt.

BRINGING IT HOME (1:21–29)

The high and lofty theology of Jesus in 1:15–20 is now brought home to the level of the local church and the individual believer. Paul tells us this very same Jesus who is Lord over creation and the church is also Lord over us.

In verses 21–23 Paul reminds them of their story. They were once spiritually dead and estranged from God, but because of Christ's redemptive work, they're alive and reconciled to Him. Salvation changes us now but it also gives us the hope one day we can stand before God holy, blameless, and above reproach because Jesus cleansed every stain of sin. Because of this, Paul admonishes us to continue in the faith and not to shift to anything else.

On the heels of looking at Jesus's supremacy and sufficiency over creation (1:15–17), over the church (1:18–20), and over the Christian (1:21–23), Paul naturally jumps to ministry within the church. If Christ is Lord over the church, then as his apostle (1:1), Paul's purpose is to point people to Jesus. This not only pictures Paul's ministry, but it exemplifies what it looks like for all of us to live with a mission of seeing others come to know Christ and mature in Him. We were made to make much of Jesus.

Paul remains focused on Christ's glory. He shocks us with the fact that because of our union with Christ, Jesus suffers when the church suffers (1:24). As the Word is made known we see God's plan for the nations fully revealed, and that plan is for Jew and Gentile alike to be in relationship with God (1:25–27). Not only does this revelation tell us Christ defines the people of God, but Christ dwells within his people (1:27). One effect is our labors of love is done in his power and not our own (1:29).

Setting our hearts on Jesus isn't something we do only on Sundays; it's what we do every day. The glory of Jesus leads to growth in our lives and good to those around us as we proclaim and image Him.

I'M NOT WHO I WAS

"And you, who once were alienated and hostile in mind, doing evil deeds, he has now reconciled in his body of flesh by his death" (Colossians 1:21–22).

Every Christian has a story of being lost and found, of newness and change.

For a mini-version of my own, I grew up in church and knew all the right things about the Bible. With the speed of a Western gunslinger I could flip open to the right chapter and verse. I was religious and involved in all the right stuff. It wasn't until high school that God opened my eyes to see I had never turned from relying upon my outward religious performances. Confessing and repenting of my sin, I completely tied my life to Jesus. Prior knowledge of Jesus became active trust in Jesus.

John Newton puts to song the amazing grace story that believers share: "I once was lost but now am found; was blind but now I see."[49]

Paul applies the theology of who Jesus is (1:15–20) in the life of the believer (1:21–23). Christ's story at some point has to become part of our story. Who I was apart from Christ is replaced by who I now am in Christ.

The Bad News

The Bible honestly describes the nature of fallen man. This is hard for modern Americans to hear. We think highly of ourselves. This is especially true today in the age where we can't say anything that might hurt someone's feelings. We live under the delusion we're basically good people, or at least we're not as bad as others, and because of that God must be pretty happy with us.

---

[49] John Newton, "Amazing Grace! How Sweet the Sound," (No. 107) in *Hymns for the Family of God* (Franklin: Brentwood-Benson Music Publishing, 1976).

But how does the Bible describe us apart from Christ? We are "alienated and hostile in mind, doing evil deeds" (Colossians 1:21). We are "by nature children of wrath" (Ephesians 2:1–3). Think of how many biblical stories show the way we run after the wrong things and do what's right in our eyes.

As much as we might not like to hear this about ourselves we need to hear it. A doctor who holds back the harsh reality of the diagnosis to spare our feelings wouldn't be good or caring. The Bible tells us how bad we really are and the terrible predicament we're in.

Because of our sin we stand condemned before a perfectly holy God. We're in the wrong lane and oncoming judgment is racing towards us at the speed of light. We're estranged from God and from one another. Our lives are full of the bitter, rotten fruit of sin: broken relationships, emptiness, idolatry, pride, rejoicing in unrighteousness, and death. We're not only told this from the outside (the Bible) but we sense it within through the feeling of shame for wrongdoing or feeling alone and alienated in the midst of a crowded world.

The Good News

That's the bad news. The good news is God intervened for us by doing what we could never do: living a perfectly righteous life and atoning for our sins. The bleak peril we live in has a solution. God became man in the person of Jesus so He might be a mediator between the two. His perfect and sinless life made Him a fitting sacrifice.

He dies on the cross not for his sins but for ours. "In whom we have redemption, the forgiveness of sins" (1:14). He is able to redeem us out of prison because He's paid our debt in full. "God has made [us] alive together with him, having forgiven us all our trespasses by canceling the record of debt that stood against us with its legal demands. This he set aside, nailing it to the cross" (2:13–14).

The gospel holds out to us a God-accomplished solution through Jesus. The one who deserved life takes our sin and death. We who deserved death receive his righteousness and eternal life (2 Corinthians 5:21; Romans 5:21).

This is the great and gracious exchange of the gospel. What was mine became his so what is his could become mine. We receive this not by works but as a gift when we trust in Jesus alone (Ephesians 2:8–9).

It's hard to believe this can be true because we know how sinful, guilty, and unlovely we are. But, when we see the glory and perfection of Jesus—as pictured in Colossians 1:15–20—we realize our sin is no match for his perfection. We anchor our salvation and life to the hope "there is more mercy in Christ than sin in us."[50]

It's astounding enough to think a holy God would offer mercy to rebellious sinners. It's even more amazing when we realize He is the one who seeks us out and pursues us back to Himself in the first place. And it's almost over-the-top when we factor in He does it to the extent of giving His Son for us. Jesus pays for our redemption with his own flesh ripped from his body and with blood that poured from his veins as He was tortured, crucified, and alienated. The Father momentarily turns His face away from Jesus so He might eternally turn His face toward us.

The "but God" moment makes all the difference as God wipes away our sin and removes our shame. Jesus extinguishes all guilt and leads us under the waterfall of grace. All of this overwhelming theology about Jesus (1:15–20) is the air of salvation we breathe in day after day.

Whatever our story used to be apart from Christ, this is our story now in Christ. I once was lost, but now am found.

---

[50] Sibbes, *The Bruised Reed*, 13.

God takes "who we once were" (1:21) and rewrites our story as He remakes us into who we "now" are (1:22) in Christ. This new story and new identity free us from the failures of our past and the worries of tomorrow. We're defined not by what we've done—good or bad—but by what Jesus did for us.

Stop replaying the tape in your head of what you should've done. Rehearsing the gospel daily is so important because we need a better memory of Jesus's perfect track record than of our failed track record. It's his righteousness we rest in, not ours.

We aren't yet who we hope to be, but by God's grace, we are not who we were.

Applying Colossians

Questions
1) What are some of the differences between your life and beliefs before Christ and what it looks like now in Christ?
2) Why do you think Paul and the Bible so clearly show us our sinful condition and our guilt before God? How is knowing who we are on our own helpful in finding joy in Christ?
3) What can you thank God for in your story?

Next Steps
- Read or sing through "Amazing Grace" by John Newton
- Write out your testimony of coming to faith in Jesus.

For Further Study
- **Before and after**: Romans 3:21; 6:22; 7:6; 1 Corinthians 6:9–11; 2 Corinthians 5:17–21; Ephesians 2:1–9; 1 Peter 2:10.
- **Grace not works**: Romans 3:21–26; Galatians 2:16–21; 3:10–29; Ephesians 2:8–9; Titus 3:3–7.

HERE COMES THE BRIDE

"And you, who once were alienated and hostile in mind, doing evil deeds, he has now reconciled in his body of flesh by his death, in order to present you holy and blameless and above reproach before him" (Colossians 1:21–22).

Two moments stand out from my wedding. The first is the climactic moment when the back doors opened and my beautiful bride made her way to me. I was stunned by her loveliness, by the brightness of the white dress, the fact that she would be mine, and the joy on her face as she walked to me. Those snapshots still stick in my mind.

The second moment was when I embarrassingly misspoke my vow to her, "You're my best friends" (plural). Obviously the first one is the better memory.

In Colossians 1:22, we're told about a bride (the church) who stands clothed in the whitest of white coverings. It's a ceremony so magnificent it will put the pomp and pageantry of any royal wedding to shame. The King of the world will join Himself to His beautiful bride forever. The words "and they lived happily ever after" will finally ring true.

Total Makeover: Wedding Edition

The gospel tells us Jesus forgives us and makes us holy, blameless, and above reproach. He's cleaned up his bride and made her beautiful. "Christ loved the church and gave himself up for her, that he might sanctify her, having cleansed her by the washing of water with the word, so that he might present the church to himself in splendor, without spot or wrinkle or any such thing that she might be holy and without blemish" (Ephesians 5:25–27). Jesus, the perfect sacrifice, can fully cleanse us down to the very core of our being (Hebrews 9:14; 10:22).

In his book *The Gospel*, Ray Ortlund reminds us we're not this kind of bride on our own.

> When men look for a bride, they often look for a beauty queen. But Christ chose the dirty one who needed his cleansing. The Son of God crossed the tracks to the wrong side of town, where we all live, to find his bride. We brought into the relationship our messy backgrounds, our ongoing problems, and our shame. But we can face all of that now because of what he brought into the relationship: cleansing enough for all our dirty guilt.[51]

We have nothing good to bring to the marriage, but Jesus has everything good and everything we need. He looks on us with love even when we're the messy, sinful, broken and dirty bride. He still graciously pursues us to Himself and takes the vows of the new covenant (Hebrews 8:8–12). In the love story we all long for, Jesus wants nothing from us; He only wants us.

If Jesus has cleansed us, declared us righteous (justified), and made us blameless, then Satan has no accusations against us. In God's court of law there's no evidence that stands against us. Our Savior paid for all our sin and wrongdoing.

Satan or anyone else can prosecute me with whatever accusations they can come up with but they have no legal case. They can scream, shout, and pound their fists on the table all day long but Jesus has completely paid for my convictions (Colossians 2:13–14) and made me free through his righteousness.

How God Sees Us

---

[51] Ray Ortlund, *The Gospel* (Wheaton: Crossway, 2014), 43– 44.

This should change how we view ourselves in God's eyes. See yourself as God sees you in Christ and how the Bible defines you. Don't live according to how you feel, what others think, or what the Enemy says about you. Live by objective truth God has said and not wishy-washy feelings from your deceptive heart.

Replace your accuser's lies with your Advocate's promises. Stop listening to yourself or your Enemy and listen to the voice of Jesus in the Word.

If Jesus says you're not guilty, believe it. If He says you are clean, know He has removed your shame. If He says you are mine and I love you, don't think otherwise. Feelings can be good but feelings mislead and prove unreliable. Your feelings are not ultimate or authoritative, so trust God's Word not the whims of your feelings.

We don't try to become something we're not or try to make God happy in the filthy rags of righteousness we cover ourselves with. We live out this holiness, but it is living out the Christ-bought, Spirit-worked righteousness in us.

Paul believes seeing who we are in Christ (identity) changes how we live (actions). Since we are made holy, live as those who are holy. Since we have been made a new person, don't live like your old self (Colossians 3:5–10). Since we are wedded to Jesus, don't go after other lovers.

His free and gracious love woos us to a life of faithfulness. Gratitude for His grace, not the weight of guilt, will propel us into living in a manner consistent with our identity.

One day the sin that still nags us will be eradicated. Our sinful hearts that run after other idols and lead us into spiritual adultery will be purified. No hint of corruption will remain.

This verse allows us to look into the future and know when we stand before God we will be found not guilty. We will be holy and blameless because Jesus made us so. No accusation will stand against us because Jesus has spoken a better word—his righteousness—over us.

> On that eternal wedding above, the bride will not need any makeup (Revelation 21:2). He will look into our eyes and say to us, 'My love, you are perfect,' and he will not be exaggerating… The real holiness Christ creates is *beautiful*. And the holiness he gives will redeem every dirty thing we have ever done to ourselves or suffered from others. We will be 'without spot or wrinkle or *any* such thing.' We will be perfect forever, because we will finally be with him and for him *only*. He will do this. He has promised.[52]

Applying Colossians

Questions
1) Do you see yourself as God sees you in Christ or as you look at yourself on your own (still sinful)? How do you preach the gospel to yourself so your identity is formed around truth?
2) What lies about your past (sins committed by you or against you) or present struggles are you believing? How can you listen to the Advocate and not the Accuser?
3) What are some of the implications of the church being Christ's bride? How might you view God more relationally because of this?
4) How does knowing Christ laid down his life to cleanse you motivate holiness?

Next Steps

---

[52] Ibid., 47.

- Make a list of any lies you're believing about yourself. Search the Bible for a corresponding promise or truth to cling to. Example: I still feel like God sees me as dirty but the Bible says He will not remember my sins (Hebrews 10:12).

- Commit to memory a gospel promises like Romans 8:1, 31; Philippians 3:8–9; Hebrews 10:22.

For Further Study

- **Christ makes us blameless**: Jude 24; Ephesians 1:4; 5:27; Hebrews 9:14; 10:10–14, 22.

- Read Hosea to see a story of how God pursues an unfaithful bride.

FINISH THE RACE!

"in order to present you holy and blameless and above reproach before him, if indeed you continue in the faith, stable and steadfast, *not shifting from the hope of the gospel that you heard*, which has been proclaimed in all creation under heaven, and of which I, Paul, became a minister" (Colossians 1:21–23).

Paul wrote Colossians in large part because of the false teaching "not according to Christ" (2:8) and that discouraged "hold[ing] fast to the Head" (2:19). Wrong views of Christ always diminish his glory and our faith. Douglas Moo comments on the connection between this bad doctrine spreading and Paul's warning to continue clinging to Christ alone in 1:23. "While it might seem at first sight, then, that the verse is a bit of an afterthought, it is, in fact, a very important indication of where the argument of the letter is going to go (see 2:6–23)."[53]

Paul cheers the church on to finish the race by continuing in their confession of Christ.

Hold Fast

The focus of the conditional "if" statement is to continue in "the faith", "implying that faith refers here not to the act of believing but to what is believed: Christian truth."[54] Throughout this letter, Paul warns them not to swerve from the gospel of Christ they've believed. The tone of the Greek in this text doesn't suggest doubting if they'll continue, but it assumes they will.

Despite the presence of some false teachers, Paul is confident they will not jump ship. He isn't suggesting salvation can be lost or we can fall away from

---

[53] Moo, *Colossians*, 143.
[54] Ibid., 145.

Christ. God keeps every one of his sons and daughters and finishes the good work in them He starts (Philippians 1:6; John 6:37). Every believer justified in Christ will be glorified (see Romans 8:29). The perseverance and glorification is so certain for the believer that Paul uses the past tense as if it's already happened.

Paul both lets them know they need to persevere and pushes them on to do so. It's not up to us in our own strength to make it but we're strengthened "with all power, according to his glorious might, for all endurance with patience and joy" (Colossians 1:11).

In this text, the foundation of assurance isn't my life or my growth but my confession of Jesus alone as Lord. The admonition should bring to repentance anyone drifting, but it's also the means God uses to keep our eyes on Christ.[55] Colossians 1:23 should scare anyone who's turned from Jesus but it should comfort anyone trusting in Him. Not because we feel up to the task or we think we're nailing it but because we trust in the sufficiency of Jesus's work for us. We rest in the promises of God to do what He said (keep us).

Live by Promise

Live by promise, not performance. This is our confidence, our hope, and the rock-solid ground we stand on. Jesus is the one who will present us holy, blameless, and without any fault (1:22) through the blood of his cross (1:20).

We know God's preservation of us includes us persevering, and that God uses warnings and encouragements from the Word to keep us persevering. What then, in Colossians might encourage us to finish the race and not let go of Christ? First, we have the prayer of 1:9–14. Paul prays for God to fill them with the knowledge of His will, cause them to walk worthy of the gospel, and strengthen them for endurance by His almighty power. Prayer keeps our

---

[55] For one explanation of how warning passages are part of the means of helping believers persevere, see Tom Schreiner's *Race Set Before Us*.

hearts tethered to God and keeps us dependent on Him to bring about our maturity in Christ.

Second, Paul says he works with all his might to proclaim Jesus (1:28) and make the Word of God fully known (1:25). Through this, Paul will present "everyone mature in Christ" (1:28). What's the point? Paul believes we will mature in Christ and hold fast to Christ *if* our eyes are set on Him.

We become like what we worship, whether that be celebrities or God. Paul sums up his ministry as growing people in Christ by showing them who Jesus is and why he's all they need. Paul stays true to his ministry plan by holding up the supremacy of Jesus above all and the sufficiency of Jesus alone throughout this letter.

Look at Jesus

If you want to look like Christ, and if you want others to see Christ in you, then give yourself over to growing in the knowledge of Christ. Open the Scriptures to see the glory of God and have you heart reoriented around Him. "A disciple of Jesus is a person who so looks at Jesus that he or she actually begins to reflect his beauty in everyday life. The gospel gives us eyes to see Jesus as well as the power to look like him."[56]

Persistently preach the gospel to yourself to rest in Jesus's work. Hold fast to Jesus by keeping your eyes on Jesus.

Our everyday decisions to seek and reflect Christ will lead to growing more like Him and enduring in Him. It's this direction, not perfection, that helps provide assurance we are His followers.

Everything we do should point us to Jesus, or be the overflow of finding our fullness in Him. In prayer, our hearts are united to his. As we serve others,

---

[56] Jonathan Dodson, *Gospel– Centered Discipleship* (Wheaton: Crossway, 2012), 56.

we experience the power of Jesus working in us. Fight sin vigorously because it steals our joy from Christ and blurs our vision from seeing Him. Feed your soul on Jesus so sin loses its allurement.

These things ignite a passion in us to know Jesus. They ground us in the gospel so we never let go of Christ. And they help us persevere even as God preserves our faith through them. Finish well. Keep going. Walk forward one day at a time, even one hour at a time.

Applying Colossians

Questions

1) What is the ground of a believer's assurance of salvation?
2) Why does resting in Jesus's work for us give us the hope that we are accepted by God now and will be accepted at our judgment?
3) How do we know God will help us endure?
4) How can you as an individual or family better set your eyes on Christ?

Next Steps

- If you're not in a community that can help encourage your perseverance then join one. If you are, ask a fellow believer to help remind you of the promises of the gospel regularly.
- Think of one thing to build into your life this week to help grow in the knowledge of Jesus.

For Further Study

- **God's commitment to us**: Isaiah 54:10; Jeremiah 32:40; Romans 8:31–39; Philippians 1:6; Hebrews 13:5; Jude 1.
- **God's preservation of us**: John 6:37–39; John 10:28–29; 17:11; 1 Corinthians 1:7–9; 10:13; Ephesians 1:13–14; 2 Timothy 4:18; Jude 1, 24.
- **Hold fast**: Colossians 1:23; 2:8; Hebrews 4:14; 6:18; 10:23.

WHAT KIND OF A PERSON REJOICES IN SUFFERING?

"Now I rejoice in my sufferings for your sake, and in my flesh I am filling up what is lacking in Christ's afflictions for the sake of his body, that is, the church, 25of which I became a minister according to the stewardship from God that was given to me for you" (Colossians 1:24–25).

What in the world does it mean that Paul's sufferings are "filling up what is lacking in Christ's afflictions for the sake of his body"? When seeking to understand what something *might* mean it often helps to begin by ruling out what it *cannot* mean.

This can't mean Christ came up short in his atoning work for sin. Colossians (1:14, 19–20; 2:13–15) and the rest of the New Testament clarify Jesus has through his one atoning sacrifice made a full and complete payment for sin. We don't add to that because nothing needs added. This is also evident because Paul never uses "afflictions" (1:24) to refer to Christ's redemptive sufferings.

The afflictions are *in regard to Christ*, or as a Christ-follower. The "filling up what is lacking" likely refers to the suffering of Christ's people completed during this age. "Thus the sufferings are the sufferings of God's people, but they are ultimately Christ's sufferings because of his identity with his people."[57]

During this age, we live under the cross as sufferers. Glory and victory are mostly for the age to come when Jesus returns. Paul sees his suffering, in part, as completing God's plan for his people as representatives of Christ.

---

[57] Kent Hughes, *Philippians, Colossians, and Philemon* (Wheaton: Crossway, 2013), 248.

You might be thinking, "I can understand that suffering is part of life, but can we really be expected to rejoice while suffering?" How did Paul rejoice in his suffering? These weren't light afflictions: imprisonments, beatings, near-death experiences, lashes, being stoned, shipwrecked, starving, sleeplessness, betrayal, and desertion from friends (2 Corinthians 11:23–28; see also 1:8–11; 6:3–10).

His joy has less to do with how things are going for him and more to do with how Jesus is being made big. How do we get a heart like Paul? How did he get there? Here are three reasons Paul rejoices amid pain. We will see there is joy in Christ, not despite suffering, but through suffering.

Suffering Purifies Us

Paul rejoices in suffering because it purifies God's people. While this isn't a focus of Colossians, it's a large part of the New Testament. "In this you rejoice, though now for a little while, if necessary, you have been grieved by various trials, so that the tested genuineness of your faith—more precious than gold that perishes though it is tested by fire—may be found to result in praise and glory and honor at the revelation of Jesus Christ" (1 Peter 1:6–7).

Living by faith while going through trials includes asking God what He wants for us and not just asking Him to take it away. Just as fire siphons out the impurities from gold, God uses trials to refine from us the sin, wrong thinking, and selfishness that cling to us (James 1:2).

Suffering, while not easy, serves a purpose. It is God's way of rounding out our rough edges as he remolds us into the image of Christ.

Suffering Draws God's Presence

Paul rejoices in suffering because God walks with us through it. We waste our suffering by avoiding it, managing it, and not letting God work through it. During our suffering we can lean, even collapse, into the sturdy arms of God. We can experience the presence and comfort of God in pain, trials, and afflictions. "The promise is not that [God] will remove us from the experience of suffering. No, the promise is that God will be with us, walking beside us in it."[58]

People often recite Psalm 23 at funerals, but these are words for the living. "Even though I walk through the valley of the shadow of death, I will fear no evil, for you are with me; your rod and staff, they comfort me" (23:4). God's presence is the balm that soothes our wounds.

"'Fear not, for I have redeemed you; I have called you by my name, you are mine. When you pass through the waters, I will be with you; and through the rivers, they shall not overwhelm you; when you walk through fire you shall not be burned, and the flame shall not consume you" (Isaiah 43:2). It is often in the dark valley we finally hear God's gentle voice or receive comfort from His presence.

"If you remember with grateful amazement that Jesus was thrown into the ultimate furnace *for* you, you can begin to sense him in your smaller furnaces *with* you."[59] The gospel assures us that in Christ God is for us and not against. He is always with us and never distant from us. It's true, we never walk alone, but we also never suffer alone.

Suffering Produces Fruit

Paul rejoices in suffering because it leads to fruitful gospel ministry. God's comfort in trials aren't to be hoarded but to be shared (2 Corinthians 1:3–8).

---

[58] Tim Keller, *Walking with God,* 227.
[59] Ibid., 235.

Paul writes to believers in Ephesus, "So I ask you not to lose heart over what I am suffering for you, which is your glory" (Ephesians 3:13). In Philippians, he finds joy in his imprisonment because it spreads the gospel. His chains and persecutions weren't an impediment. They were the means by which God multiplied the gospel all the way to Rome (Philippians 2:12–26). This is why Paul can say, "In all our affliction, I am overflowing with joy" (2 Corinthians 7:4).

If we long to be ambassadors of Christ, then part of the job requirement is suffering. We will always be in short supply of compassion or the experience of God's comfort without it.

In this fallen world, we are always either headed towards some form of suffering or we are in the thick of it. Paul finds joy not despite suffering but through suffering because his life is bigger than himself. Anything that leads to experiencing Christ in deeper ways and being able to share Christ with others is fuel to the fire of his passion.

We can find joy in suffering if Christ is our source of joy, not comfortable circumstances. Look to Him today. Ask yourself, what might God want for me in my pain? How can I turn to Him? How might God want me to use my own experiences to comfort others?

"Fear not, for I am with you; be not dismayed, for I am your God; I will strengthen you, I will help you, I will uphold you with my righteous right hand" (Isaiah 41:10). Know and believe this for yourself, and then remind and comfort your fellow believers with it.

Applying Colossians

Questions
1) When was a time God used suffering or trials in your life? How was it for your good?
2) How have some of the hardest experiences in life helped you have empathy, compassion, or be of help to other people?
3) How can we walk with God through suffering and not turn to anger or despair?

Next Steps
- Is there a friend who is suffering and in need of encouragement today? Share with them how God is with us in our sufferings and pray for them.
- Write down some of the ways you've seen God's goodness, how He's blessed you, and ways He's faithfully preserved you through hard times in the past.
- Read the lyrics to the hymn "How Firm a Foundation" or "Never Once."

For Further Study
- **Christ suffering with his church**: Romans 8:17; Acts 9:4; 2 Corinthians 4:10; Philippians 3:10.
- **God walks with us:** Psalm 23:4; Isaiah 41:10; 43:1–2; 63:9; Daniel 3:25–27; Matthew 28:20; Hebrews 13:5.

UNLOCKING THE MYSTERY

"the mystery hidden for ages and generations but now revealed to his saints. 27To them God chose to make known how great among the Gentiles are the riches of the glory of this mystery, which is Christ in you, the hope of glory" (Colossians 1:25–27).

A good mystery movie or novel surprises us in a way that's simultaneously fitting and yet so different from what we expected that it delights something deep within. It tells a story where all the seemingly random pieces link together. When you watch it again, you now see all the clues pointing to the big disclosure. What felt like a surprise the first time now makes perfect sense as you retrace the story and see the breadcrumbs leading you along.

"In Pauline terminology, a mystery was a truth which lay hidden in the pages of the Old Testament, and its explanation awaited another day."[60] For Paul, "the mystery" (Colossians 1:27; 2:2; 4:3) isn't absent from the Old Testament but it's something hidden which is now made clear. It might not have been obvious as the Old Testament unfolded but now it's nearly impossible not to see. The mystery isn't a riddle to solve or a puzzle we figure out. God reveals it to us. It isn't held secret for a few gurus with extra knowledge but it's made known to all, Jew and Gentile.

God's Great Mystery Story

If we're drawn to mystery stories, we should be on the edge of our seats to see what mystery God revealed. The mystery involves at least three components. In Jesus, God became man to die for men. Second, this salvation in the gospel of Christ is available to all people. And third, Christ not only saves his people but He unites Himself to them.

---

[60] Melick Jr., *Colossians,* 241.

Christians talk a lot about the first aspect, Christ's death for us, but they often neglect the other parts of the mystery. The New Covenant's power not only justifies us individually but it has corporate significance.

The Gentiles are now made equal citizens of the New Covenant (Ephesians 3:9; Romans 11:25). All can sit around God's table. God's New Covenant doesn't give a higher priority to any group. It's for all people of any race, color, ethnicity, or social class who turn *from* sin and *to* Jesus alone.

Not only does Jesus open wide the doors for all to come on in, but their inclusion comes from their identification with the Messiah and not from becoming an Israelite. The hope for the world isn't "Jews among Gentiles" but "Christ among the Gentiles." [61]

Things like racism, elitism, and sexism are gospel issues. All people are created in God's image. All sinners are equally condemned and undeserving of God's mercy. And all believers are united as one so that the color of our skin, the size of our house, the country of our origin, and our gender cannot separate us or divide us.

In Christ, we are one. And our oneness in Christ is the most defining thing about us. While our God- designed diversity should be embraced and celebrated, we have more in common in Christ than we do apart from Him. To act otherwise is to deny the mystery of the gospel that Jesus is for all, and all who are united to Him by faith are made one in Him.

The Mystery Revealed

Where did God provide clues to this mystery? Speaking about the Christ, God says: "I will make you as a light for the nations, that my salvation may reach to the end of the earth" (Isaiah 49:6). God promises about the coming Servant,

---

[61] Ibid., fn. 151 on p. 242.

"I will give you as a covenant for the people, a light for the nations." (Isaiah 42:6; see also Isaiah 52:10; 60:3; Psalm 98:3).

This is good news for Gentiles. We who were on the outside have now been brought inside (1 Peter 2:9–10). This gospel makes us people who don't create barriers or keep people out. We are to be "includers" and "inviters" who see all people as equals: sinners desperately needing God's grace.

Gentiles aren't only invited into God's people (Israel) but they're united with God: "Christ in you, the hope of glory" (1:27). The defining reality isn't Jewishness—or any other man-made distinction—but our union with Christ, which signifies both that we're in Him and He's in us.

Like all beautiful things, this is one of those phrases that stops us in our tracks and bids us to take a second look. "Christ in you, the hope of glory." Jesus *with* us but He's also *in* us. He indwells us through the Spirit He poured out on His church.

Jesus is my life and he lives through me (Galatians 2:20). "When Christ, *who is your life* appears, then you also will appear with him in glory" (Colossians 3:3–4). The free gifts of God to us—stubborn sinners who resist Him—remind us He's way too good to us. Christ is in us. Christ is our life. Christ is ours. We are in Christ.

The Christian doesn't lead a trouble-free life. We receive the full-court press from a fallen universe. People mistreat and misunderstand us. Our bodies bewilder and fail us. Jobs are lost and money seems to evaporate. Tragedies strike and pain cuts deep. So, why do we follow Jesus if it isn't all rainbows and sunshine like we want? If we still suffer, what's the difference between those in Christ and those apart from Him?

The difference is we get out of bed and are united to Jesus Christ, the Lord of all (1:15–20). What we don't have in this life pales in comparison to what we have in Him.

We have the joy of being reconciled back to a God who loves and cares for us. We're joined to God in a personal and life-giving relationship. We have the solacing peace that Jesus now sits in the director's chair and runs our life, scripting only what's good for us. We have the hope that there's a whole lot more for us than this fleeting, immortal life.

"We are invited to live our whole life under his benediction, his smile, his love."[62] Our union with Christ should put a spring in the step of the Christian, even the ones taking baby steps and the ones barely on their feet.

Applying Colossians

Questions
1) How does God's work of bringing Jew and Gentile together in Christ help us think about our unity in Christ?
2) What are some reasons a Christian has hope, now and forever?
3) How would you explain the different nuances between Christ being in us and us being in Christ?
4) How does the nearness of Jesus encourage you?

Next Steps
- Write down five reasons to hope in Christ now, and five hopes awaiting you after this life.

For Further Study
- **Mystery**: Matthew 13:11; Colossians 1:26, 27; 2:2; 4:3; 1 Corinthians 2:6–7; 15:51; Ephesians 2:11–22; 3:9; Romans 16:25–26.
- **Christ in you**: Romans 8:10; 2 Corinthians 13:5; Galatians 2:20; 4:19; Ephesians 3:17.
- **The hope of glory**: Romans 5:2; 8:10; Ephesians 1:18; 1 Timothy 1:1; Titus 2:13.

---

[62] Elyse M. Fitzpatrick, *Found in Him* (Wheaton: Crossway, 2013), 140.

BECOMING LIKE HIM BY LOOKING AT HIM

"Him we proclaim, warning everyone and teaching everyone with all wisdom, that we may present everyone mature in Christ. 29For this I toil, struggling with all his energy that he powerfully works within me" (Colossians 1:28–29).

Since Paul's conversion, everything changed. Jesus moved from an enemy he shook his fist at to the Lord who mercifully redeemed Him. For the rest of his life, Paul's day-to-day existence orbited around one central thing: Jesus.

Even life and death were viewed in relation to Jesus. If he was killed, he'd be in Christ's presence. If spared, he would preach Christ for the joy of others (Philippians 1:21–26). It's a win-win scenario for Him.

Having arrived at the end of chapter one, we can see Paul's unshifting focus on Jesus.

- He rejoices in their faith in Jesus and the fruit they're bearing in Him (1:3–8).
- He prays their walk would reflect the King who redeemed them from darkness (1:9–14).
- He lifts Jesus higher and higher so we rightly recognize Him as the Lord over all (1:15–20).
- He encourages them with the promise that Jesus's death bought their holiness (1:21–24).
- He reminds them God's mystery revealed is "Christ in you, the hope of glory" (1:24–27).

Paul will put on gloves and step into the ring with anyone undermining the person and work of Jesus (Colossians 1:28; 2:8; Galatians 5:7–12). He pours out his life, struggling with every God-given ounce of energy to see people understand and love Jesus more (1:29).

Paul's letters are thick with the aroma of Christ, not as an intellectual ideal but as his Lord. All of this has an end-goal of seeing believers "mature in Christ." He tells us about Jesus so we might become like Him.

In a parallel passage, Paul writes about reaching "mature manhood, to the measure of the stature of the fullness of Christ…we are to grow up in every way into him who is the head, into Christ" (Ephesians 4:13, 15). It's through the knowledge of Jesus we mature into being like Jesus (4:13–15).

Romans 8:28 not only assures believers that "all things work together for good" but it tells us what our greatest good is: "to be conformed to the image of his Son" (Romans 8:29).

In a similar passage, Paul writes, "And we all, with unveiled face, beholding the glory of the Lord, are being transformed into the same image, from one degree of glory to another" (2 Corinthians 3:18). Unlike how Moses had to cover his face, God has revealed Himself in Jesus and told us to take a look. The Spirit gives us eyes to see Jesus and through seeing Him in all his glory we are magnetized, drawn in, and changed.

Beholding Leads to Becoming

In *We Become What We Worship*, G.K. Beale summarizes his book: "All humans have been created to be reflecting beings, and they will reflect whatever they are ultimately committed to, whether the true God or some other object in the created order. Thus, to repeat the primary theme of this book, we resemble what we revere, either for ruin or restoration."[63] Beale traces the history of idolatry in the Bible and how when people elevate creation they image their idols. This always devastates us and turns us into something ugly.

---

[63] G.K. Beale, *We Become What We Worship* (Downers Grove: InterVarsity, 2008), 22.

Consider what images you elevate and give attention to with your eyes or mind. Women, do the images portrayed on TV and magazines shape your vision for what a woman should be? That idol could come in the form of the super-skinny women jammed in front of our faces or it could be the ideal mom with a clean house, smiling kids, and a fridge stocked full of organic food.

Men, do the images of guys with ripped abs or the portrayal of the successful business man inform your vision of manhood? Do we spend hours staring into the television, forming idols in our hearts we will reflect?

The images we spend our time looking at will become what we idolize and imitate. And no doubt about it, this will be for our ruin, not our restoration. "Sin will never deliver what it promises. Our idols never love us in return, always disappoint, and their aim is our destruction."[64]

A Reflection that Restores

There is one person who we were created to reflect, and as we reflect Him, it will be for our restoration. Paul knows this and his heart beats to the drum of Christ's glory. Again and again, Paul comes back to talking about Jesus. What we all need most is to have the eyes of our heart fixated on the glory of Christ. We need to know Him so we can follow Him.

Whatever you're going through, whether the highest– highs or the lowest– lows, we need to know the God-man, Jesus. We need to fellowship with Him and feast on Him. Our lives will display the beauty of holiness as we image Jesus. Our words will reflect the fullness of grace and truth as we hear his words in Scripture. Our affections for sin will be extinguished not by more

---

[64] Chris Beals, "He Came and Bought Her" College Park Church Fishers September 17, 2017. Accessed August 5, 2018 https://fishers.yourchurch.com/sermon/fishers-he-came-and-bought-her/.

discipline alone but by the rekindling of intimacy through quality time with Him.

This is true for you, for your church, and for the people in your life. What they need most is for you to redirect their eyes to the goodness and the glory of Jesus shown to us in the gospel.

Put away distractions stealing your focus away from him. Avoid promoting anything above Him or making your hobby-horse issue more important. Nothing motivates maturity in Christ like the right knowledge of Christ. We become like Him by looking at Him.

Applying Colossians

Questions
1) How can you make looking at Jesus the priority in your life? How will seeing Him and then imaging Him be for your restoration?
2) Where have you seen this principle lived out: we become what we revere?

Next Steps
- Write out two or three of the idols you're tempted to conform to. Write out how that will ultimately ruin you. Then write out two or three things you've seen about Jesus in Colossians. Write out how reflecting what you see in Him will lead to your restoration.

For Further Study
- **Mature in Christ**: Ephesians 4:13–15; Hebrews 5:12–14.
- **Reflecting Jesus**: Romans 8:28–29; 2 Corinthians 3:18–4:6; Romans 12:2; Colossians 3:10.

FULLNESS IN CHRIST (2:1–9)

In the prior section (1:21–29), Paul spoke of his ministry. In God's strength (1:29), Paul works with all his energy to proclaim the name of Jesus. It's seeing Jesus that leads to growing in Jesus. Paul would be surprised by contemporary "Christian Living" books with seven simple steps to maturity focused more on the individual than on Christ. It's not that we don't have things to do, but we can never mature in Christ (1:28) unless we see Him and know Him. Paul *warns* against anything that takes us away from Jesus. And Paul *teaches* us about Jesus, in all the glory of his person and work.

As Paul continues in 2:1–9, he doesn't exit his line of thinking but keeps in the same lane. He will alternate warning and teaching (cf. 1:28). He teaches about the sufficiency and supremacy of Jesus and warns against anything drifting away from Jesus.

This gives us clear guidance about how we grow personally, as well as how we do evangelism, discipleship, and ministry to one another. The heart of all we say and do is pointing people to the fullness of Christ (2:8) and the fullness they have in Him (2:9). Keep walking in Him (2:6).

We refute what's false and dangerous, but even more importantly, we teach the glory of Jesus. Although others might offer their own theories of wisdom or claims to knowledge (2:4, 8) Christ is the one in whom all wisdom, knowledge, and understanding is found. He doesn't just offer wisdom and truth; he *is* wisdom and truth (John 14:6).

Christians are those with their minds set on Christ. Revering Jesus in our hearts leads to reflecting Jesus in our lives. It's also how the body of Christ is united in love and strength (2:2–3). If we want our hearts and our lives to be full, then we must fill up on Christ (2:8–9).

UPHELD AND UNITED

"For I want you to know how great a struggle I have for you and for those at Laodicea and for all who have not seen me face to face, that their hearts may be encouraged, being knit together in love" (Colossians 2:1–2).

Growing up as a rambunctious boy, bouncing or throwing a ball most of the day, I broke my fair share of household items. Where would I have been without the rescue of super-glue? Whether it was a snapped chair-leg, a shattered mug, or broken toys that got into my tornado-like path, the power to put things back together was found in that tiny tube of glue.

Sin splintered humanity like a vase smashing against the floor, but in Christ a new humanity is being pieced together. We might paraphrase Colossians 2:2 to say: that their hearts may be reinforced like steel welded together in love. Or, that their hearts may be made stronger than ever, being super-glued together. Jesus knits his people together through the fabric of his love.

Here we see the difference between a *crowd of individuals* in one place and a *community of believers* belonging to one another. The Colossians have been comforted and encouraged collectively. Love unites them. They're discovering together the riches of God's great revelation: Jesus.

It is the mutual support of the body that instills courage and comfort in their hearts. Elsewhere, Paul describes this as being strengthened with power in our inner being (Ephesians 3:16).

Love for One Another

Love weaves us together (2:2), including love for each other and the love of Christ toward us. We'll start with how love within the body unites us. "And above all these put on love, which binds everything together in perfect harmony" (Colossians 4:2). While an inward focus and selfish lifestyle *repel* people—like two positive ends of a magnet—selfless love *unites* people in powerful and long-lasting ways.

A community of believers living life together will love one another. They'll be there to mow the grass when someone is sick, sacrifice time when somebody moves, watch the kids in a pinch, enjoy meals together around the table, and to take one another back to the pages of Scripture.

How are you doing when it comes to loving Christ's church? Are you joined to a community of believers and committed to them, or do you show up to church and leave like you would the movie theater? If you're struggling in your walk with Christ, one reason might be you're doing it alone when you were designed to do it in community.

> It is hard for us to grasp the significance of this community identity, because we live in a radically individualistic culture. We bring this worldview with us into the church so that it shapes our understanding of the gospel. So we have a loose connection with Christians on Sunday, but then largely we go back to living our everyday lives on our own. No wonder we struggle to thrive. Our faith is animated on Sunday mornings as we sing God's praise and hear his Word. But it limps along during the week when we live apart from the body of Christ.[65]

The Source of Such Love

---

[65] Steve Timmis and Tim Chester, *Everyday Church* (Wheaton: Crossway, 2012), 53–54.

What turns a crowd of individuals into a community? What separates Christ's church from any other club or organization trying to rally people together?

The super-glue of all super-glues is the love of Christ. The church isn't the church without the love of God pouring into us. We're a divinely created community united as one by the unsurpassed love of God. None of us deserve it, but all of us receive it in Christ.

Paul tethers being strengthened in heart to Christ's love. "that you, being rooted and grounded in love, may have strength to comprehend with all the saints what is the breadth and length and height and depth, and to know the love of Christ that surpasses knowledge" (Ephesians 3:17–19). Christians delight to sing about God's love. We grasp for words to describe this measureless, powerful, never–ending love.

"The love of God is greater far Than tongue or pen can ever tell… Oh, love of God, how rich and pure! How measureless and strong!"[66]

"O the deep, deep love of Jesus, Vast, unmeasured, boundless, free! Rolling as a mighty ocean In its fullness over me! Underneath me, all around me, Is the current of Thy love;"[67]

This divine love sees us for who we truly are—in all our sin and brokenness—and yet loves us without restraints and requirements. The love of Christ soothes our aching hearts, strengthens our feeble bodies, stirs our passions to live for Him, and ties us together as sharers in such grace.

Our hardened and hurt hearts might have been boarded up for years, but Christ's love removes barriers and opens up new channels of love in us. "Christ's love for them provided a basis for unity and formed a common bond between them. Christian growth is a group task! The individuals of the

---

[66] Ibid., Frederick M. Lehman, "The Love of God" (No. 18)
[67] Samuel Trevor Francis, "O the Deep Deep love of Jesus" (No. 24).

church needed each other."[68] God's love towards them and their love for God created a mutual love for one another.

Christ's love bonds the church at the deepest of levels. No differences should push us apart when Christ has brought us together.

Paul struggles with all his might to see the church mature in Christ (1:28). This includes maturity in a community of believers where hearts are encouraged together as they're united around the love of Christ.

How do we become this type of people who love like Christ? It happens as we experience the love of Christ firsthand. Study the Scriptures on the lookout for the love of God toward you, and open your heart to receive His love. You might struggle to believe you can be loved so freely and graciously, but believe it and drink deeply of it. As we daily taste and see Christ's love for us anew, we'll be changed and compelled through God's love and we'll become conduits who carry His love to others.

Applying Colossians

Questions
1) What are some ways God has demonstrated His love towards you?
2) How are believers united by Christ's love for them? How are they united for their love for one another? How does experiencing Christ's love propel us to love others better?
3) Why is a community of believers in the local church so important for our maturity?
4) When do you doubt God's love? What promises need remembered in those moments?
5) How can you extend Christ's love to those in your own church?

Next Steps

---

[68] Melick, *Colossians*, 245.

- Read/sing one of the hymns quoted above.
- Pray Colossians 2:2–3 over someone and then tell them you're praying these verses for them.
- Take any next steps needed to be involved in your church so that you experience genuine community where you can be encouraged and encourage others.

For Further Study

- **Encouraged in heart**: 1 Corinthians 16:13; Ephesians 3:16; 6:22; Philippians 4:13; Colossians 1:11; 2:5 4:8.
- **United in love**: Philippians 2:1–2; Ephesians 3:14–4:16; Colossians 3:14; 1 Peter 4:8.
- **God's love for us**: John 3:16; Romans 5:5–8; Ephesians 2:4; 3:16–19; 2 Thessalonians 2:16; 1 John 3–4.

NO ADDITIVES NEEDED

"that their hearts may be encouraged, being knit together in love, to reach all the riches of full assurance of understanding and the knowledge of God's mystery, which is Christ, 3 in whom are hidden all the treasures of wisdom and knowledge. 4 I say this in order that no one may delude you with plausible arguments" (Colossians 2:2–4).

In the TV show *Treasure Quest* a large and technologically decked-out boat full of archaeologists, sailors, and treasure hunters scans the ocean bottoms for sunken ships. They look for buried treasure: gold, silver, and historic artifacts. Every episode pulls me in with tales of lost treasure and the adventure of finding what so many legends had spoken of. As a boy who read *Treasure Island*, and then as a teenager watching *Pirates of the Caribbean*, the hunt for treasures has always fascinated me.

Throughout history, people have with equal vigor searched for wisdom and knowledge. Every religious or philosophical seeker is on a personal pursuit of understanding. Countless pilgrimages are undertaken to find true wisdom, whether through a guru, a book, or an intellectual discovery. Paul tells us Jesus Christ is the one in whom *all* the hidden treasures of wisdom and knowledge are found (2:2–3). Jesus is the mother lode and God-sized treasure-chest of all wisdom and truth.

Believers don't need to look anywhere else for knowledge. There's no higher or hidden knowledge beyond Jesus. Part of the false teaching in Colossae suggested Jesus is the starting point but eventually other philosophies need sprinkled in. Paul counters such claims throughout the letter by repeatedly arguing for the supreme sufficiency of Jesus alone. Christ's sufficiency includes salvation but it also extends to wisdom and knowledge. There's no time or area where he's not enough.

All the treasures of wisdom are found in Him.

The Wisdom of God

Jesus doesn't just *dispense* wisdom, knowledge, and truth; He *is* wisdom, knows all things, and is the truth. Christ is the power and wisdom of God (1 Corinthians 1:24, 30); not a slice of wisdom but the whole kit and caboodle.

John describes Him as full of grace and truth. Jesus' states "I am the truth" (John 1:14; 14:6). Elsewhere Paul calls the Holy Spirit the "Spirit of wisdom and of revelation in the knowledge of him" (Ephesians 1:17). The "him" at the end is Jesus, meaning the wisdom the Spirit gives is wisdom and revelation in the knowledge of Jesus. When we find Him, we find the jackpot for everything we could ever need or want: righteousness, wisdom, sanctification, and redemption (1 Corinthians 1:30).

This clarifies why Paul writes "to reach all the riches of full assurance of understanding and the knowledge of God's mystery, which is Christ" (Colossians 2:2). He has confidence that wisdom and truth in its fullness belongs to them because Christ's words abide in them. Every one of us desires to increase our understanding and discernment. The answer isn't found simply in watching more Jeopardy, reading books, or absorbing content from the internet. Gain wisdom by growing in the knowledge of Christ.

Truth in A World of Opinions

This is encouraging news in a world publishing information at a blistering pace. You don't have to stay up to speed with all the wisdom the world offers or read what's on the best-sellers list. All the wisdom you need for knowing God and living faithfully and joyfully in this world is in Christ (2 Peter 1:3–4).

If we trust Paul's words in Colossians 2, we should be the most energetic and diligent treasure hunters on earth. In the treasure map of God's world,

Christ is the only X you need to look for because *all* wisdom, knowledge, and truth is found in Him.

We also trust Christ's wisdom above our own. If Jesus is Lord, He's more than capable of leading us, not only because He's sovereign and good but because He guides us in all wisdom. We would do well to regularly check our hearts with this proverb: "Trust in the LORD with all your heart, and do not lean on your own understanding." (Proverbs 3:5).

The all-knowing, all-seeing, perfectly good, absolutely sovereign, truth-telling, grace giving, and supremely wise Lord is the one we entrust with our lives. Take that worry, anxiety, stress, confusion, or fear you're carrying today to the great Counselor of our souls (Isaiah 9:6; 12:2–3).

Put your hope in *His* wisdom and knowledge, not in what you think. Just like I as a parent know better than my two-year old—despite that look she gives indicating she knows best—God always knows what's best for us. He can be trusted. He should be trusted.

We sometimes don't go to Jesus for wisdom because we've become self-sufficient. To say it bluntly, too often I'm guilty of being a know-it-all and I tell God what He should do. It's tempting for Christians to act as if God has gotten caught up with other business, so we need to figure things out. Or in our pride, we think our understanding is enough to get us through. But the little wisdom and knowledge we have pales in comparison to Christ's wisdom. It's like holding a flickering match up against the midday sun.

God desires for us to seek His wisdom rather than relying on our own. This is in part why He allows trials to come. In the discomfort of those trials, we feel how bankrupt our wisdom is and how much we need God's help.

The wisest man who ever lived, Solomon, tells us to pursue wisdom above all things (Proverbs 2:2–6). "Seek it like silver; and search for it as for hidden treasures, then you will understand the fear of the LORD and find the knowledge of God" (Proverbs 2:4–5). Jesus Christ, the treasure-chest of God's infinite wealth of wisdom, will teach us everything we need to know.

Where have you drifted from trusting God's plan and wisdom by pursuing your own thoughts and plans? If honest, are you tempted to lean on your own ability to come up with a solution, figure things out, or try to control the desired outcome? What are ways you're seeking to know Christ in His Word so He is your source of knowledge and understanding?

Our lives will flourish in wisdom—which rewards us with joy—when we set out on the mission of growing in the knowledge of Christ. We'll dig deep into this well of truth the rest of our lives, but the further we dig the more gold we strike.

Applying Colossians

Questions
1) How do wisdom and knowledge lead to faith and love?
2) What are sources of knowledge today that might draw you away from the truth? How do we make sure our thoughts line up with the Word?
3) How does growing in your knowledge about/of Jesus give you wisdom to live as an image-bearer of God?
4) What are symptoms of leaning on your own understanding?

Next Steps
- Spend a couple of minutes considering what other sources might influence your thinking and how to carefully guard your mind.
- Read Scripture this week with your eyes on a search mission for knowledge of Christ.

For Further Study
- **Wisdom:** Proverbs 2:2–6; Isaiah 11:2; 45:3; 1 Corinthians 1:24, 30; 2:6–7; Colossians 1:9–10; 2 Peter 1:3; 1 John 5:20.

KEEP GOING IN THE LORD

"Therefore, as you received Christ Jesus the Lord, so walk in him, rooted and built up in him and established in the faith, just as you were taught, abounding in thanksgiving" (Colossians 2:6–7).

In N.T. Wright's book *Following Jesus: Biblical Reflections on Discipleship* he entitles the chapter on Colossians "The Battle Won"—emphasizing the truth and the implication of Jesus being Lord. He's the King who went to war against death, the devil, and the dominion of sin.

Language of Lordship

Common words like "Lord" can become the biblical wallpaper we never even see as we walk through the Bible. We can't let that happen. "Christ Jesus the Lord" is no mere religious cliché to skim over. Nor is it a religious nickname making Jesus recognizable. It is a divine title drawn from the imagery of war, dynasty, and dominion.

Jesus has won the decisive battle against the rulers of this age (Colossians 2:15), demonstrating his absolute power over all things and his authoritative right to rule the entire universe. He reigns over all. Over everything. And everyone. And every square-inch of the universe He created.

Like soldiers reflecting their leader or citizens reflecting their king, we are to walk in a manner worthy of the Lord (1:10). This is especially the case for Christians since Jesus paid for our freedom with his life. We used to belong to the kingdom of darkness, but through Christ's redemptive blood, we've been *bought out* and *brought into* the kingdom of the Son (1:13–14). He's both the king who has conquered evil and the king who cares for his own.

The hymn of Colossians 1:15–20 trumpeted the universal Lordship of Jesus so we would see Him in a category all by Himself. This Lordship includes the defeat of evil spiritual forces that might threaten harm against us. As the rightful ruler, Jesus now reigns from the throne of heaven on the seat of power (3:1).

Jesus is not a tyrant but a kind King. He proved his love and selflessness by laying down his life for us at the cross. He leads us and rules us for His glory and our good. He acts with our best in mind and works with his might and mercy in hand. Jesus is the caring, conquering, and life-changing Lord.

Trust His Rule

What are a few ways this truth connects to your reality? How do you start another day with the banner under which you live being "Jesus is Lord?" Since Jesus is Lord you can trust his rule. Don't second-guess Him and the plans He has for you. He *is* good and *does* what is good.

Are we trusting His rule? Are we exchanging our anxieties and worries for rest? Do we believe His plans for us right now are for our best?

A Lord—biblically speaking—is not a harsh ruler but a shepherd-king. His rule involves his care for those He rules, even ruling with their interests above his own. He's tough enough to fight our enemies for us, and tender enough to care for us when we're hurt.

"Behold, the Lord God comes with might, and his arm rules for him; behold, his reward is with him, and his recompense before him. 11 He will tend his flock like a shepherd; he will gather the lambs in his arms; he will carry them in his bosom, and gently lead those that are with young" (Isaiah 40:10–11).

The arms of the Lord that fight back our enemies and rule in power are the same arms of the Shepherd that carry us, hold us close to his heart, and lead us when we're weak. Jesus the Lord is mighty and merciful, tough and tender, glorious and good, powerful and yet patient. He is trustworthy, in all things and at all times. Trust Him.

Find Refuge from Fear

Since Jesus is Lord we have safety in Him. A big part of Colossians' context is Paul writing to those in spiritual warfare, many who used to be in bondage to dark spiritual forces. Paul assures them Jesus has conquered evil.

They no longer need to fear, and they certainly no longer should submit to anyone besides Christ. If any country ever felt safe because the power and leadership of their king, imagine the security Christians should feel under *their* King. The enemy might rage but he is conquered and stripped of all real power.

Are we letting a defeated foe accuse, tempt, or rule us? If Jesus has control over everything as Lord then can't we give Him our fears?

Follow His Lead

Since Jesus is Lord, we lay down self-rule over our lives. Paul seamlessly moves from a theology of Jesus as Lord into the Christian life where we then walk according to his leadership. If Jesus redeemed us from the darkness at the cost of his life, and if through the resurrection-ascension he was enthroned with authority over all, then our lives must reflect that Lordship.

The Christian life is not one of autonomy but it's a life of letting Jesus call the shots. When Jesus is large and in charge, it always works out for our good. When we get in the way things go south quickly.

If Jesus is Lord, what in our lives do we need to surrender? What little kingdoms have we tried to keep as our own that Jesus needs to reign over?

Jesus as Lord is the Christian life. At conversion, we come to Jesus as our Lord in desperation, aware that we've made a mess of our lives and can't dig ourselves out. We start out the Christian life by coming to Jesus as Lord and that never changes. The Lord who saves is the Lord who sanctifies.

What Erik Raymond says about conversion also applies to the ongoing Christian life. "Conversion is not about adding Jesus to an already crowded shelf of idols. May it never be! Conversion is about sweeping clear the shelves of our heart and pledging supreme love and loyalty to God—and God alone."[69]

Just as you received Jesus as the Lord continue walking in Him (2:6). Keep going. Don't give up. Don't change courses. Keep following who you're following. The Jesus you planted your roots in at conversion is the same Jesus who nourishes and grows you.

Let his lordship direct your thinking, acting, being, and walking. Lordship isn't an idea or a relationship tucked away. It is the controlling and consuming influence of the all-sufficient and joy-producing Christ over all of your life.

Live in the light of his lordship today. Let Him lead you. Let Him fight your battles. Rest in His care.

---

[69] Erik Raymond, *Chasing Discontentment* (Wheaton: Crossway, 2017), 45.

Applying Colossians

Questions

1) How should Jesus's lordship affect our day to day lives?
2) What are some areas of your life Jesus has changed, even if the change has been small and is still a work in progress? How has that worked out for your good?
3) How can we start seeing the world around us through the lens of Jesus's lordship?
4) What is one thing you need to trust Jesus with more this week?

Next Steps

- Read Colossians again in another version of the Bible (try the NLT or NET) and see if anything stands out differently. Look especially for words or images of lordship.

- Consider a scary next step and ask a trusted friend if they see any areas of your life that don't seem to be submitted to the lordship of Jesus.

For Further Study

- **Jesus is Lord**: Romans 10:9; 1 Corinthians 12:3; 2 Corinthians 4:5; Philippians 2:11.

- **Jesus as Lord in Colossians**: 1:3, 10, 13, 15–20; 2:6, 14–15; 3:1, 13, 17, 20, 22, 23, 24; 4:1; 4:7, 16.

- **Walk**: Galatians 5:16, 25; Colossians 1:10; Ephesians 4:1; Psalm 1; 1 Thessalonians 4:1.

DEEP ROOTS MAKE HEALTHY PLANTS

"Therefore, as you received Christ Jesus the Lord, so walk in him, rooted and built up in him and established in the faith, just as you were taught, abounding in thanksgiving" (Colossians 2:6–7).

As a great teacher, God filled the earth with physical illustrations of spiritual realities. Creation points us upward and conveys God's truth in endless ways. Consider grape vines. The vine's health depends on the roots. Droughts force the roots to go deeper and deeper into the earth, which both enhances the earthy flavor of the grapes and enables the plant to withstand future droughts or other problems. The deeper and stronger the root the healthier the fruit.

Not only does life and health come from the roots, so does the flavor. The roots carry the flavor of the soil into the vine and out through the taste of the grape itself.[70] This concept known as "terroir" applies to many delicious foods and drinks: wine, coffee, chocolate, and even meat. The product put on the shelf begins with and depends upon good soil. Since God designed creation to reflect His glory and teach us, I believe there's a built--in lesson here.[71]

Deep roots in the soil of Christ produces healthy fruit on the vines. It's the lesson Jesus taught when he said, "Whoever abides in me and I in him, he it is that bears much fruit, for apart from me you can do nothing" (John 15:5).

---

[70] Genesis 2:9 says God gave fruit-bearing trees that are both pleasant on the eyes and profitable as a sustainable food source. We might deduce from this God gives us creation, including food and drink, both for a purpose (nourishment and health) and for pleasure (enjoyment and wonder). Even high-quality cheese and cured meats are ultimately influenced by the environment—the grass eaten by the animal, the air in the room of the aging food, the temperature and humidity. Every time you take a drink or bite of something flavorful and delicious you can thank God for designing such a world.

[71] For verses on how creation teaches us, or how God points us to creation to learn spiritual truths, see Job 12:7–10; 38–41; Romans 1:20; Psalm 8; 19:1–2; 104; Matthew 6:25–30.

Christians rooted in Jesus bring to surface the health and beauty they tap into in Christ. The fruit we seek as Christians isn't a checklist of good behaviors tacked onto our lives. Fruit blossoms when we're so rooted in Jesus that He blooms out our life (John 15; Galatians 5).

The indwelling Spirit transforms us into the image of Jesus so His love, joy, peace, kindness, and goodness ripen in us. As we'll see in Colossians 3:5–15, when we put off sin and put on righteousness, we take on our God-given task of imaging God as we reflect Jesus (3:10). Christians offer the world a vintage taste of being human when we carry the flavor and aroma of Christ. And this only happens as our roots go deeper in Him. Our geography, our climate, and our soil all come from the ideal conditions of being "in Christ."

Abiding

In 2:6–7, Paul tells the people living in Colossae to keep walking—steadily continuing forward—in the same Lord they received. Remain and continue. "Together, these participles emphasize that believers can live lives that exemplify the Lordship of Christ only by remaining, like branches, firmly attached to the vine in which God has himself placed them (Cf. John 15) and by continuing to allow God to integrate them, like stones, into the new structure that is nothing other than Christ himself."[72]

We remain in the one we received. The temptation is to run frantically from one thing to another. Our culture is fixated on fads. What's the latest trend, gadget, or promise to make us wealthier, skinnier, healthier, or happier? It doesn't take long before the grass is greener syndrome kicks in and we want something else. This mentality moves into our spiritual lives and we—even if unconsciously—wait for the next big thing in bold letters and shiny lights to fix our problems.

---

[72] Moo, *Colossians*, 181.

Jesus tells us to abide, to remain and continue in Him, and that as we abide in Him, He will bear fruit in us. If Jesus causes their growth, maturity, and fruitfulness, why would we look to other sources for our nourishment and progress? Throughout Paul's letters (see 1 Thessalonians 4:1), he encourages believers that growth comes not by moving beyond Christ to something else—self-help, spiritual guides, deeper knowledge, additional religions, etc.—but by growing deeper in Christ.

Trials Strengthen Roots

The beating sun of daily life either dries us out or strengthens our roots by forcing us to stretch deeper into the soil. Trials can extinguish our faith by turning us away from God or enhance our faith as we have nothing to cling to besides God. Whether in the shaky moments of despair, feeling alone and rejected or misunderstood, having life sweep your legs from under you, in loss or tragedy, or even during temptation, we can turn to God.

In desperation, we lean into knowing Jesus and cling to Him alone as our hope. We pour out our hearts to Him in raw honesty instead of a veiled transparency. It is in these moments we draw near to God and He draws near to us in unique and special ways.

The things of life that threaten to destroy us end up being the things that enrich our fellowship with God. Deepen your roots of faith by digging down into the soil of your relationship with God. As this happens, not only will we not dry out from drought and heat or be swept away by rains and floods, but there will be a time where the deepened roots lead to healthy fruit on the vine. Our lives will flourish because we have gone further into the soil of life in Christ. In ever greater degrees we will reflect the beauty and goodness of Jesus Christ.

What is one thing you can do today to root yourself in Jesus? (That's not a rhetorical question. Pause to answer it.) Now let the roots run deep.

Applying Colossians

Questions
1) Is there anything going on in life right now that might be an opportunity to deepen your roots in Christ? How do you let that happen as opposed to just "drying out" or staying put?
2) How did you answer the question in the last paragraph: what is one thing you can do today to root yourself in Jesus?
3) What are ways you can lead your family or the small group you're in to be more rooted in Jesus together?

Next Steps
- Write down five things you've seen in Colossians that you admire about Christ. Pray into those things both to worship Jesus and to ask for God's Spirit to transform you into Christ's likeness.

- Think of one specific way this week you want to take steps in knowing God more. Make sure it leads you to Jesus and then do it daily this week.

- Write down and share with an individual or your small group two things you'd like to do this year to keep growing in the faith. Ask them to pray for you and encourage you in it.

For Further Study
- **Rooted and built up**: Ephesians 3:17–18; Isaiah 42:4 & Jeremiah 12:2; 17:8; Acts 20:32; 1 Corinthians 3:10, 12, 14; Ephesians 2:20; Jude 20.

- **Continuing in what you've been taught**: Philippians 4:9; Colossians 1:3–8; 1 Thessalonians 3:11–4:1.

- **Fruitfulness**: John 15:1–16; Romans 7:4; Galatians 5:22–23; Ephesians 5:9; Philippians 1:11; Colossians 1:6, 10.

WARNING! WARNING! WARNING!

"See to it that no one takes you captive by philosophy and empty deceit, according to human tradition, according to the elemental spirits of the world, and not according to Christ" (Colossians 2:8).

Christianity, in every culture, faces a common challenge: syncretism. Syncretism happens when religious ideas, practices, or truth claims mix together. It might feel like a hybrid of two religions or it might continue to look a lot like Christianity with other ideas slipped in. The problem is even the smallest sprinkling of false ideas corrupts. It creates something that sounds and looks like Christianity but it's opposed to what Christianity is at its core. If you've ever accidentally replaced salt with baking powder in a recipe, you know a small change can ruin everything.

Paul shepherds the Colossians by pointing out the poison being smuggled into their church. He urges them to filter out anything that's not 100% pure, undiluted gospel of Jesus Christ. Beliefs matter. Theology about Christ affects our worship, ethics, identity, and how we live out our faith. Doctrine either leads us towards Christ or away from Christ.

That's why Paul uses the war-language of "captivity" to describe what happens when a person swallows down false beliefs about Christ. Throughout his epistles, Paul sounds the alarm when false teaching invades the church.

Good vs Bad Tradition

Traditions and handed down knowledge aren't bad.[73] The question is, "what's the source?" As we've seen, the Colossians received the gospel message from

---

[73] Traditions can actually be a great thing when rooted in the Bible, or when it's understood the traditions and practices are meant to be helpful but not authoritative. As human beings, we value a connection to our past, remembering and being placed in a

Epaphras (1:7) who most likely received it from Paul who received it from Jesus. This is tradition at its best which Paul commends throughout his letters. It is the faith being passed down from one generation to another and from one person to another (2 Thessalonians 3:6; 1 Timothy 6:20). Gospel-doctrines are the best kind of hand-me-downs.

False teaching, however, does not lead back to Christ and His Word but to some man-made way of thinking. Paul warns against false teachings that find their sources in a deceptive spiritual (angelic) being claiming to speak truth (Galatians 1:8–10; 2 Corinthians 11:14). A river might look appealing, but if its source is a toxic dump, it's deadly. Take every tradition handed down to you and trace it back to the source. Where is it coming from and what's being mixed in?

Jesus rebuked the Pharisees and teachers of the law for following their tradition more than God's truth revealed and passed down (Mark 7:1–23; Matt 15:1–20). They taught the doctrines of men as if they were the commandments of God (Mark 7:7–8).

Be careful of anything that finds its origin in man and not in God. Watch out for those who ignore, deny, twist, or add to the Bible. Be on guard against those who talk a great deal about "spiritual things" but don't focus on Jesus. And be cautious not to elevate traditions, opinions, convictions, and morality alongside the authority of the Word.

Use the Right Filter

God's Word is the filter by which we sift out theological pollution. Paul doesn't go in-depth about the false teaching or heresy in Colossians but he makes the problem clear: it was "not according to Christ." Evaluate every "Christian" sermon, song, church, or book with that test.

---

story, and having meaningful practices to share with people we love. For a good book on family traditions that honor Christ, see *Treasuring Christ in Our Traditions* by Noel Piper.

A lot of what is branded "Christian" in our culture today is unsafe and toxic because it presents a different Jesus than the one revealed in the Bible or no Jesus at all.

> Any teaching that in any way detracts from Christ's exclusive role is by definition both wrong and ineffective. The teachers themselves are probably not denying that Christ was central to God's saving purposes. They seem rather to be arguing that certain practices must be added on in order to achieve true spiritual fulfillment. But, for Paul, in this case, addition means subtraction: one cannot 'add' to Christ without, in effect, subtracting from his exclusive place in creation and in salvation history.[74]

The problem with the false teachers creeping into Colossians isn't that they deny Christ or want to get rid of Him but that they want to add to Him. They want something beyond Him that feels special and sophisticated, but in fact it is empty and vain.

There is always an appeal to something "out there" that feels hidden, secret, or beyond the knowledge of what most people have. But, "extra knowledge" that's not according to Christ or found in the Word is "extra" in the worst sense. It's human-manufactured and of no real value.

This takes us back to the supremacy and sufficiency of Jesus. He's not only over all powers, rulers, and created beings but He stands alone when put alongside other philosophies and sources of wisdom. All understanding is found in He who is the treasure chest of all wisdom and knowledge (2:2–3). Saturate your mind with Jesus as revealed in the Bible and you'll sniff out false teachings about Him.

---

[74] Moo, *Colossians*, 193.

Add more Jesus into your life, but don't add more to Jesus. If Colossians has made anything clear, it's that Jesus is enough. He's the fullness of God who can bring fullness to your life.

Wisdom, rest, peace, joy, blessing, healing, and contentment can be found in Jesus. He is and has and offers everything we need.

Applying Colossians

Questions
1) What are examples of how our beliefs impact the way we live, positively or negatively?
2) How might we evaluate traditions, practices, and ideas that are presented or passed down to us—even if they're from good sources like family, friends, or a church?
3) Not everything packaged as "Christian" is truly biblical or according to Christ. How do you test what you hear, read, watch, or see to see if it's "of God" or "of man"?

Next Steps
- Many people around you have a wrong view of Jesus so be on the offense and share with someone this week who Jesus is and what He's done.
- Pick out a favorite hymn or song that focuses on the person and/or work of Christ. Sing or meditate on those words as a way to worship Him.

For Further Study
- **Beware of false teaching**: Mark 7:7; Galatians 1:8–10; 1 Timothy 6:20; 2 Timothy 3:1–9; Titus 1:14.
- Pick up a book on the person and work of Jesus, like John Piper's *Seeing and Savoring Christ*, Jared Wilson's *Gospel Deeps*, Bruce Ware's *The Man Christ Jesus*, or Dane Ortlund's *Gentle and Lowly*.

GOD WITH US

"For in him the whole fullness of deity dwells bodily" (Colossians 2:9).

The Bible is the story of all stories. As J.R.R. Tolkien said to C.S. Lewis, it is the "true myth." It is audacious in its claims and anything but dull or trite.[75] It's a story of mythical proportions that is historical and truthful.

Scripture's story includes the themes of God dwelling with His people and God's plan to redeem sinful people back to Himself. Both will only happen through the incarnation of the Son of God as he takes on a human nature and body. The songs we sing at Christmas aren't cute and innocent little ditties. They tell the beautiful but shocking story of God becoming man in order to be killed by man to save man.

The gospel-story is God becoming one of us so we could become one with Him. He stoops down to lift us up.

Redemption, the ascension, the resurrection, the cross, none of those things happen unless God incarnates Himself as the God-man. Jesus takes on a human nature—without giving up or compromising His divine nature—so He can become humanity's mediator. God comes down to us to bring us back to Himself. God comes to us so He might be seen and known in the clearest of ways: as a human person. In all of this, He remains God, losing nothing but taking on humanity (Philippians 2:5–11).

This is what Paul means when he says in Jesus, "the whole fullness of deity dwells bodily" (Colossians 2:9). Jesus is not close to God or part of God; He is the fullness of God in the person of the eternal Son (Colossians 1:15–19) who becomes man and lives among us. This is what we celebrate and

---

[75] In her essay, "The Dogma is the Drama," Dorothy Sayers teases this out.

rejoice in at Christmas time. God is with us because He became one of us. Jesus is our Immanuel.

By our union with Jesus, the God-man, we are saved and sanctified. Jesus reveals God to us, redeems us to God, and unites Himself with us as one.

Jesus Reveals God to Us

In the incarnation, Jesus reveals God to us in the most personal and clearest of ways. "And the Word became flesh and dwelt among us, and we have seen His glory, glory as of the only Son from the Father, full of grace and truth" (John 1:14).

Jesus came to make God known to us, not as the first revelation but as the final and complete revelation. "He is the image of the invisible God."

Part of what makes our study of Colossians so rich is seeing the glory and beauty of all Jesus is as the God-man and allowing it to shape our understanding of God. It's one thing to look at creation to see God's power—which we should do—but God's power is on display uniquely when we see Jesus speak and bring a dead man to life (John 11:43). We see God's attribute of compassion as Jesus looks at hurting and sorrowful people and He weeps with them (John 11:33–35). Jesus shows us God.

Jesus Redeems Us to God

Jesus becomes a human person, including taking on our human nature and our fleshly body, so He might truly become one of us. From the moment of Christ's birth, He was born for the purpose of His body being broken and His blood being spilled to save us from our sins. It's because Jesus is God in flesh (Colossians 1:19) He can make peace through the blood of His cross (1:20) and the body of flesh (1:21). Because Jesus is fully God and fully man, He's the only one able to bridge the gap between the two.

Paul moves from the incarnation (2:9) to our union with Him as head—which is only possible because He took on humanity (2:10ff). This union is the means by which we participate in His death and resurrection and receive the benefits of redemption (2:11–15). "If he had not been man, He could not have redeemed men. If He had not been a righteous man, He could not have redeemed unrighteous men. And if He had not been God's Son, He could not have redeemed men for God or made them the sons of God."[76]

Jesus Unites Himself to Us

This takes us to a third reason the incarnation matters. Our union with Christ is not only the basis of our salvation, but it's the basis of our communion with Him.[77] The bond of union is so strong that Paul summarizes it by saying "your life is hidden with Christ" (3:3) and "Christ is your life" (3:4).

Paul's language of the head and the body (1:18; 2:10, 19) is union language. It not only refers to Christ's authority *over* us but his nearness, care, and oneness *with* us. When Paul speaks of his sufferings he can refer to them as Christ's sufferings because of this union (1:24).

In the incarnation, God proves His desire to be known by us, and known rightly, as Jesus reveals who God is to us. Jesus becomes human so He can be united to men and women, not only for our salvation but for a union that creates fellowship and sanctification. He continues even now in heaven to dwell bodily, meaning He remains the God-man who can intercede for us and be united to us.

---

[76] John Stott, *The Message of Galatians* (Leicester: Inter Varsity Press, 1986), 105.

[77] There are other benefits, including receiving the Spirit who causes us to look at Jesus so we will look like Jesus.

Colossians offers us hope and reason to rejoice as the glory and supremacy of Christ awes us. It not only shows us who God is but it unites us with Him. Jesus is God with us as one of us.

This encourages us in the midst of pain, weariness, suffering, loneliness, or any other struggle that we can draw near to a God who understands because He lived the human life. He is the perfect high priest who sympathizes with us so He might draw near to us (Hebrews 4:15).

Because Jesus draws near to us in compassion, we can draw near to Him in confidence.

Applying Colossians

Questions
1. Which of the three purposes listed for the incarnation most applies to where you are today? Why?
2. If Jesus is so glorious, and us seeing and savoring His glory is essential to growing in Him, why do you think we struggle to think about and delight in the glory of Christ throughout our day?

Next Steps
- As you talk to people this week, point them to specific truths you've learned about Christ and how he is present, sovereign, and sufficient in their life. Be praying about and then looking for opportunities to share the things you're learning about Jesus with those around you.

For Further Study
- **Christ's divinity**: John 20:28; Romans 9:5; Philippians 2:5–7; Hebrews 1:3; 2 Peter 1:1.
- **Christ's humanity**: Philippians 2:5–7; Galatians 4:4–5; Matthew 4:2; 1 John 1:1–3.

NEW LIFE (2:9–23)

Though we can't separate the person of Jesus from the work of Jesus, so far Paul has concentrated on the person of Jesus. Though Paul mentioned what Jesus accomplished at the cross (1:13–14, 21), he's spent more time exalting who Jesus is. He's the King of Creation, the image of God, all wisdom and knowledge are in Him, and he's the fullness of God.

A slight shift in focus takes place in 2:11–15. Paul celebrates the new life, forgiveness, freedom, and victory through the death, resurrection, and ascension of Jesus.

As we dwell on the redemptive work of Christ, we discover all we now have in Him. Christ's victory becomes our victory. Christ's resurrected life becomes our new life. Christ's payment of sin becomes our full pardon from sin. If your spiritual-tank is running on empty, Paul's about to pour in fuel for refreshment and rejoicing.

There's much to cling to and find hope in from this section of Scripture. The beautiful gospel plays out in such an ugly event: the cross. We see the gospel not only saves us but it sanctifies (matures and grows) us by making us new. Our life is so wrapped up in Jesus that His death is ours and His resurrection is ours. Our sin and old identity are exchanged with who we now are in Christ. He is our head, salvation, forgiveness, life, Lord, and the soil in which we flourish.

Paul then moves from teaching to warning in 2:16–23. Having considered the fullness of life, forgiveness of sins, and freedom through victory in Christ, Paul can't help but shake his head at the thought of turning to other things. He's out to convince us of the power of staying put in Jesus. He confronts those things in their church detracting from Christ's glory. We already have everything we need in Christ and are growing because of Him (2:19), so don't drift to experiences, visions, rules and asceticism, or legalism.

Everyone else will want to add to Christ. We must be the people who understand His supremacy and sufficiency, and are convinced there's no room for improvement. How do you add to the fullness of God (2:8) that fills us (2:9)? You can't. Rehearse all you have in Christ and stay rooted in Christ.

FEASTING ON HIS FULLNESS

"For in him the whole fullness of deity dwells bodily, 10and you have been filled in him, who is the head of all rule and authority" (Colossians 2:9–10).

I love a good feast. It's not the most important thing about holidays or celebrations, but part of what makes these times so good is the meal shared. Who doesn't want a banquet of food spread before them, full of smells and tastes delighting the senses? In our family's kitchen, we have Psalm 104:14–15 framed in chalk art. "You cause the grass to grow for the livestock and plants for man to cultivate, that he may bring forth food from the earth and wine to gladden the heart of man, oil to make his face shine and bread to strengthen man's heart."

Notice that food and drink aren't just a provision so we survive. They evidence God's goodness in giving us food to add to our happiness. But, we might ask, what else does God intend to point to or teach us in our feasting?

In John 6, Jesus feeds over 5,000 people. He later explains it was meant to point them to a greater reality: He's the one we need to feed and drink on to be made full. Only a chapter later, He uses the imagery of water. "On the last day of the feast, the great day, Jesus stood up and cried out, 'If anyone thirsts, let him come to me and drink" (John 7:37; see also John 4:14). Jesus was saying to pull up a chair and feast yourself on the fullness that He is. Your soul's appetite is too big for finite things. Only the infinite and eternal can quench it.

The Fullness of Jesus

Circling back to Colossians 2:10, Paul tells us we have been filled in Christ. We're called to feast on Jesus and to let our soul's hunger be satisfied by Him.

Paul had just said in Jesus all the fullness of God dwelt bodily (2:9). We feast on He who is the fullness so we are fulfilled (fully filled) by Him. John meant as much when he wrote, "And from his fullness we have all received, grace upon grace" (John 1:16). This has been Paul's point throughout Colossians. Christ is enough.

If Jesus led to us "bearing fruit" and growing, why find life anywhere else (1:6)?

If Jesus delivered us from darkness and redeemed us, why slip back into bondage (1:13–14)?

If through Jesus we inherit all that belongs to God, what else do you need (1:12)?

If Jesus rules over all of creation, why try to take control of things (1:15–17)?

If Jesus made us holy and blameless, why put your hope in anything else (1:22–23)?

If Jesus dwells in us and is the one changing us, why work in our own strength (1:27–29)?

If Jesus is the one in whom all knowledge is found, why go after empty opinions of men (2:2–6)?

If Jesus is the fullness of God, what do we lack outside of Him (2:9)?

This is just a sampling from the first thirty-eight verses of Colossians. In all this, Paul puts the beauty, glory, and sufficiency of Jesus before our eyes so we might see all we have in Him.78 Like a food magazine that draws you in with the zoomed-in picture of a decadent dessert on the cover, Paul gives us a close-up of Christ so we might feast on Him. Fill up your plate and come back for seconds.

In Him is life. In Him is salvation, freedom, power, hope, and wisdom. In Him is reconciliation back to our Creator and renewal in the image we were created to bear. In Him our roots go deep so fruit might blossom.

Filling Up on Jesus

We must ask ourselves this: Where are we seeking to find *ultimate* fulfillment and satisfaction? The temptation is to appraise good things—blessings like relationships, success in your work, and activities—as ultimate things. We then hope they will fulfill us and satisfy us in a way that only Christ can. What feels unfulfilled by Christ in your life? Or, what are areas are you tempted to seek something else to fulfill you?

Paul assures the Colossians anything other than Christ will leave their hunger unsatisfied and their thirsts unquenched. Our hearts have big desires and thirsts. Our desires aren't the problem, but the direction we point them gets us into trouble or leaves us empty. Aim your hungers and thirsts at Jesus. You can be full by feasting on His fullness.

As we read through Colossians meditate on God's love for you, His gifts to you in Christ, all you have through union with Christ, and all you have because of Christ's work on your behalf. As you see the glory and sufficiency of Jesus, let your heart be made full by worshipping Him and getting to know Him. Feast on His fullness.

---

78 In the parallel passage of Ephesians 3:14–21, Paul prays that we'd be filled by God's love for us in Christ. "And to know the love of Christ that surpasses knowledge, that you may be filled with all the fullness of God" (3:19).

Applying Colossians

Questions

1. What are things you're tempted to find fulfillment in or think you're completed by?
2. What are specific ways you might feast on Christ?
3. Over the next six months, what might be one goal for you to better feast on Jesus in a consistent, intentional, and deep way?
4. Over the next six months, what might be one goal for your family, house, or small group to better feast on Jesus in a consistent, intentional, and deep way?

Next Steps

- Set aside time in your mornings to feast on Christ through the Bible.
- Be on the lookout for how you might point others to find fulfillment in Jesus. Do this in a caring and sympathetic way, not an annoying and controlling way.
- As you eat your meals this week, enjoy them to the glory of God. Also reflect on how our taste-buds, appetites, and stomachs point us to our need be satisfied and fed by God.

For Further Study

- **Fullness language**: John 1:16; Colossians 1:19; 2:9; Ephesians 1:22–23; 3:19; 4:10.
- **God filling His temple or people**: 2 Chronicles 7:1; Ezekiel 44:4; Ephesians 5:18.

OUT WITH THE OLD, IN WITH THE NEW

"In him also you were circumcised with a circumcision made without hands, by putting off the body of the flesh, by the circumcision of Christ, 12having been buried with him in baptism, in which you were also raised with him through faith in the powerful working of God, who raised him from the dead. 13And you, who were dead in your trespasses and the uncircumcision of your flesh, God made alive together with him" (Colossians 2:11–13).

In many regions, there's an annual tradition called "spring cleaning." As winter's gloom gives way to spring's warmth, people clean and purge their homes and garages. Whether it's creating room to get new stuff, making sure neglected areas are dusted and wiped at least once a year, or identifying prospects for an upcoming garage sale, we're eager for things to seem new again. We love a clean house, an organized garage, and a closet where shoes and clothes aren't pouring out like a volcanic reaction. Every year, this spring cleaning excites us with new beginnings and a fresh start.

While a fresh coat of paint and a few open windows might brighten things up, it's still the same house. If there are bigger problems—like a cracked foundation or a dead AC unit—you need bigger and more substantive solutions. If this is true in our homes, it's even more true in our lives. Every person needs a fresh start. But sin goes so deep and is so pervasive we don't just need a little tidying up or a quick coat of paint to cover the blemishes. We need a complete renovation of the heart. We need to be made new not just made a little better.

Jesus does exactly that for His people in Colossians 2:11–13. He gives us a totally new life, not just an improved one. He doesn't come to us as a repairman to fix a few problems; He comes to rebuild things entirely. It's out with the old me and in with the new me.

A New Person

Few things are as exciting as someone's baptism because it tells the story of dead people coming to life. I love when people are baptized at our church. We hear the story of how God brought them from death to life, and then we see a visual reenactment as they go down into the water and come up with great joy. The church celebrates their baptism because we rejoice in their union with Christ and their new life through Christ. Baptism doesn't save them but it's a powerful sign and seal of the resurrection life received in Christ. In Christ we die, and in Christ we come alive.

Paul explains Christ's fullness for us by pointing to the shadows of circumcision and baptism that have their substance in our new life in Christ. Similar to how people today wear wedding rings to cement and convey their union with one another, circumcision reminded Israel they belong to God and were in covenant with Him. The act of cutting off the flesh had a clear spiritual representation. "Circumcise therefore the foreskin of your heart, and be no longer stubborn" (Deuteronomy 10:16; see also 30:6; Jeremiah 4:4). Their hard hearts needed cut away so a heart of flesh would remain. It pictured receiving a new heart, or a person becoming new.

The shadow pointed to the reality found through union with Christ. Jesus makes us new from the inside–out. The Spirit's work of regeneration gives us new hearts. Paul picks up this language and calls Christians, those in the new covenant, the circumcised at heart. "But a Jew is one inwardly, and circumcision is a matter of the heart, by the Spirit, not by the letter" (Romans 2:29). Paul says we are the circumcised (Philippians 3:3) because the body of flesh has been put off and we are made new (Colossians 2:11; 2 Corinthians 5:17).

Baptism is the sign the new covenant people, circumcised in heart, now undergo to symbolize they have died and are risen with Christ. While circumcision pointed to the promises and obligations the Jews had by being in

Israel, baptism points to the promises we receive in Christ (2:12). God does the work of making us alive through our participation in Christ, and we receive it only through faith. Baptism therefore doesn't do the cleansing or recreating work but it symbolizes what God accomplished when we joined ourselves to Christ by faith (see also 1 Peter 3:21; Titus 3:5–6).

In Romans 6:1–11, Paul assures the believers they have died to sin because of their baptism into Christ. "We were buried therefore with him by baptism into his death, in order that, just as Christ was raised from the dead by the glory of the Father, we too might walk in newness of life" (Romans 6:4). Christ's crucifixion not only pays for our sin, but through our union with Him, we participate in dying to sin and a resurrection to life with God.

The Old Me is Buried and Gone

Jesus is the fullness for us and we see it here as He releases us from the bondage of sin, our old self is put to death, our heart is renewed, and we're made alive in Christ. Jesus doesn't merely buy or earn a different life for us. Jesus *is* our life. We are made new *in Him*. Our regrettable, shameful pasts are buried with Him and our identity is remade *through Him*.

Pause to reflect on the fact that your past was buried with Christ. Your shame was taken into the grave when He died, and when He rose it was left behind. You aren't defined or dominated by past sins or former struggles. They might still rear their ugly heads, but put them back in the grave where they belong. The old you died with Christ, and a new you rose with Christ.

The waters of baptism declare that we have passed through judgment and came out alive. Part of Christ's sufficiency, supremacy, power, salvation, glory, and fullness invading and changing our life includes making us a new person who is transformed into His likeness. His work accomplishes our redemption and resurrection. And His work, applied by His Spirit does the work of regenerating, renewing, and remaking us. To experience this kind of life, a resurrection life, we don't look beyond Jesus but to Jesus.

If you have died with Christ, then the shackles of your sin and corrupted nature don't have to imprison you anymore. If you have been raised with Christ, the same power that triumphed over the grave offers you the power to walk in newness of life today. Live out of His fullness; not your own and not anyone else's. He is who He is in His fullness so He might give all these things to those united to Him.

What are areas in your life right now that feel dead or hopeless? Is it a relationship, singleness, your prayer life, health, attitude, or something else? Where do you need the resurrection power of Christ bursting life into your world? Christ rose, lives, and reigns so His fullness can fill your life. Let Him do so by asking Him to bring new life to yourself or to something in your life that needs renewed.

Applying Colossians

Questions
1. What are some ways you've seen God make you new?
2. What does baptism signify or portray?
3. Where do you need Christ's resurrection power in your life today?
4. When were you baptized and what was the significance of that event?

Next Steps
- If you haven't been baptized and are a believer, now is a great time. Talk to one of your pastors about your desire to be baptized.
- Write out your testimony of how God brought you from death to life.
- Share with someone this week how God has worked in your life and brought His resurrection power into areas of your life that felt dead or hopeless.

- **Circumcision of the heart**: Deuteronomy 10:16; 30:6; Jeremiah 4:4; Acts 7:51; Romans 2:29; Philippians 3:3.
- **Made alive**: John 3:3; Romans 6:4; 8:11; 2 Corinthians 5:17; Galatians 2:20.
- **Baptism**: Colossians 2:12; 1 Peter 3:21; Galatians 3:23–29; 6:1–11; Acts 8:12–13.

ANGLES ON THE CROSS

"And you, who were dead in your trespasses and the uncircumcision of your flesh, God made alive together with [Jesus], having forgiven us all our trespasses, by canceling the record of debt that stood against us with its legal demands. This he set aside, nailing it to the cross. He disarmed the rulers and authorities and put them to open shame, by triumphing over them in him" (Colossians 2:13–15).

Everyone views the cross from a different angle. Rome saw the cross as a crushing blow to the Jewish King. The Jews saw it as the end of Jesus the blasphemer. We could move from person to person and from group to group to see how perspectives on Jesus and the cross differed. Think of how the soldiers, the two criminals, Jesus's mother, His followers, or Gentile visitors to the city would have viewed the cross differently. With so many outlooks on Jesus and perspectives on the cross, who sees things rightly? Paul gives us the view from above as he recounts the universal significance of Jesus's sacrifice.

Just and the Justifier

Colossians 2 draws the picture of God sitting as the court's Judge upholding justice in the world. Paul describes our sins as a record of debt speaking against us. Just like a convicted criminal's charges are read to testify against him, so also the legal demands of our law-breaking are recorded as debts that must be paid. We live on death-row, awaiting the rightful punishment of creatures who spit in the face of their Creator by choosing their way over His. The Judge cannot and does not overlook the charges because the debt from law-breaking absolutely must be paid.

The good news of the gospel is the extent and debt of our sin is outmatched by the purity of Christ's blood and the magnitude of God's mercy. In an act of astonishing mercy God takes our list of guilty charges and writes on them, "PAID IN FULL."

God is just, and in the death of Jesus our guilty charges are nailed to the cross. Jesus dies. not for Himself, but to exhaust the legal demands against us. Our criminal record built up over a lifetime is nailed to the cross of Jesus, and it's only the pure blood pouring from His holy veins that erases the debt.

In these amazing verses of Colossians 2:13–15, Paul announces the forgiveness, freedom, victory, and new life accomplished by Jesus's work on the cross. This is not only the hope that draws an unbeliever in repentance to God for salvation but it's the daily anchor of believers who still struggle. When I resist God, there's a temptation to give in to defeat or to think I stand condemned. But we return by faith to Jesus's cross and remember Jesus paid it all. My legal verdict in Jesus is now "there is no condemnation" (Romans 8:1), not guilty, and freed!

Run to the Cross

This is how Jesus "disarmed the rulers and authorities and put them to open shame, by triumphing over them in him" (2:15). The very moments that Satan would like to use against me to bury me under guilt are the very moments that lead me back to the cross. I don't deny my sin but confess it.

Instead of puffing up my chest because of any innate goodness, I humbly lean upon the mercy of God demonstrated in sending His Son for me.

We don't just believe this once for salvation; we believe this again and again to rest in God's grace through the gospel. Satan will whisper to your ears reminders of past sin and present failures. Don't respond by giving in to his discouragement but by believing in faith Jesus has fully paid for all your sins and failures: past, present, and future.

Not separating the cross of Good Friday from the empty tomb of Resurrection Sunday, Paul ties together forgiveness through Christ's death to freedom through Christ's resurrection. Being "alive" signifies we have life through the Spirit. Because of Christ's work, our thick file listing our debts is replaced with adoption papers granting us an inheritance.

We're not just declared "not guilty" by the Judge and set on our way. We're adopted by the Father and now loved more than we could ever imagine.

No wonder Paul repeatedly sees reason to rejoice. To return to another hymn, the words of "It Is Well with My Soul" reminds us Jesus bore our sins once so we never have to bear them again. "My sin, oh, the bliss of this glorious thought! My sin, not in part but the whole, Is nailed to the cross, and I bear it no more, Praise the Lord, praise the Lord, O my soul!"[79]

Applying Colossians

Questions
1. Have you placed your faith in Jesus alone for forgiveness, salvation, and reconciliation?
2. How does this powerful gospel message help you fight unbelief, condemnation, regret, sin, and Satan's attacks?
3. What are some reasons you have to rejoice today?

Next Steps
- Share with one person how the message of the cross shapes how you view your past, your sin, and your relationship with God.

For Further Study
- **The cross**: Romans 3:21–26; 2 Corinthians 5:20–21; 1 Peter 1:19–21; 2:24–25.

---

[79] Lyrics to "It Is Well with My Soul" by Horatio Spafford found at: http://en.wikipedia.org/wiki/Horatio_Spafford. Accessed on May 10, 2018.

SHADOWS VS SUBSTANCE

"Therefore let no one pass judgment on you in questions of food and drink, or with regard to a festival or a new moon or a Sabbath. 17These are a shadow of the things to come, but the substance belongs to Christ. 18Let no one disqualify you, insisting on asceticism and worship of angels, going on in detail about visions, puffed up without reason by his sensuous mind" (Colossians 2:16–18).

Before any family vacation I like to research our potential destination. I'll buy a few travel books, learn the history of a place, figure out what makes it worth visiting, and determine the must–see sights or must–do experiences. The more I research, the more excited I get to be at this place in person, which always exceeds the limits of what's seen on a flat image through my screen. I don't just enjoy the vacation but I enjoy "nerding out" in the research phase.

Imagine my wife and I fly to our destination, let's say it's the coast of Northern California. What if, on that first morning, I woke up and explained that instead of going out and experiencing the breath-taking hike in Point Reyes so we can smell the air, feel the breeze, and see the glorious view, we'll stay in the hotel and look at pictures.

Would it not be insane to sacrifice the experiences, smells, memories, and views of the rocky coast of California to stay in my hotel and look at two-dimensional images? We all know our pictures—before or after a trip—don't compare to the actual experience. The travel book's whole purpose is to point you to a place and get you on your way.

Paul appeals to the Colossians not to settle for shadows when Jesus is the substance. The religious practices, festivals, and observances of the Old Testament pointed to the coming of the Messiah who could provide complete redemption, perfect righteousness, and a final rest. To lean on or look to incomplete shadows whose purpose is directing us to a bigger and brighter substance—Christ—is even crazier than me ignoring my vacation because I have a little travel book to gawk at.

In 2:6–15, Paul unpacked the fullness we have in Christ. He admonished them not to be taken captive by false teaching or human tradition not according to Christ (2:8). He compelled them with the fullness they have in Jesus (2:9–10), the forgiveness and freedom they have in Jesus (2:13–15), and the new resurrected-life they have in Jesus (2:11–13). You who were dead have been made alive *in Christ*. When you have this kind of fullness in Jesus, why look somewhere else?

Subtraction by Addition

Paul continues by honing in on subtle ways they've put their hope in things besides Jesus. Fulfilling his own charge in Colossians 1:28, Paul proclaims Jesus alone and warns against anything that adds to or takes us beyond Christ.

Paul warns against getting stuck on religious rituals that exist for something beyond themselves, and he teaches that Jesus is the fulfillment of what was looked for. He rebukes empty "spiritual experiences" that only puff up, and he teaches us that only experiencing Jesus grows people. He reproves reliance upon man-centered rules and self-generated efforts that are powerless, and he teaches us that only living in view of our new identity in Christ will overcome the old flesh. "Because it is in Christ that you have spiritual fullness, Paul is saying, do not let anyone impose upon you a program of spiritual development that does not have Christ at its heart."[80]

"Let no one" judge, condemn, or disqualify you (2:16, 18). Paul's not simply saying "don't let anyone think less of you." He's making it plain you should not be condemned for resting on Jesus and His righteousness alone. Now that Jesus has come and fulfilled all the laws, types, festivals, and ceremonies pointing to Him, we have everything needed and longed for in

---

[80] Moo, *Colossians*, 218.

Him. He alone provides righteousness. He alone assures us we are God's sons and daughters, loved and accepted. He alone nourishes our faith and our hearts as we follow Him.

Lethal Legalism

There are many legalistic churches today still requiring people to obey man-made rules or to keep religious practices from the Old Testament that Jesus fulfilled. We need to be on guard against teaching, or following any teaching, not firmly grounded in the Bible and according to Christ alone. But we can't put this verse or put a works-oriented bent only on "those legalists" since we all are prone to drift this way. Even the most gospel-centered, grace-loving Christian must fight against the internal urge to think God will smile on my attempts at goodness.

We all must check our hearts and ask if there are any things besides Christ we will think get us in, make us good, clean us up, win God over, or make us a little better off. Even good things, like going to church or committing to praying daily, can be wrongly used by our deceptive hearts. We easily slip into a lethal legalism that trusts in our works.

Anytime other things—good or bad—chip away at the fullness we have in Jesus then we've started living by works and not by faith. We've started to live by performance, not grace. We've started to lean on self, not Jesus. Like in Colossians, this is often subtle, slow, and it can be deceptive because our self-righteousness is wrapped in good intentions and religious fervor.

Our drift towards relying on works is why we need to daily preach the gospel to ourselves, and then walk in it. We must daily die to self, both the self that resists God outright and the self that tries to justify ourselves because of the stuff we do for God. We need to daily confess sin, not just the wrong we've done but the good we've done for the wrong reasons. Every morning we must place our faith, hope, trust, and confidence on Jesus alone.

View yourself through the eyes of God. He looks at you through the lens of who you are now "in Christ." This means your sins are not held against you (see Colossians 2:13–14) and your good deeds can't make you any more acceptable before God than you already are in Jesus (2:16–3:4).

If you trust in your own works or goodness, you'll burnout from running on the treadmill of performance. But if you trust in Jesus's righteousness and work for you, you can rest on the sofa of God's grace. Grace doesn't make us lazy when it comes to obedience, but it does help us last as our endurance isn't from our own energy.

The gospel shifts our gaze away from our own goodness or badness and onto the fullness and glory of Jesus. Looking *in* leads to a wrong despair or a false pride but looking *up* leads to the freedom and joy found in Jesus.

Applying Colossians

Questions
1. Does your religious background make legalism, works-righteousness, or a performance mentality more of a temptation? Why or why not?
2. What are things in life—good or bad—you sometimes do to make God happy with you?
3. How do you need to fight any reliance on self-righteousness and instead find Jesus's righteousness to be sufficient?
4. If you have children or are close to any kids, how can you help them rest in the grace of Jesus? What are ways we might do the latter unintentionally?

Next Steps
- Share with a believer close to you (family member, small group member, disciple, etc.) the things you sometimes lean on when you

should lean on Jesus alone. Ask them to help you remember the freedom in the gospel and to fight any performance-oriented bents.

- Think about what you find most meaning or fulfillment in. Consider ways they can be enjoyed but also how they point to the greater substantive fulfillment found in Jesus.

For Further Study

- **Parallel verses**: Romans 14:1–17; 1 Corinthians 8–9; Mark 7:14–23; Ephesians 4:11–16.
- **Food and drink**: Mark 7:14–23; Romans 14:3–17; 1 Corinthians 8–9; Hebrews 9:10.
- **Calendar**: Romans 14:5; Mark 2:28; 1 Chronicles 23:31; Nehemiah 10:33.

FEEDING ON REAL FOOD

"Let no one disqualify you, insisting on asceticism and worship of angels, going on in detail about visions, puffed up without reason by his sensuous mind, 19and not holding fast to the Head, from whom the whole body, nourished and knit together through its joints and ligaments, grows with a growth that is from God" (Colossians 2:18–19).

Despite pervasive secularism in our culture, religious and spiritual experiences are as popular as ever. Stroll through any bookstore or flip through your television's self-help shows or religious channels (actually, I don't recommend that second one) and you'll see how much weight people put into what they think are spiritual experiences. Because it's exactly that, an experience, we're prone to think experience is either the trump card over beliefs or the goal we seek in our beliefs.

Paul doesn't advocate an experience-less Christianity devoid of emotions and affections. As we'll see in 3:1–4, Paul encourages emotion, passion, and the role of our affections. But in 2:18–19, he does warn against experiences opposed to Christ or that take our focus off Christ. The temptation when reading through this part of Colossians is to get sidetracked by what Paul's against here and miss what he's for. But since Paul found it more worth his time to go into detail about Jesus than the weird and false religious views, we'll follow Paul's example. Focus on what's clear, not what's curious.

What Not to Pursue

Paul first puts out an alert against "asceticism" (ESV) or "false humility" (NIV) or "pious self-denial" (NLT). It's the kind of self-abasement that comes from denying something to the body (2:20–23). Many commentators think it might even be tied to a severe form of fasting or self-deprivation that leads to the visions and experiences mentioned. They see visions, but those religious visions are more likely due to a brain starved of good health than a heart flourishing with the Spirit's presence.

The next phrase, "worship of angels," indicates some were over-emphasizing spiritual beings. This isn't a "back then" practice. If you visit other cultures, you might be shocked by how much their daily life involved thinking about spirits, angels, demons, or gods. This is spreading rapidly to the West. Paul already assured the Colossians that Jesus's death and resurrection defeated all such authorities and powers (2:15).

Paul also warns against those "going on in detail about visions." These might feel powerful and vivid, but that experiential feeling does not mean it is of God or according to Christ. Even today a host of "Christian books" or "Christian movies" go into detail about experiences in heaven or hell. The fact that they are so willing to speak where the Bible has not and to focus on "things" over Christ should give us great caution.

Paul writes to people full of themselves, "puffed up," who have no reason to be so. In fact, their attention on "spiritual things" and not the things of the Spirit (or "Spiritual things") indicates their mind is set on things opposed to God (the "flesh").

Paul's message forces us to ask tough questions. What tempts me away from looking to Jesus alone? What experiences do I give weight to that are contrary to Christ? What things do I invest in or give attention toward to grow instead of being nourished by Christ? We need to examine our hearts and lives and let any idols be exposed so we can worship Jesus and Jesus alone.

What to Pursue

In verse 19, Paul moves from spiritual experiences that don't lead to discipleship to how we truly grow. It doesn't come from anything apart from

Jesus. Since Jesus alone is the Head of the body, He alone is the one from whom we receive life, growth, and nourishment. To rely on things other than Jesus—whether religious rituals, rules, or experiences—is to be a body without a Head.

How does a body without a head grow? How long will a body with a missing head last? Will it be healthy, happy, and well fed? Paul's image is straightforward. Any part of the body detached from the head is destined to quickly die. Jesus is the head of the church, His body, and we will only grow, be nourished, and find life when fed by our firm connection to Him (not experiences, rules, or religious practices).

Jesus alone is the authority in our lives. Jesus alone is the one we've been intimately united with. Jesus alone is the one who provides genuine growth. Hold fast to Jesus, and Jesus alone.

Knit Together for Growth

The imagery beautifully pictures how the church grows in Christ *together*. As the last phrase of 2:20 says, our growth is "from God." God knits, unites, and holds us together in Christ. Similarly, Ephesians 4:12–16 says we're "joined and held together by every joint with which it is equipped, when each part is working properly, makes the body grow so that it builds itself up in love" (Ephesians 4:16).

In chapters 3–4 of Colossians, we'll see how the body can act in this way, building one another up and serving one another as brothers and sisters under the same Lord. For now, consider these questions. Are you connected with the head (Jesus)? Are you also joined to and built up by the rest of the body (the church)? Those are God's means of growth.

What Paul's after is genuine growth in the lives of those following Jesus. There's no shortcut to maturity. It happens over a lifetime of faithfully following Jesus and submitting to His Lordship. That growth might even be slow, at least slower than we would like, but it will be genuine. It might not be as exciting as the visions and experiences, and it might not give us as much room to boast in ourselves, but it will be from Christ.

If we want to grow, we don't need the next thing, the new thing, or the latest thing. We need an ordinary faith that continues to pursue Jesus in the context of His people living in the gospel together.

Applying Colossians

Questions
1. Are there any "experiences" that you think you need to *really* grow in Jesus? Do you rely upon mountain-top experiences or rely on a firm faith in Jesus to grow spiritually?
2. What are ways you're allowing others in the body to help you grow in Christ? How are you helping others in the body grow in their walk with Christ?
3. Are there any things you need to give more time, energy, or attention to so you can be firmly rooted in Jesus and growing in Him?

Next Steps
- If you're not currently regularly attending a local church, that would be a great first step to being "knit together" with others. If you are, consider joining a small group, bible study, or discipleship group.
- Write down two things you can do to build someone else up. Serve or care for someone, write an encouraging note, visit a church member who might be alone, or choose another way to love others in the body.

For Further Study
- **Worship of angels**: Hebrews 1:1–2:4.
- **A growing body**: Colossians 1:3–8; 3:13–17; Ephesians 4:11–16; 1 Corinthians 12.

THE POWERLESSNESS OF SELF

"If with Christ you died to the elemental spirits of the world, why, as if you were still alive in the world, do you submit to regulations—21"Do not handle, Do not taste, Do not touch" 22(referring to things that all perish as they are used)—according to human precepts and teaching. 23These have indeed an appearance of wisdom in promoting self– made religion and asceticism and severity to the body, but they are of no value in stopping the indulgence of the flesh" (Colossians 2:20–23).

Colossians 2:23 and its context (2:20–3:4) is a well-worn section in my Bible. It rebukes a notion of Christian maturity built on the shaky grounds of "self-made religion." This text always helps me, whether fighting my own reliance on self and rules, or when talking to another believer about how to battle sin.

Our rules, our vigor, our denial of what's "taboo," and our reliance upon works has "no value in stopping the indulgence of the flesh" (2:23). Those are strong words by Paul. They have the potential to smash the beliefs and practices we can succumb to in sanctification (Christian growth). Not only that, but his words raise the important question he answers in chapter 3. If these regulations have no value (ESV) or provide no help (NLT) in stopping the powerful desires of my fallen flesh, then what *is* of value or what *does* help me fight my sinful desires? Can you think of a more practical question to ask and answer?

We've already seen Paul speak against putting stock in religious rituals that were shadows pointing to Christ (2:16–17) and spiritual experiences and visions that puff up rather than build up (2:18–19). In 20–23, he continues by denouncing a rule-making, man-centered, pleasure-denying, self-empowered way of living for God. Any self-sufficient Christianity is a Christ-less Christianity.

Fleshly Fighting

Paul summarizes the made-up rules of the false teachers. These rules banned certain foods and drinks. It emphasized human rules and teachings (2:22), especially those that appear pious in denying the body from pleasures in this world. When we read 2:6–23, we see an emphasis on asceticism—saying no to creation—and man-made rules and prohibitions. These false teachers were saying "the world is bad" so godly ones will deny everything in it.

A good rule of thumb is to be careful of anyone who talks more about what they're against than what they're for. Or, when it comes to local church and individual believers, watch out for those more passionate about self-made commands than Christ. Keep the main One the main thing.

Asceticism, rules, rigid discipline, and extreme self-denial might appear wise and "spiritual" at first glance, but they're opposed to God—who created good things in the world—and a gospel-centered view of following Jesus.[81] "They wanted to measure their Christian progress by things of this earth."[82] But the human heart is much more complex, deceptive, and difficult to measure than that.

It's easy to do a few activities, follow a few rules, attend a couple of meetings, cut out some vices, and then be able to hold my head high because of what I've done. In that process, we avoid rooting up the idols of the heart and cultivating genuine worship and obedience to Jesus Christ. It's easy to construct rules about what not to eat or drink or touch (2:21) without addressing the bitterness, gossip, lust, and materialism entrenched in our hearts. And yes, it's easy right now to think about ways other people ignore

---

[81] This helps us to see that Paul's language in 3:1–4 about the things above and the things are on earth is not against the material stuff of creation. Since he is here rebuking a spirituality that denies the goodness of creation, we should understand Paul as referring to "things that are on earth" (3:2) as the things that belong to this fallen world. See Joe Rigney's *Things of the Earth* or Trillia Newbell's *Enjoy* for more on this.

[82] Melick Jr., *Colossians*, 276.

their own heart issues instead of admitting where we fall prey to legalism and pride.

It's likely Paul has in mind here Christ's teachings. In Mark 7:1–13 Jesus confronts the Pharisees for observing the rules and traditions of men but ignoring the commandments of God. In verses 14–23, Jesus says what defiles a person isn't the food they put into their body but what's in their heart. It's the evil within that defiles more than the evil outside of us. While there's wisdom needed so we resist evil in the world we also must see the evil in our own hearts.

Dealing with Desires

Part of the problem is rules might help us avoid bad behaviors—for a while— but they don't deal with the heart's hungers. Rules and willpower don't overcome the powerful, sometimes seemingly all-consuming passions of the heart.[83] Desire itself is not a bad thing. We were created to desire and to desire with passion. The problem is that we desire things opposed to God and His good designs. We're enticed by the fallen desires of our flesh and can easily be ruled by those desires. Even good desires are commandeered by the enemy to be misdirected towards the wrong things.

If we have one king, Jesus, then we shouldn't be dominated by our selfish or sinful desires. Our desires are powerful but we can and must subordinate them to the will of our Maker and Redeemer. When we fight sinful desires not by the power of Jesus but by appointing another master, we only compound the problem. Rules or laws can become a master we think can direct our lives and give us freedom. Or, we assign ourselves as co-ruler as we try to run our

---

[83] As we will see throughout chapter three of Colossians, this is not to say we don't fight sin, obey God's commands, or instill discipline into our lives. But there's a big difference between the self-empowered efforts and man-made rules Paul attacks in chapter two and the Spirit-dependent power and God-given commands Paul embraces in chapter three.

own lives, live in our own power, please God with our checklist, and put on a religious performance.

Both legalism (reliance on the rules) and moralism (reliance upon my works or my effort) promise freedom but only end up offering more bondage. Walking in and with Jesus is the only thing that has power to help us fight the passions of our flesh (2:23). In fact, when we walk in Christ by the Spirit our desires can actually change.

Desires cannot simply be told to be quiet or stop. I mean, you can try that but it will be like telling your dog to settle down when someone just dropped a juicy steak on the floor. Good luck. Desires need fulfilled, but they need fulfilled in a God-ordained and God-directed way.

If I'm hungry and tempted by an enticing plate of warm cookies in my kitchen, I can't avoid them by just saying to myself "Don't eat the cookies. Don't eat the cookies. Don't eat the cookies." Unless I quench that hunger with something else, my desire will always be there. Desires and hungers are quenched only through their fulfillment, not by merely denying them.

While Colossians 2 gives warnings of what to avoid and what doesn't truly change us, Colossians 3 offers clear and practical answers on where to aim our heart for satisfaction and sanctification.

As chapter 3 makes clear, desires must be fulfilled by the right things. Jesus is the right thing to set our desires on. Any substitute—good or bad—is the wrong thing and will fail us and frustrate us. What are the desires, longings, and hungers of your heart? How can those be deeply and truly fulfilled by Jesus alone?

Applying Colossians

Questions

1. What are ways you rely upon self or the structures of rules to pursue holiness?
2. Why do rules, laws, and even self-discipline (apart from Christ) ultimately fail to change our hearts or overcome our strongest desires?
3. What are some of the longings of your heart that might lead you into temptation or idolatry? How do you think they might point you to Jesus?
4. What are some differences between self-empowered effort and Spirit-dependent effort? How do you know when you're resting in the self's power or the Spirit's power?

Next Steps

- Spend some time doing an evaluation of the desires in your heart. What do you find yourself truly desiring, wanting, or thinking about when you have time? What things do you pursue to fulfill those desires? What idols might need rooted out? How can you submit your desires to Jesus and see them fulfilled in good and godly ways?
- Ask a spouse or friend to help you think through these questions and dial into your heart's desires. Pray together and ask for encouragement as you fight idols and pursue Jesus.

For Further Study

- **Against man-centered religion**: Isaiah 29:13; Mark 7:1–23; Galatians 3:1–9.
- **Passions of the flesh**: Romans 6:12; Ephesians 4:22; 1 Peter 1:14; 4:2; Titus 3:3.
- Read Trilia Newbell's *Enjoy* or Joe Rigney's *Things of the Earth*.

RAISED WITH CHRIST (3:1–10)

In chapter 2, Paul held up the glory of Christ's work for us to marvel at. The grace of Christ rewrites everything about us because we're united to Jesus. Union with Christ comes with a lot of perks. It creates intimacy with Christ and a new identity in Christ. We are "filled in him" (2:10) so there's absolutely nothing we lack. We pass from death to life through the resurrected Christ (2:11–13). God forgives all our sins, fully and forever (2:13). And Jesus triumphs over evil so we share in this victory and freedom (2:15).

Not only is that true of us as individuals, but Christ is who He is as the Head of the church. Christians united to Jesus are united together by Jesus (2:19).

Not to be outdone, chapter 3 starts with equally astounding truths of who we now are in Christ. We're raised up with Him and seated with Him (3:1). Our life is hidden with Christ in God (3:2). Christ is our life (3:4). And one day, we will appear with Him in glory (3:4).

Consider who we used to be and who we now are in Jesus. Dwell upon all you possess in Christ. Soak up these life-changing identity statements so they can be squeezed out as we go through our day. These truths remind us the gospel is not only about Jesus forgiving our past but it's about Jesus giving us life in the present and a whole new future.

Since this *is* true, don't lean on or look to anything other than Jesus. Don't live out of old identities, replacement identities, or false identities. Live out of your identity in Christ, formed by looking at and knowing Christ. A.W. Tozer wrote, "While we are looking at God we do not see ourselves—blessed riddance. The man who has struggled to purify himself and has had nothing but repeated failures will experience real relief when he stops tinkering with his soul and looks away to the Perfect One."[84]

When we look at Jesus and know Him, we will over time become like Him. As we put off who we used to be and put on the new me, the real me in Christ, we see our identity and image come together. We are in Christ and we start to image Christ through the knowledge of Christ (3:10). All this theology and knowledge about Christ seen in Colossians is leading us to action. It leads to ridding ourselves of anything that doesn't look or smell like Jesus. Seeing Jesus so clearly in Colossians gives us discernment for what in our life does and doesn't reflect Him.

---

[84] A. W. Tozer, *The Pursuit of God* (Camp Hill: Christian Publications Inc., 1993), 85.

CHRIST IS OUR LIFE

"If then you have been raised with Christ, seek the things that are above, where Christ is, seated at the right hand of God. 2 Set your minds on things that are above, not on things that are on earth. 3 For you have died, and your life is hidden with Christ in God. 4 When Christ who is your life appears, then you also will appear with him in glory" (Colossians 3:1–4).

Who Are You?

Imagine you and I meet for the first time. As we exchange introductions, what would you tell me about yourself? Take a minute and think of three things you'd tell me about who you are.

We all describe and define ourselves around something. At first, we think these are small matters and that the way we think about who we are has little to do with our identity. But each person has something they define themselves by. There's something they live their life around, to be or become. This might be gender, ethnicity, vocation, personality, religion, looks, geography, socio-economic status, gifts or talents, relational status, family, values, religion and beliefs, political leanings, and on and on. We might find our identity in what people think of us, our accomplishments or failures, how we think God views us, our worst moments, or even the pain we've experienced.

All those might be part of who we are and aspects of our identity. But what we see in Colossians 3:1–4 is only one thing is so big, so central to who we are, so long-lasting and deep-rooted that it can be the core of our identity. What we find our identity in shapes how we understand the world we live in (including ourselves, God, others) and how life should be lived.

For example, if you find your identity in people thinking highly of you, you will think, talk, and do whatever it takes to be approved by them. This becomes an enslaving force (an idol). The moment you feel as if someone is unhappy with you, you either become angry or sad. You change to become what you think will make you accepted. Before long you don't like the "new you." The idol swallows up and spits out any meaning and wholeness to your identity. In her excellent book on identity, *Made for More*, Hannah Anderson writes:

> When we turn to other things for knowledge, when we define ourselves by things like our work, our relationships, our giftedness—we create an alternative source of identity. And as we image this false god, our very personhood crystallizes around it. Instead of being fully formed, multidimensional people who radiate the complexity of God's nature, we become one-dimensional caricatures, as limited and superficial as the thing that we have devoted ourselves to. And we actually begin to resemble it.[85]

We were created to find our identity in something we worship. While God's good design was that we would image Him (Genesis 1:26–28) sin so marred and corrupted us we now image the idols we worship (Romans 1:22–25). This loss of a true, fulfilling, lasting, and sustaining identity where we can flourish in God's good designs for us is no small loss.

Idolatry and Identity

There is a cyclical relationship between idolatry and identity. Because we worship (live for) idols, we form an identity around those idols. The more we define ourselves by something the more prone we are to idolatry. Because those idols disappoint, there is an unhappiness deep within because we've laced who we are (identity) with what we live for (idolatry). The idolatry and misplaced identity impoverish our soul and hollows us out.

---

[85] Hannah Anderson, *Made for More* (Chicago: Moody Publishers, 2014), 50. See also, Richard Lints, *Identity and Idolatry* (Downers Grove: InterVarsity Press, 2015).

The good news is this can lead to seeing the bankruptcy of idols. It can point us to Jesus. The bad news is that our hearts are darkened and deceived so we often just move from one idol to the next.

This is, in part, why Paul says don't fight desires at the level of rules, religion, will-power, and strict discipline (Colossians 2:0–23). If your idol remains in your heart, you'll continue to desire what the idol promises to you and you'll center your identity on it. But, if you displace idol worship with a heart set on Jesus (3:1–4), you'll find your identity in Him. Your desires *and* actions will then reflect Him (3:5–25). "In discovering Him, the source of all existence, you will also discover yourself. In finding Him, you will find the answer to the question 'Who am I and why am I here?'"[86]

Indicatives and Imperatives

Paul almost always announces what is true about believers before he tells them how to live. As we grasp our identity, we have a better understanding and motivation for walking in it. For those who have turned from sin and self and trusted in Jesus alone for their salvation, they are so united with Jesus Christ that they are *in Him* (Romans 6; John 15). This union is such that God now sees us as one with His son, so what is true of Jesus becomes true of us and what belongs to Him belongs to us and defines us.

Being "in Christ" is our fundamental, life-shaping, joy-producing identity. As we saw in the very first verse of Colossians, who we are is defined by whose we are.

Listen to what Paul says about us in Christ in the opening of Colossians 3. You have been raised with Christ (3:1). You have died with Him (3:3). Your life is hidden with Christ in God (3:3). Christ is your life (3:4). When He appears, you will appear with Him in glory (3:4).

---

[86] Anderson, *Made for More*, 27.

This identity conversation continues in the next section as the church is told to live in the light of their true identity. Be who you really are by putting off the old self (3:9) and putting on new self (3:10). This new you is being renewed into the image of Christ. As you worship Jesus and find your identity in Him, that identity moves from the inside-out as the Spirit helps us reflect Jesus.

When we consider the line of logic that began with the powerlessness of self in 2:16–24 to a life reflecting Jesus in 3:5 and following, the key link is the power behind worshipping Jesus and rooting your identity in Him. Worship informs our identity, and a Christ-centered identity (3:1–4) empowers Christ-exalting living (3:5–25).

In the coming days, we'll flesh this idea out more as we think about how the put off and put on exhortations tie back to identity. For now, pause to consider where you've placed your identity. It's easy to say it's in Jesus, but is that true? Does that define you? Is that reality so core to how you see yourself that your responses to people, your priorities, desires, thoughts, and actions all flow from your identity in Christ? Or do you first define yourself by something else? Is your identity rooted in some idol? Do you live out of something you think is more central to who you are: personality, career, relationships, gender, ethnicity, past behaviors, pain experienced, or status in life?

We are all searching for an answer to the question, "Who am I?" We don't just want to know things describing us; we want to know what truly defines us. Christ claims us and defines us. We are who we are in Christ and because of Christ. This changes everything about us. It redirects our purposes and mission. We belong to a people as we're placed into a community. It tells us how God sees us and relates to us.

Union with Christ is the anchor stabilizing our lives, the engine motivating us, and the wheel directing us. Live out of your identity in Jesus.

Applying Colossians

Questions

1. Why is identity so important for the believer?
2. What do you tend to find your identity in?
3. If your identity is in Jesus through union with Him, what does this mean about your unity with other believers who might seem different from you?
4. What are things your family values and celebrates? If you have children, are there pressures put on them, things you often talk about, things affirmed in them or emphasized that might lead them to finding their identity in something other than Jesus?

Next Steps

- Write down ways you're tempted to define yourself. After writing a few things, cross them out and write next to them what is true of you in Jesus Christ.

For Further Study

- **Union with Christ:** John 15:1–11; Romans 6; Galatians 2:20; Ephesians 1:3–14.

TOO HEAVENLY MINDED
OR NOT HEAVENLY MINDED ENOUGH?

"If then you have been raised with Christ, seek the things that are above, where Christ is, seated at the right hand of God. 2 Set your minds on things that are above, not on things that are on earth. 3 For you have died, and your life is hidden with Christ in God. 4 When Christ who is your life appears, then you also will appear with him in glory" (Colossians 3:1–4).

Have you ever heard the phrase someone is "so heavenly minded that they are of no earthly good"? It's not a compliment. The jab suggests the person is aloof from the concerns and daily realities of the rest of us. You've likely met this kind of overly pious person (think of Ned Flanders from *The Simpsons* or Angela from *The Office*). They're always ready to be the rain-cloud in the room or rigidly steer all conversations towards religion. Don't be that guy or gal.

Paul isn't against us being passionate about our faith. It's good to see all of life through a bigger story than what our eyes observe. We are dual-citizens. We possess a heavenly citizenship in Christ that's lived out in our earthly citizenship. Our earthly life matters, from the mundane to the momentous. Those who set their mind and heart on Jesus (3:1–4) will be renewed into His likeness (3:10) so they can live good and loving lives (3:5–11) for the good of those around them (3:12–17). That's here and now.

Dual-Citizenship

This means the truth is we can only be of earthly good if we are heavenly minded, in the right way. And the right way to be heavenly minded is to not to separate your spiritual life from your physical life.

Recalibrate your values, affections, desires, beliefs, and manner of living around your citizenship in Christ's kingdom (see Matthew 6:25–34). But as you follow Jesus, He leads you into an earthy life. He leads Christians into renewed living in the normal spaces of home, work, school, church, cafes and restaurants, and neighborhoods.

Jesus will lead you into bloody battles against your sin (3:5–9). He will lead you to take on new ways of relating to others (3:11–17). He will lead you to do all things as His image-bearer who reflects His character, purposes, and values to those around us (3:10, 17).

It's important not to misunderstand Paul's language of "things on earth" versus "things above." He spent time in 2:20–23 fighting against any ascetic mindset that views created things as wrong and "spiritual" things alone as good. Paul explains these terms in 3:5 when he says to "put to death what is earthly in you" (3:5) and then he defines "earthly" as sins of the flesh.

He's not advocating escaping from this world or being "of no earthly good" by neglecting our earthly citizenship. He's urging us not to get swept up in the priorities and pleasures offered by this fallen world.

Even in the good things of this world, we must not worship anything alongside of Christ. It's easy to let family, relationships, careers, possessions, pleasures, desires for happiness or belonging, or any other good gifts become idols we bow down to and live for in Jesus's place. For example, countless "Christian homes" tell their kids God is most important, but practically, they're ruled by the idols of popularity and achievement. Jesus only occasionally makes a cameo in family conversations, while the cultural gods of grades, sports (or another extracurricular activity), college, and careers make a daily appearance.

Because of our indwelling sin and the pull of the current of living in a fallen world, we drift towards idolizing even good things. Paddle towards Jesus as fast as you can, whatever else might be screaming for attention.

Seek and Set

Notice the two verbs Paul uses. He tells us to *seek* after and *set* our minds on Jesus (the substance of things above). Paul doesn't use "seek" to mean go find something or obtain something but to wrap your mind around this. Richard Melick Jr. writes: "The term implies more than a way of thinking; it includes values and loves as well. It could well be translated as 'delight in things above.' In contrast with this second command, which speaks of values, the first command refers to desires."[87]

You might also recall the words of Jesus, "but seek first the kingdom of God" (Matthew 6:33). Or elsewhere, "You shall love the Lord your God with all your heart and with all your soul and with all your mind" (Matthew 22:37).

What are Jesus and Paul calling us to as Christians? What is the heartbeat of following Jesus? It's about aiming hearts and minds towards Jesus and pursuing Him above everything else. It's seeing Him as the greatest treasure and delighting in Him. It's pointing your thoughts, affections, desires, loves, words, and life towards Jesus so you follow Him with everything you have in every area of life. It's about worship. Walking with Jesus is about finding delight, joy, and rest in Jesus—both above all things of the earth and in every earthly gift.[88]

Before moving to the applications of how to live out our new life in Jesus (3:5ff), we might ask why Paul takes us in this direction. Why point us to Jesus? Why not just tell us what to do, what sins to stop and what good things to start?

---

[87] Melick Jr., *Colossians*, 280.

[88] I recommend reading Joe Rigney's book *The Things of Earth* to better understand how to delight in God through enjoying His earthly gifts.

It's only when we allow ourselves to linger over who Jesus is that we see His glory and worth. It's only when we understand who Jesus is that we realize He is not to be thought about briefly on Sunday or only sought occasionally when we need Him to answer prayer.

Jesus is our wisdom in everyday decisions, our redemption when we sin, our strength when weak, our hope when sorrowful, our power when tempted, our joy above and in all joys, the one holding everything together, ruling from His throne, reconciling us to God and to one another, giving life to His church, making us new, and giving us a fresh start and new identity. He is our everything.

It's only when we see Him like this we will follow *Him* more than our fallen, fleshly desires (2:23). Only when we have large, sweeping thoughts of Jesus will we trust Him when life is falling apart. Only when Jesus is known both for His transcendent glory and nearness will we run to Him for strength and help. Only when we believe Jesus can really deliver us and make us new will we put to death the old self and live as a new creation in Christ.

What are you doing today or this week to aim your heart and mind towards Jesus? What are you doing to slay any idols that threaten to steal your affections away from Him? How can your time in the Word and prayer, your time with God's people, or your thoughts throughout the day point toward the glorious Jesus seen throughout Colossians?

When we take time to reflect on the fullness of who Jesus is, we realize He can fulfill all we need and desire. Here again we see the message of Colossians. Jesus alone is worth beholding with the full weight of our mind and heart's attention. And it is in beholding Jesus we become like Jesus.

Applying Colossians

Questions

1. What do the action of "seeking after" and "setting your mind on" make you think of? What might this look like in your life?
2. How can you seek Jesus *above* everything? How can you seek Jesus *in* everything?
3. What are things (good or bad) that keep you from pursuing Jesus with more of your heart and mind? What distracts you from pursuing knowing Him more?

Next Steps

- Come up with one way you can intentionally seek after Jesus this week. Ask someone to pray for you and encourage you as you seek to do this.
- Ask another believer(s) for how they've seen God's glory, faithfulness, grace, and goodness show up in their life. Be encouraged and worship through them remembering God's work.

For Further Study

- Read Colossians again and notice everything you see about the person or work of Jesus.

BE KILLING SIN

"Put to death therefore what is earthly in you: sexual immorality, impurity, passion, evil desire, and covetousness, which is idolatry. ₆On account of these the wrath of God is coming. ₇In these you too once walked, when you were living in them. ₈But now you must put them all away: anger, wrath, malice, slander, and obscene talk from your mouth. ₉Do not lie to one another, seeing that you have put off the old self with its practices" (Colossians 3:5–9).

Do you ever notice little inconsistencies or disconnects in your life? Maybe you're like me and you've been guilty of watching a healthy cooking show on TV while munching down chips as you're parked on the couch. You might even watch a fitness show, like American Ninja Warrior or sports, and you tell everyone else how you could do what they're doing while you finish another pint of ice-cream. It's easy to live one way even though we might talk about, value, or desire something else. As they say, actions speak louder than words.

If honest, we notice this kind of disconnect in our life when we say we're followers of Jesus but we don't follow Him in our desires, thoughts, words, actions, and relationships. Following Jesus and being a Christian isn't about general ideas we're meant to nod our heads at in agreement only to go back to living for self. Just like how a show on healthy food should help you replace the loaded-fries with asparagus, so also Paul's teaching on what it means for Jesus to be Lord should lead to replacing living for self with living for Christ.

Let's review where we're at in Colossians 3. Paul calls believers in Colossae to be disciples of Jesus who live out what's true of them. Through faith they've been united to Jesus. They've died to their old life and have been raised to a new life in Jesus (2:11–3:4). Now, because this is what's true of them (identity), they need to walk in it.

Discipleship includes trusting in Jesus and following Jesus. It's finding eternal life in Jesus for the future but also finding life now in Jesus as He leads us to live differently in a thousand ways. We are to seek after Him (3:1) and to set our heart and minds on Him (3:2). We are to root our identity in Him. (3:3–4). And then we're to live this out by putting off sin—those thoughts and behaviors inconsistent with Jesus (3:5–9)—and putting on ways that reflect Him (3:12–17).

This mosaic of maturing in Christ has several interlocking pieces to it: worship, identity, theology, fighting sin, cultivating holiness, loving one another, pursuing Jesus, and imaging Jesus. If you only focus on one aspect of the picture—such as fighting sin—you might miss the bigger story going on. Noting all these pieces helps us know that maturing is much more than stopping our sin, but it's not less than that. Following Jesus means following Jesus into war against our sin.

Paul's wartime or fight-club language regarding our sin reminds us how hard this will be. It's not as simple as deciding not to sin and then it magically goes away to live in a land of unicorns, rainbows, and butterflies. Sin remains within believers until we're fully resurrected and glorified one day.

Though we've been liberated from sin (Colossians 1:14; 2:13–15) and we don't have to walk in it, we regularly give in to selfishness, our fallen flesh, worldly influences and temptations, and attacks from spiritual enemies. We still are caught in a battle against sinful urges, desires, thoughts, patterns, words, behaviors, and actions. We're still wounded and reeling from ways others have sinned against us.

Temptation and sin are real. It's a battle and war. Do you believe that? Do you experience that? Paul knows this is the case, so he uses war-language when he says put to death what's earthly in you.

Following Jesus means following Jesus into battle against your sin.

Know Your Heart

In order to kill sin, we have to see it. You can't fight an invisible enemy. Part of our strategy in the war against sin (in the flesh, from the Enemy, in the world) requires us to do some things that are a bit uncomfortable. We let the Bible corner us with tough questions. We ask God for Spirit-opened eyes to see our sin and not to be deceived by a heart saying that's "no big deal." We look into the deep, dark, dank cellar called our heart where all kinds of icky things hide. Let the light of God's Word shine into your thoughts and desires and all kinds of critters will be seen running, trying to hide.

The goal then isn't to read a passage like Colossians 3:5–9 and receive a hall pass by justifying why these sins aren't a part of your life. It's better to submit yourself in the midst of this passage and let God reveal how these sins might manifest themselves.

- Does my speech include gossiping, controlling people, discouragement, attempting to look good, or delighting in filth? What's this say about my heart and who I'm living for?
- Does anger show up through outbursts, my thought life, annoyance with others, frustration at God for not fixing things, or in my words?
- Are there things God has not given me that I daydream about, lust over, get jealous when others have, and covet whenever I think about it? How do greed or covetousness show up in the areas of wealth, health, relationships, status, beauty, etc.?
- Do I condone my sin and deny Jesus's authority by saying it's just my personality, it's part of my upbringing, it's who I am, it's never going to go away, or it's not that bad?
- When I put my life next to Jesus, what are desires, thoughts, words, and behaviors that wouldn't reflect Him? Is there a hint of impurity anywhere? Am I willing to put those things to death or do I really want to keep them around?

If we would pause, honestly and humbly letting God's Spirit shine a spotlight into our heart, we would see areas we need to put to death. These sins of thought, desire, word, or deed should not be toyed with and kept around. They are not tame or safe. You can't stop a little bit or on occasion. Paul intentionally says, "put it to death." Kill the whole thing. Just like you rip up the entire weed in your yard, and not just what's above the ground, we must uproot sin in its entirety and not just the visible, external actions.

What does that look like in your life today? What about the old you, the you where sin rules, have you let stick around? What does Jesus want to free you from? What bad habits and sins does Jesus want to replace with good things leading to your joy and peace?

Both today, and in the following sections, let God's Word do its work in our hearts. Let it shine a light on your enemy—indwelling sin—and then attack that enemy with all the forces at your disposal through Christ.

Don't be caught off-guard. Be on the lookout for temptation and sin. Be ready to battle it in the Spirit's power. Fight the good fight of daily war against your flesh.

Applying Colossians

Questions
1. Why is it important to begin with your identity in Christ and right relationship with God as you fight sin? What happens if you try to fight sin in order to gain God's favor instead of fighting from a position of God's favor?
2. What desires, thoughts, words, decisions, actions, habits, and behaviors in your life don't reflect Jesus? Think through a day or week in your life to see how our sin might show up.
3. What are underlying idols behind the sinful thoughts, feelings, words, and behaviors in your life?

4. In your family or friendships, how can you both give grace to one another in struggles and sins, but also encourage one another in following Jesus? How can you encourage without controlling?

Next Steps
- Spend time reflecting on and confessing sin. Read through 3:5–17 allow God's Spirit to help you see how your life matches up. Ask a friend to speak into areas of your life they might notice sin.

For Further Study
- **Parallel passages**: Galatians 5:19–26; Ephesians 4:22–5:2;
- **Put to death/put off**: Romans 6:13; 8:13; Galatians 5:24; Ephesians 4:22; Colossians 2:11.

WHEN SEX ISN'T SO SEXY

"Put to death therefore what is earthly in you: sexual immorality, impurity, passion, evil desire, and covetousness, which is idolatry. 6 On account of these the wrath of God is coming. 7 In these you too once walked, when you were living in them. 8 But now you must put them all away: anger, wrath, malice, slander, and obscene talk from your mouth. 9 Do not lie to one another, seeing that you have put off the old self with its practices" (Colossians 3:5–9).

One TV show it's hard for me to turn away from is *When Animals Attack*. Each segment is similar. There's a person of questionable intelligence who thought it would be a good idea to have a dangerous, lethal animal around as a pet. Or in other instances, a person makes an equally bad decision by getting too close to violent and volatile animals in the wild. In both cases, the human treats the wild animal way too casually for what it is, and the result is (no surprise) the animal turns on them and attacks. Sometimes it leads to death, but almost always it leads to lifelong damage and trauma for the individual. The show's allure isn't so much the animal attacks but the shocking and dangerous situations humans put themselves in. The program could easily change its name from *When Animals Attack* to *When Humans are Idiots*.

As the viewer, it's easy to mock the people's judgment. "I would never do that," we say. "Of course the wild animal will do that." And yet, we have to be honest in admitting we are just as casual with sin and Satan, with equally devastating harm being suffered. The Bible warns us our enemy sneaks around like a lion looking to devour us (1 Peter 5:8). The Bible tells us that sin will allure us, seduce us, and deceive us until we're snared (Proverbs 7).

Sin is serious. It's deadly. It's sly and deceitful. Like those animals that seem so friendly one minute, alluring you to take a closer look, sin entices us to come a few steps closer. Then it sinks its teeth into us.

Taking Temptation Serious

This is why the Bible uses such clear language about how we should approach sin and temptation. Paul says put it to death. Kill it. Put it away or rid yourselves from it.

Jesus sees temptation and sin to be so dangerous He tells us an eye or hand that leads us to sin is better to be cut off than kept while our soul is led into hell (Matthew 5:27–30). We are not to play games with it or tip-toe as close to the line as we can. We should never try to cage it or tame it, thinking we can keep it around at a safe distance without it eventually turning on us.

In Colossians 3:5–9, Paul provides two lists of sins, each set with five vices. The first list primarily deals with sexual sin (3:5) and the second set seemingly revolves around speech (3:8). The nearer we get to the holy Jesus, the more any unholiness in our sexual purity or speech is likely to be seen and felt. If we are now in Christ and are being made into His image (3:10), anything that looks unlike Jesus needs uprooted.

Because these aren't consistent with Jesus's life they are now inconsistent with our life in Jesus. Let's briefly consider the "old ways" mentioned.

- Sexual immorality: a general term for any sexual sin (Ephesians 5:3–5). It includes crossing boundaries, seeking sexual fulfillment outside of the ways and means God has commanded and provided, or finding pleasure apart from God's good designs (and timing) for us.
- Impurity: any kind of moral corruption, but often linked with sexuality (Galatians 5:19). Impurity can involve our deeds, thoughts, desires, wants, and words.
- Passion: lust or inordinate affections (1 Thessalonians 4:5). Wanting things for the wrong reasons or wanting them in a fleshly (sinful) way. This might include a good desire (sexual intimacy in marriage) that becomes an idol in how all-encompassing it is.

- Evil desire: this might mean sinful desires generally, but often wrong sexual desires (Galatians 5:16). Whereas passion can be desiring right things wrongly, evil desire likely has in mind those desires that are wrong from the start.
- Covetousness: Wanting more of what you have, wanting what you don't have, or wanting what others have (Ephesians 5:3; Romans 7:7).

Putting off Impurity

All of us struggle and are tempted somewhere in the area of sexuality. For some this might be more apparent than for others, but each of us need to allow the Spirit to search and convict us. To walk in Christ we can't reject His authority over our sexuality.

It's not only the adulterer or the person addicted to pornography that needs this text (though they do need it). This warning and call to action is for any believer who struggles with impure thoughts, who is flirtatious when they shouldn't be, who allows their mind to engage in fantasies for comfort or pleasure (not just "sexual" but emotional), who becomes discontent with God's plan and timing, who stretch healthy lines for physical purity in dating or engagement, who cross God's designs for sexuality for what feels natural or seems right, who use sex selfishly with their spouse, or for anyone who lingers just a little too long over the wrong image, social media post, internet ad, or scene in a movie. This list could go on.

Ask yourself regarding anything that seems questionable, does this thought/act/desire/feeling reflect the image of Christ or does it reflect the image of my fallen, old self? Would this thought/act/desire/feeling portray to others Jesus or some false idol I'm worshipping and reflecting? Is it consistent with worshipping Jesus and finding my identity in Him, or with idolatry and finding my identity in something apart from Jesus? Does it increase my affections for Christ or diminish them?

Paul orders us to kill anything in us unlike Jesus; anything that doesn't reflect Him to the world and is opposed to His plans for us. And this call is to do so immediately, fully, and intentionally.

Don't put it off any longer. Before the beast turns on you with a vicious attack, kill it. What images do you put in front of your eyes you need to flee? What thoughts, emotions, and desires do you keep around that steer your heart away from contentment in Jesus and towards covetousness and sexual impurity? What are ways you've ignored the Bible's demands for holiness and embraced what "feels good", seems acceptable, or is done by others? Where have you used physical intimacy to get what you want?

These are the things we need to confess and repent of, to kill immediately and not feed any longer. And the good news right now is Jesus will help you. He died not only to set you free from the guilt of sin but from the power of sin (Colossians 2:11–15). Jesus offers forgiveness where you've failed and freedom so you can walk in new ways.

Applying Colossians

Questions
1. What are ways we treat sin casually?
2. What do you think it means to put sin to death? What does this look like for sins or temptations that will continue to come up throughout life (such as coveting)?
3. What are ways sexual impurity might exist in your life? Are there any thoughts, desires, feelings, beliefs, words, and actions that don't fully line up with Christ's designs, commands, and plans for us?
4. If as believers we bear the image of Christ, how does our life tell others about Jesus? How does sin in our life then misrepresent who Jesus is and who we now are in Him?

Next Steps

- Spend time in prayer asking God to help you see, now and this week, anything not consistent with Christ in your life. Consider having a friend help you process potential blind spots in the areas of sexuality or speech.
- If you have any friends, small group members, or those at church you are now are trying to fight against sin in any area, offer to meet with them on a regular basis for a while for mutual encouragement. Simply meet to dig into God's Word, pray for one another, and encourage one another in how you can pursue Jesus and fight sin.

For Further Study
- *Counterfeit Gods* by Tim Keller; *Intoxicated with Babylon* by Steve Gallagher; *Sex and Money* by Paul David Tripp

DAMNING SPEECH

"But now you must put them all away: anger, wrath, malice, slander, and obscene talk from your mouth. 9 Do not lie to one another, seeing that you have put off the old self with its practices" (Colossians 3:8–9).

Last time, we looked at the first of two "vice lists", each with five related sins. We saw the first five (3:5) revolve around sexual immorality, and the next five (3:8–9) connect to speech. In both arenas, sex and speech, Paul calls us to put to death any sins of our old life apart from Jesus. Since we are now in Christ, we are seeking to live a life reflective of Christ. As the Spirit helps us put to death the deeds of sinful flesh (Romans 8:14), the Spirit also helps us put on deeds of new life in Jesus (2 Corinthians 3:18).

You might think of it like an athlete who signs with a new team. Once he's on a new team it would be inconsistent—not to mention offensive—to continue to wear the jersey of the team he left behind. The athlete gets rids of the gear associated with his old team and starts wearing the jerseys and clothes of his new team.

As believers, there are sinful deeds representative of our old life we simply cannot wear now that we're in Christ. Jesus aims to clothe us in new ways of thinking, speaking, desiring, and acting that are true to being the people of God. Our speech glorifies God not only when we talk *about* Jesus, but our speech glorifies God when we talk *like* Jesus.

One hurdle for us is seeing sin for what it is. When you read Colossians 3:5–9, Christians often emphasize the dangers and devastating consequences of sexual sin, but we are much slower to denounce sins tied to the tongue. Yes, premarital sex and pornography are warned against, but are we as quick to point out how ungodly and destructive gossip and grumbling can be?

All sin is serious. We must feel the force of verse five and plead with God to lead us into sexual purity in our thoughts, desires, and deeds. I hope our last entry prompted us to do that. But we must also engage in a war against our words. We must be just as diligent to battle sins of the tongue as we are to battle sexual sins.

A War with Words

Paul isn't letting off the gas as he moves from sex to speech. Both are rooted in idols of the heart that move their way into our desires and thoughts, which come out in words and actions. Let's consider this second list of five, and how we might tame the tongue.

The last phrase of verse eight, "from your mouth" or "from your lips" seems to not just refer to obscene talk but to the entire group of sins. It's similar to how in verse five, idolatry is connected to the whole set of sexual sins and not just covetousness. In verse 8, Paul mentions the following vices in the context of speech that doesn't bear Christ's image.

- Anger: strong displeasure or annoyance with someone or something (Ephesians 4:31; Matthew 5:22).
- Wrath: rage or outpouring of displeasure or hostility, often coupled with anger (Ephesians 4:31).
- Malice: an evil disposition or wicked behavior, often tied to speech (Ephesians 4:31; 1 Pet. 2:1).
- Slander: Speech that defames, undercuts, or harms someone. This can include gossip, lying, damaging speech, profanity, or blasphemy (Ephesians 4:31; 1 Timothy 6:4).
- Obscene talk: Talking in the wrong way or about the wrong things, including "dirty talk" or "angry talk" (Ephesians 4:29).

The next verse (3:9) about not lying to one another seems to be an example or an elaboration of such sins of speech. While it's easy to see ungodly talk as a "respectable sin," Paul warns us to get rid of and put away anything out of line with who we now are in Christ. We need to not assume our speech is okay or not to downplay ways we sin with our words. Let the mirror of God's Word help us see sin as God sees it.

Tough Questions

Ask yourself, how seriously do I fight gossip, crude joking, discouraging words, controlling comments, lying or bending the truth, words said in anger, sarcasm meant to put someone in their place or put them down, or things said out of selfish protection or selfish desires? Is my speech full of gratitude or full of grumbling? Do I say things out of an idolatrous desire to be liked or approved by others? Are my words like honey that's sweet to others, or are they bitter with every drop? Do I just have to give my opinion, get a dig in, or add my two cents?

When we see these things in our heart or hear them come out of our mouth, do we see how unlike Jesus they are? Do we put to death any speech that doesn't reflect the love, holiness, goodness, kindness, gentleness, and selflessness of Jesus? Are we willing to spar with our patterns of speech like we do with sexual immorality? Are our words full of Christ and the Word (3:16)? Our words will either point people to Christ or away from Him. Our speech can hurt or heal, build up or tear down.

Speak with the goal of encouraging and building others up (Ephesians 4:29; Colossians 3:16). Paul later writes, "Let your speech always be gracious, seasoned with salt, so that you may know how you ought to answer each person" (4:6). How could your speech be more gracious today? What would it look like for your conversations to be encouraging and Christ-like?

Listen to how James talks about the power of the tongue. "And the tongue is a fire, a world of unrighteousness. The tongue is set among our members, staining the whole body, setting on fire the entire course of life, and set on fire by hell… It is a restless evil, full of deadly poison" (James 3:6, 8). Scripture shows us the power of our speech.

The way we talk about others and talk to others is extremely significant. Our words can either be refreshing and life-giving or they can be a fire setting things ablaze. Our words will either help others see Jesus or get in the way of others seeing Jesus. Words will either bring about peace or they will cause division. Conversations will either glorify God and be for the good of others, or they'll dishonor God and harm others.

This is scary but also exciting. As we try to live out our God-given purpose to be image-bearers of Christ, representing Him in our world and reflecting Him to our world, this can be done in many ways. While we might rarely think about how influential our conversation and speech is, it's one of the most powerful weapons for or against Christ.

If you've ever met an affirming or encouraging person, you know how their simple words can be like wind in your sail. If you spend much time around grumblers, gossips, and critics, you know their words suck the life right out of you.

Before moving on, reflect on these questions. What are ways your conversation, speech, words, and tongue still look like the old you apart from Jesus? How might your words and tone discourage others or dishonor Christ? How can you affirm and encourage others with words today (be specific)? How can you let God's Word spill off your tongue? How can your speech today refresh others?

Applying Colossians

Questions
1. Why do we sometimes neglect how dangerous and deadly speech sins can be?
2. What do you think it means to put sin to death in our speech?
3. What are ways you're tempted to sin with your tongue?
4. What are ways you can image Christ with your speech?

Next Steps
- Spend time in prayer asking God to help you see, now and this week, anything not consistent with Christ in your life. Consider having a friend help you process potential blind spots in the areas of sexuality or speech.
- Come up with two ways you can intentionally use your speech to encourage or build someone else up today.

For Further Study
- Read *War of Words* by Paul David Tripp or *Practicing Affirmation* by Sam Crabtree.
- See Proverbs 16:24; Matthew 15:11; James 3:1–12; Ephesians 4:29; Colossians 4:6; 1 Peter 3:10

PUT ON THE NEW YOU

"Do not lie to one another, seeing that you have put off the old self with its practices 10 and have put on the new self, which is being renewed in knowledge after the image of its creator" (Colossians 3:9–10).

In C.S. Lewis's *The Voyage of the Dawn Treader*, there's a boy named Eustace who is a cousin of the four main (human) characters. Early on, he's quite an annoying character; not the sort you root for. He's whiny, demanding, peevish, cowardly, generally obnoxious, and self-centered to the core.

To summarize one part of the story (go read the book!), a golden bracelet tempts Eustace. After slipping it onto his arm and falling asleep, he wakes up as a dragon. Though powerful, a dragon isn't a creature one wants to be. It's a very lonely life, not to mention subject to skirmishes. Eustace the dragon eventually comes face to face with Aslan the lion. Aslan—the greatest fictional character of all time—is the Christ-like figure ruling the land of Narnia.

The dragon wants to bathe in a beautiful well of water to ease his pain caused by the bracelet digging into his leg. To get into the water and be healed he must "undress." As Eustace takes off several layers of his scaly, snake-like skin he sees how nasty it is. But he also discovers he can't get out of his "clothes" or skin. He can't take off his dragon-ness on his own and make himself clean enough for the pristine pool. Aslan must do it to him. Eustace feared the lion's sharp claws tearing into his skin, but he was desperate in his pain and loneliness. Eustace relays what happened to him next.

> The very first tear he made was so deep that I thought it had gone right into my heart. And when he began pulling the skin off, it hurt worse than anything I've ever felt. The only thing that made me able to bear it was just the pleasure of feeling the stuff peel off…Well, he peeled the beastly stuff right off—just

as I thought I'd done it myself the other three times, only they hadn't hurt—and there it was lying on the grass: only ever so much thicker, and darker, and more knobbly-looking than the others had been. And there was I as smooth and soft as a peeled switch and smaller than I had been. Then he caught hold of me—I didn't like that much for I was very tender underneath now that I'd no skin on—and threw me into the water. It smarted like anything but only for a moment. After that it became perfectly delicious and as soon as I started swimming and splashing I found that all the pain had gone from my arm. And then I saw why. I'd turned into a boy again.[89]

Though painful, Aslan tears the dragon skin off, making way for a new Eustace. After Eustace gets out, Aslan dresses him in new clothes proper for a boy. We see that an inside-out change took place as Eustace apologizes to Edmund. For the rest of the book we see a different Eustace (thankfully).

New Life

As a follower of Jesus, when you read this, you're reading your own story. The removal of our old flesh was painful, but the sting doesn't compare to the sweetness of new life in Christ. Paul's charge to put off sin (3:5, 7, 9) and put on Christ–likeness (3:10, 12) is set in a context of having been made new in Jesus. We are not the ones who make ourselves new. Jesus has done that for us (2:13). We are not the ones who forge a new identity for ourselves. Jesus has done that for us (3:1–4).

---

[89] C.S. Lewis, *The Voyage of the Dawn Treader* (New York: Harper Collins Publishers, 2000), 107–110.

In 3:10 we see that the new self is put on as it's "renewed in knowledge after the image of its creator." We know from Colossians 1:15 that the Maker whose image we bear is Jesus.[90]

Growing in Christ involves looking like Christ. And this happens by seeing Christ; by knowledge of Him. This connects us back to 3:1–4 where we saw how change happens when we pursue, worship, and follow Jesus. We set our hearts and minds on Him. We seek knowing Him.

Knowing by Knowledge

Not all knowledge leads us to Christ. The false teachers in Colossae loved "knowledge", but it was a speculative, philosophical knowledge separated from Christ (2:8). Being interested in debating religious ideas or discussing spiritual matters isn't always the same as wanting to know God. It's only the knowledge of Jesus that wows us into worship and woos us into friendship. This being laid low in worship and wanting to draw near in friendship provides a sustainable, lasting power to walk in Christ and not resort back to our old ways.

Section after section of Colossians grabs us by our cheeks so we can focus our eyes on Jesus. Paul's not telling us things about Jesus so we can skim past them or add them to our shelf of doctrinal beliefs. He talks in specifics about Jesus so we know who He really is. Looking like Jesus requires first knowing what He looks like, something we need the Bible to show us. When we get to know Him, we learn He affects everything. As Paul said earlier, knowledge of Jesus leads to fruit in our lives as we walk with Jesus (1:9–10).

Paul wants us to know Jesus was strong enough to deliver us from the domain of darkness, to kick down the doors of our bondage, to defeat our enemies, and to bring us into His kingdom (1:13–15).

---

[90] See also Romans 8:29; 2 Corinthians 3:18; 1 Corinthians 15:49.

He wants us to be caught up in the glory of Christ as the perfect image of the invisible God (1:15).

He wants us to rest in and trust the one who rules all things and holds everything together (1:16–18).

He wants us to know true life, a satisfying and empowering life different from what we've ever known, comes through Jesus (1:18). He is our authority and Lord, but also our strength.

He wants us to enjoy the reconciliation back to God that only Jesus our mediator could provide through His bloody cross (1:20).

Those are only a few things Paul mentioned in a span of seven verses (1:13–20). Just like a kid who idolizes his dad or a famous athlete starts to dress, talk, and look like that "hero," so we image Jesus when know Him well enough to be caught up in the worship of Him. Is Jesus someone you want to truly know or is He only someone you intellectually believe things about?

As sins crop up in your life should you repent and forsake those things? Yes. Should you try to cultivate virtues like humility and patience (3:12)? Yes. But above all, set your gaze on Jesus. Place the focus first on the root (Jesus), not the fruit (behavior). It helps us be satisfied in Christ so we don't go running after idols to fulfill our longings, hopes, and desires.

The battle takes place on the field of worship versus idolatry. You won't worship Jesus until you see Him and know Him. And you won't see Him and know Him apart from seeking Him.

What are you doing today to seek Christ? How does your Bible reading, prayer, fellowship, and anything else you do as a Christian lead you to knowing and treasuring Jesus? There is a new you hidden in and united with Christ (3:1–4). And the more you see Him and know Him the more you'll look like Him. Knowing Jesus leads to being renewed in the image of Jesus.

Sometimes we do need to look in—and the last few days in Colossians have helped us do so—but even more often we need to look up. Many of us need to focus less on analyzing all our behaviors and emotions and we need to focus more on adoring Christ. Look up.

Applying Colossians

Questions
1. In a couple of sentences, how does the knowledge of Jesus lead to being remade in His image?
2. How do we grow by pursuing the knowledge of Jesus (3:10) *and* by putting off and on (3:5–9)?
3. How can you more intentionally seek knowing Jesus this week? What distractions and temptations tend to get in the way of this for you?

Next Steps
- Determine to do one thing to pursue knowing Jesus better this week. Maybe it's adding something to what you're doing or just going deeper. It could be reading a Gospel and meditating on what you learn about Jesus, praying over the attributes of God, or reading a book solely about Jesus.
- Start a conversation this week with an unbeliever about Jesus. Ask questions and listen to learn what they think about Jesus. Share what you know about Him in a personal way.

For Further Study
- *Seeing and Savoring Jesus Christ* by John Piper or *Rejoicing in Christ* by Mike Reeves.

TOTAL MAKEOVER (3:11–15)

Paul's theology established in chapters 1–2 is a theology that lives and breathes in chapters 3–4. It's not a theology of works but a theology that works.

Seeing Jesus not only provokes worship but it produces maturity. Since our identity is tied to Jesus, as our knowledge of Him expands so does our understanding of ourselves. Our theology of Jesus directly informs our identity in Jesus which drives how we then live. Paul anchors our ethics in our identity in Christ (3:5–17). The community we belong to is based on our identity in Christ (3:15–16). And our mission (4:2–6) is based on our identity in Christ.

This new identity results in freedom from old ways and fuel to live a new way. As we put forth effort and fight with all God's might in us (1:29) to resist sin and obey Jesus, we do so knowing he has already done everything so we *can* obey. In the last section (3:5–10), we looked at the put off commands. We'll now consider the flip side as we're told to replace old ways with new ways. Jesus doesn't just tell us to "stop it" when it comes to sin but to replace it. He points out what's wrong but shows us what's right.

The command to "put to death" our sinful nature and old self (3:5) is doable because our old self *was* put to death with Jesus (2:11–13, 20). So also, the command to "put on" (3:12) practices that rightly fit with our new identity in Christ is doable because we were made alive with Him (2:13; 3:1).

The Christian life—or sanctification—is a matter of living out what is true of us. It is a life of learning to walk in our new identity. This makes Christians take sin and holiness seriously while resting on God's grace and not our works. We confess our sins and repent of (turn from) practices, thoughts, deeds, and sins that are part of our old self. We do so with assurance the sins we confess are forgiven and the sins we repent of can be stopped by the Spirit renewing us into Jesus's image (3:10).

We want sin out of our life not to get God off our back but so we possess a clearer vision of Him. Our goal as a Christian is not avoiding sin but pursuing, knowing, and reflecting Jesus. Sin will keep us from that goal but we can't lose the greater aim—seeing Jesus—in all our skirmishes with sin.

The amazing thing is seeing Jesus is not only the goal but it's also the means by which that goal is accomplished. It's only as we look to Jesus we begin to look like Jesus. It is through seeing Him and knowing Him the Spirit restores us into His image (3:10).

A NEW PEOPLE

"Here there is not Greek and Jew, circumcised and uncircumcised, barbarian, Scythian, slave, free; but Christ is all, and in all" (Colossians 3:11).

In the beginning, God created the heavens and the earth (Genesis 1:1). And it was good. He then filled it with other good things. It wasn't until the sixth day God created people. Mankind was unlike the rest of creation. There was something special about us. God designed humans to accomplish a specific purpose. Listen to how Genesis 1 describes mankind being made in God's image.

> Then God said, 'Let us make man in our image, after our likeness. And let them have dominion over the fish of the sea and over the birds of the heavens and over the livestock and over all the earth and over every creeping thing that creeps on the earth.' 27 So God created man in his own image, in the image of God he created him; male and female he created them. 28 And God blessed them. And God said to them, 'Be fruitful and multiply and fill the earth and subdue it, and have dominion over the fish of the sea and over the birds of the heavens and over every living thing that moves on the earth.' (Genesis 1:26–28)

The end-goal of multiplying and filling the earth was that God's image-bearers would saturate the planet with His glory. Image-bearers represent someone. They work for their purposes and convey their words and actions. We were to be those who stewarded the earth like our God, in holiness, righteousness, and love. We were to have fellowship with God and one another as we did so.

It's a beautiful picture. People caring for creation, building up civilization and culture, fulfilling God's good designs, united and in friendship with one another, all under the favor of God. The prophet Habakkuk describes this vision of God's glory filling the earth through image-bearers. "For the earth will be filled with the knowledge of the glory of the Lord as the waters cover the sea" (Habakkuk 2:14).

And yet, we know Adam and Eve disobeyed God and sought their own way. Their sin plunged the cosmos into corruption. Relationships are ruined. Harmony with one another was replaced by hostility. Every possible difference is now a source of division. Our ability to image God is damaged and we now look little like Him. We are alienated from Him and under judgement. Sin sent shock waves of destruction into every corner of earthly life, especially our relationship with God and with one another.

Jesus came to reverse the curse. His birth, life, death, resurrection, and ascension are part of how God undoes sin's damage. We only see this in part now as His kingdom extends by bringing people into a new humanity, the church, and making them part of the New Creation. One day, all things will be made new as the new humanity lives on a new earth without any of the old effects of sin.

God's Family

Redemption then isn't only personal or individualistic, nor is spiritual growth. God justifies individuals as they repent and believe in Jesus, but redemption involves a larger humanity reconciled to God (Ephesians 2:1–10) and to one another (Ephesians 2:11–22). We are not only made children of God in Christ but we become spiritual siblings. We belong to Jesus and we belong to everyone else in Jesus.

In Colossians 3:10–11, Paul reminds us God's idea of filling the earth with image– bearers who reflect Him is still His plan for the world. This is now happening through the church as the Spirit restores us into the image of Jesus (3:10), individually and corporately. As God's people, we fill up the earth with spiritual fruit. We reflect God, following His design and purposes for us, and live in unity as His people.

We've already said being in Christ gives us a new identity (3:1–4). Verse 11 makes sure we don't miss that it also makes us a part of a new community or people, Jesus's church of redeemed sinners. Our identity is in Christ and it is the defining marker of who we are. Since this is true of everyone in Christ, this means we are now united and reconciled to other image-bearers of Christ. For believers in Jesus, the most important thing about us isn't what makes us different, but what unites us.

Differences still exist and these differences are part of God's very good design for how we image Him in many ways.[91] But these differences aren't to be a source of division. Ethnicity, gender, class, education, employment, and nationality don't remove the equality and unity in Christ. Jesus unites us. Jesus rules us. Jesus fills us. Jesus is remaking and renewing us.

God's plan for us includes our individual salvation and sanctification (growth), but it's part of a bigger story of God saving *and* sanctifying a people together for His glory. It is through our unity and love for one another that His glory is displayed (John 13:35; 17:23) and His image is made visible to the world.

Why It Matters

Consider a few implications of being in this new humanity. God never gives up on what He starts. His plans are never thwarted. The Bible tells the story of God rescuing a people to Himself, and no earthly or angelic evil can stop Him. This should bolster our confidence in God and our gratitude to God.

---

[91] A great book for kids on celebrating diversity is *God's Very Good Idea* by Trillia Newbell. And for adults, see her book *United: Captured by God's Vision for Diversity.*

Second, we must see all division, arrogance, or hostility based on race or ethnicity, gender, class, education, wealth, or anything else as sin. You cannot love God and hate those in His image (1 John 4:20). Too many times the church has wanted union with Christ without union with Christ's people. Too many times the church has fallen into division because of differences instead of fostering dependence on one another because of those differences.

Not that we lose all differences in Christ. Paul clearly sees men and women as different genders created to image Him through our God-designed differences. There are cultural and ethnic differences that show aspects of God in a myriad of ways. Rather than these causing us to distance ourselves from one another or exalt ourselves over anyone else, we should see how God is glorified through our diversity. This is part of what will make the new earth so glorious (Revelation 5:9–14).

Third, our holiness isn't lived out in the solitude of our daily devotions but in the world and the church. Notice how the Christ-like qualities we put on in 3:12–17 are interpersonal. You cannot live out Paul's charge to put on Christ apart from doing so with people. You can't be compassionate, kind, forgiving, forbearing, loving, and encouraging by yourself. We not only need one another so other believers can encourage and strengthen us, but we need them to best image Jesus through our mutual love and selfless service.

We can't live a "Christian life" apart from other Christians. We need to be members of Christ's body committed to living this kind of Christ-exalting life together (Colossians 2:19). We need one another to show the world what Jesus is like as we image Him together. Christ is Lord of your life, so you follow Him. But Christ is all and in all so we follow Him *together* as one people. If you want to love Jesus well you must love His followers well.

Applying Colossians

Questions

1. How does the gospel or being in Christ unite us with other believers? What are ways Christians don't reflect this unity, and what are ways Christians do reflect this unity?

2. What are practical ways you can help cultivate unity and love among other believers who might be different from you?

3. We often think of holiness or growth in terms of something done alone or in private, but many of the New Testament commands for us are things done in relationships (see Colossians 3:12–4:6). Why might remembering this be important for what we lean into as Christians trying to mature?

Next Steps

- If you're not currently a member of a local church, find and commit to one. If you're already a church member, how can you better live out your Christian discipleship and mission with others (examples: join a small group, serve, give financially, be discipled or disciple someone, etc.)?

For Further Study

- **Growing Together**: Acts 2:42–47; 20:28; Romans 12:4–5; Hebrews 10:24–25; 13:17; Ephesians 2:10; Colossians 2:19; 1 Corinthians 1:2.

- Read *United: Captured by God's Vision for Diversity* by Trillia Newbell or *One New Man: The Cross and Racial Reconciliation* by Jarvis Williams.

- Read Colossians 3:12–4:18. Make note of all behaviors, commands, or encouragements from Paul that are interpersonal or relational in nature.

GOD'S PEOPLE

"Put on then, as God's chosen ones, holy and beloved…" (Colossians 3:12).

How would you describe the church? Is it mainly positive or negative? What experiences are you basing that description on? Do you think about her like God does?

The church is not (yet) a perfect bride. The church is a "beautiful mess." Seeing the mess is easy, but do we notice her beauty? Do we consider that Jesus is working through her today? Do we think about what it means for us if we are in the church?

It's a significant question, and if we move past the phrase "as God's chosen ones, holy and beloved" too quickly, we'll miss it. We'll find ourselves lost amidst all these verses of impossible challenges (forbear, love, seek peace, be meek, etc.) and not even know why or how we should live this kind of selfless life.

Chosen Ones

God chose the church to be His people. The church is holy, separated out of the world and set apart to God. And the church is loved, not in some vague way but with all the care and commitment of an infinitely loving God. We're chosen to be loved by God and chosen to be lights for God.

When we're called God's "chosen ones" it's not like He's the basketball captain picking His squad. God doesn't look at who's impressive. He doesn't scout out the standouts, look at our spiritual stats, consider who can add the most to the team, and then pick those players. That's not what the New Testament means by "chosen ones" or "God's elect."

To be chosen means God graciously sets His love upon us and commits to making us His own. It's God's initiative and pursuit of us that explains how we became His people. Left to ourselves, we would have remained hostile enemies and spiritually lifeless sinners far from Him (Ephesians 2:1–3). But God, out of His gracious, sovereign, and merciful purposes rescues a people from the world to Himself.

God used this language about His people in the Old Testament.

> For you are a people holy to the LORD your God. The LORD your God has chosen you to be a people for his treasured possession, out of all the peoples who are on the face of the earth. 7 It was not because you were more in number than any other people that the LORD set his love on you and chose you, for you were the fewest of all peoples. (Deuteronomy 7:6–7)

God reminds Israel He chose them out of all the nations to be His people. And just in case they've forgotten or not looked in the mirror lately, this has nothing to do with their goodness, might, fame, intentions, or anything else. The source of their being God's people and God rescuing them is in God, not them.

In the New Testament, Jesus goes global with His people, saving men and women from all nations and including them into the people of God. The church, all those in Christ, is called God's chosen, holy, and loved people (Romans 1:7; Colossians 3:12; 1 Peter 2:9–10).

God, out of His own perfect and wise purposes, chooses a people He can bring out of the world and to Himself. We then get to know God. God remakes us so we display Him to the world. We get God, and God gets us. (You hopefully see how we got the better end of that deal.) We are like a bride God sees among all other women, and for whatever reason, He makes us His own. He chooses us to be with Him.

It's stunning. The God of the universe, eternally existing in all His glory and perfections, chooses us to be His people. You.

You know all the baggage in that *us*; all the sin, stubbornness, and selfishness in us. And yet God makes us His own. He calls us to Himself. You can imagine how a people steeped in the awareness of their privilege as the chosen ones of God might be humble (3:12) and grateful (3:16, 17, 18).

Holy

The next two words build on this idea of being chosen. The first is holy (3:12). While we often think of holiness in terms of moral purity or a life of righteousness, it primarily conveys belonging to God.[92] "With regard to God's people, holiness means being set apart for a relationship with the Holy One, to display His character in every sphere of life."[93]

To be holy is to be set apart (sanctified), from something and to something or someone.

We are God's. We belong to Him. He calls us His treasured possession. He brought us out of the world and into friendship with Himself. Christians aren't just saved *from* sin and the world but they're saved *to* God. He looks on us and calls us His people, the people He loves.

Our identity in Christ as God's holy ones emphasizes two sides of one reality. We no longer belong to the world and we now belong to God.

---

[92] See David Peterson, *Possessed by God: A New Testament theology of sanctification and holiness* (Downers Grove: InterVarsity Press, 1995).

[93] Ibid., 24. Moral purity is one thing given or that comes after the fact because God makes us into His image, but the word isn't first about our behavior but our status.

Loved

Paul, like other biblical authors, links holy and beloved. We aren't just God's possession (holy) but we are His *treasured* (loved) possession. We belong to Him (holy), not as property but in relationship (loved).

When God calls us to Himself, He does so to love us. We know this theologically but we struggle to believe it for ourselves. It's hard to imagine that God loves us, not just puts up with us or remains faithful to us, but He delights in, treasures, and deeply loves us. Yet this is the language God uses again and again (Deuteronomy 7:6; Hosea 2:23; Romans 5:8). Not because we're worthy of His love, have earned it, or even know how to enjoy it and appreciate it. He loves us because we're His. He loves us because He's chosen us and called us to Himself. "We didn't ruin God's plan; we *are* his plan, his eternal plan to love the undeserving, for the display of his glory alone."[94]

Your Bible reading might not take you to the book of Zephaniah often, but know how God describes His love for His people in 3:17. "The Lord your God is in your midst, a mighty one who will save; he will rejoice over you with gladness; he will quiet you by his love; he will exult over you with loud singing." He rejoices over us with gladness. He quiets or calms us by His love so we're at peace. He exults or delights in us with loud singing.

You are God's beloved, God's dearly loved ones. He loves you. He chose you to be His own, and He set you apart to Himself.

Are you living as if salvation is a transaction done for you or do you live in relationship to God as His people? Do you live under the knowledge you are His? He pursued you out of His own grace. He treasures you. You belong to Him, and you are His beloved. Live in light of that love today.

---

[94] Ray Ortlund, *The Gospel*, 42.

Applying Colossians

Questions

1. If we understand these privileges and gifts as God's people, what are
    ways we might be different? How might we respond to God, and how
    might we respond to others differently?
2. Why do we struggle to believe God loves us? How do we fight this
    with Scripture?
3. What are ways you are living the Christian life within the church as
    opposed to on your own?
4. What are ways we know God loves us?

Next Steps

- Read through 3:12–15 about how we are to love one another.
  Consider how God has acted with patience, forgiveness, love, and
  peace to you.

For Further Study

- **Chosen**: Deuteronomy 7:6–9; 10:15; 14:2; Ps 105:6; Isa 43:20; 45:4;
  65:9, 15; 1 Chronicles 16:13; Romans 8:33; Luke 18:7; 2 Timothy 2:10;
  Revelation 17:14; 1 Chronicles 16:13; 1 Thessalonians 1:4; 2
  Thessalonians 2:13; Jude 1.
- **Treasured**: Exodus 19:4–6; Deuteronomy 7:6; 10:14–15; 14:2; Isaiah
  43:21; Jeremiah 31:3; Hosea 2:23; Ephesians 3:17; Malachi 3:17; 1
  Peter 2:9–10.
- **Loved**: Deuteronomy 14:2; Psalm 86:15; 136:26; Ephesians 3:17;
  Jeremiah 31:3; Deuteronomy 10:15; John 3:16; Romans 5:8; 8:31–39; 1
  John 3:1; 4:9–11.

I WANT TO BE LIKE . . .

"Put on then, as God's chosen ones, holy and beloved, compassionate hearts, kindness, humility, meekness, and patience, 13 bearing with one another and, if one has a complaint against another, forgiving each other; as the Lord has forgiven you, so you also must forgive. 14 And above all these put on love, which binds everything together in perfect harmony" (Colossians 3:12–14).

Scrap any notions of holiness lived in isolation. You can't obey Scripture or reflect Jesus apart from relationships. Practicing humility, meekness, kindness, patience, forgiveness, and love doesn't happen in the mirror. They're done to and with other flesh-and-blood people; people who are sinners like you. Despite our culture's anti–organization sentiments, commitment phobia, and infatuation with individualism and autonomy, you can't follow Jesus apart from other followers of Jesus.

Paul told us to put off our old ways (3:5–9) but he now tells us what to put on (3:12–17). New habits displace old vices. You don't just stop sinful patterns and behaviors; you must replace them with Christ-like ones. Put off *and* put on. Put off *by* putting on. This is the *what*.

The *where, when,* and *who* is we put on Christ in human relationships. A God-glorifying, Christ-centered, Spirit-produced life of holiness takes place in the church (3:12–17), in the home (3:18–21), at work (3:22–4:1), and in the world (4:2–6).

Yes, it would be easier if holiness took place on my couch, in the solitude of peace and quiet, with a Bible in front of me and coffee next to me. Instagram and Facebook might convince us this is the ideal Christian life. But the biblical vision of growing in Christ by imaging Christ happens in the trenches of personal relationships with other stubborn, sinful, stress-inducing, struggling people.

People are messy and difficult. You are messy and difficult. But Christ's glory shines in the muck and mud of relationships as we image Him to one another. This is the *why*. The daily sowing of righteousness among our relationships leads to the world seeing the beauty and glory of Jesus.

Identity

But what about the *how*? How in the world can we live out this overwhelming stack of virtues? On my own, I'm anything but humble, patient, long-suffering, and forgiving. Paul offers two sources of motivation. First, as we looked at last time, we take part in the people of God and together share an identity. God chose us, called us to Himself, and loves us (3:12). Paul shares who we are before telling us how to live because actions are rooted in identity.

Knowing who we are (identity) allows us to look into the closet of behaviors to see which clothes fit us. For people showered with God's grace and love, our old raggedy clothes of pride, grumbling, and self-centered living just don't fit anymore. But, the clothes of humility, meekness, harmony, and gratitude are the exact outfit capturing our identity, so we put them on. Being His people leads to looking like Him (individually and collectively).

Love

Not only does our new identity motivate change, but remembering how God has saved us helps us love others. God calls us to Himself so He can lavishly love us. He delights in us, and we delight in Him. "For you are a people holy to the LORD your God, and the LORD has chosen you to be a people for his treasured possession, out of all the peoples who are on the face of the earth" (Deuteronomy 14:2). We fix our minds on who—*whose*—we are, and only then can we be that kind of person. We remember how God treats us and it transforms how we treat one another.

God's love for us enables us to love God's people (3:14). If you know God loves you it makes possible loving the unlovely. Despite how challenging it might be, we *can* love people as inviting as a cactus because we've seen and experienced undeserving love. Paul anchors how we are to live in how we've been loved. Belonging to God leads to knowing God which leads to becoming like God. Identity paves the way for imaging.

Worship

Colossians is all about becoming like Jesus by beholding Jesus, or reflecting the one we revere. Growth happens as we're renewed in knowledge after the image of Jesus (3:10). Sanctification is the Spirit transforming us into Christ's likeness (2 Corinthians 3:18). We reflect Jesus by seeking after and following Jesus (Colossians 3:1–2). We put on Christ as we pursue Him (Romans 13:14). Or, if you're less and less awed by Jesus as other things capture your attention, those other things will become idols you image.

When I was a kid, I looked up to Michael Jordan. I was more than happy to sing along with Spike Lee that "I want to be like Mike." Basketball was what I thought about all day. If I wasn't watching it, I played it. I bought Air Jordans (his shoes). I wore Nike clothing. I had the Bulls jersey. Because I idolized and looked up to Michael Jordan, that showed up in my life through my clothes, love of basketball, and in how I tried to mimic his fade-away jumper. I looked like MJ because I looked up to MJ.

This happens for us as we worship Jesus. When you read the Bible and you see Jesus, he shows us what it means for us to be fully alive. He demonstrates in tangible ways how we can image God as human beings. He puts flesh on what it means to be godly.

Jesus does more than provide a model for us, so we don't reduce the person and work of Christ to only being our WWJD example. But as the incarnate God, He does reveal how to live. We are drawn to His glory and compelled by it. We follow His lead.

His compassion to the hurting moves us (Luke 7:13). His kindness endears us (Matthew 8:1–4). His love woos us and compels us (John 11:35–36). His humility and meekness astound us (John 13:1–20). His forgiveness to the least deserving floors us (Luke 23:34). His patience and long– suffering fill us with gratitude (Mark 10:35–45). We know Him by seeing Him in Scripture.

The more we get to know Him the more we love and worship Him. And it's in this, our worship and looking up to Jesus, that we look like Him. We put on Christ-likeness by putting Jesus in front of our eyes (3:1–4). Knowing leads to showing. This happens individually as we follow Christ and collectively as churches follow and image Jesus together.

As you read the Bible, be on the lookout for Jesus. Make seeing Him and loving what you see the first priority of your time in the Word. Repent of ways you've rejected Christ-likeness. Seek to live out the compassion, humility, patience, forgiveness, and love of Jesus to the people He puts in your path each day. Get to know Jesus, and then help others get to know Him by telling them about Him and showing what He's like.

Applying Colossians

Questions
1. How does knowing who we are as God's people lead to the characteristics of 3:12–15?
2. What are examples where Jesus showed compassion, kindness, humility, meekness, patience, long-suffering, forgiveness, and love?
3. How do our behaviors, words, and lifestyle say something about Christ?
4. What are ways you can live out the character qualities in 3:12–14 this week?

- Spend some time slowly reading, meditating on, and praying about 3:12–15. Ask God to reveal any ways you don't image Jesus and to help you think of ways you can image Jesus. Ask a Christian who knows you well if any of these virtues you model well or if any need some work.

- Affirm another believer for any ways you've noticed them image Christ along the lines of 3:12–15. Encourage them by helping them see God's work in them.

For Further Study

- Read through one of the gospels, noticing how Jesus lives out these beautiful and righteous virtues.
- **Put-on**: Ephesians 4:17–5:2; Romans 13:9–21.

PUT ON CHRIST (PART 1)

"Put on then, as God's chosen ones, holy and beloved, compassionate hearts, kindness, humility, meekness, and patience, 13 bearing with one another and, if one has a complaint against another, forgiving each other; as the Lord has forgiven you, so you also must forgive. 14 And above all these put on love, which binds everything together in perfect harmony" (Colossians 3:12–14).

Magazines, TV commercials, internet pop-ups, advertisements on billboards, and even those pesky radio and streaming commercials all sell you a version of the good life. They're not solely telling you about a product that can help in one area of life. They're selling you a kind of life or a way of living, something with the promise of happiness. It's the cosmetic product or clothing store promising you a life of beauty, assuring you everyone will think you're attractive.

The big truck tells men they can be a dude's dude. A sleek new minivan allures moms and dads into the dream of a perfect family. The high-end sports car is marketed towards middle-aged men holding on to the belief they're still young and cool. Advertisers aren't just selling you a car; they're selling you an identity. I'm tempted to buy more North Face clothes to convince myself I'm outdoorsy and adventurous—assuming I can snap a good selfie wearing them with a beautiful backdrop of creation.

Just as Paul provided two vice lists with five characteristics (3:5, 8), his virtue list also contains five characteristics: compassion, kindness, humility, meekness, and patience (3:12). It's then followed by two actions that exhibit these virtues: forbearance and forgiveness (3:13). Finally, it's summed up with the admonition to put on love, the chief Christian virtue putting all the pieces together (3:14).

As we briefly consider each virtue, an item of clothing from Christ's closet we can put on, we'll see how Jesus lived it out. The person we are to become isn't the self-made you but the Christ-like you. And we put on Christ by putting on the characteristics of Christ.

> A significant aspect of these virtues is that they are often attributed to, or associated with, Christ. It is as if Paul is saying in the words of Romans 13:14, that we are to 'put on Christ.' And, of course, this Christological focus neatly elaborates the key idea in vv. 10–11. Having put on 'the new self,' identified with Christ himself, it is necessary at the same time to put on those virtues that characterize Christ.[95]

Compassion

Put on compassionate hearts (3:12). Other places use this word to refer to tender mercy (Luke 1:78), affection (2 Corinthians 7:15; Philippians 1:8; 2:1), comfort (Philemon 7), heart (1 John 3:17), and tenderhearted (Ephesians 4:32). To put on a compassionate heart means to allow yourself to feel concerned with the needs and burdens of others. Through compassion, we put on someone else's shoes and enter into their life and struggles with them.

Jesus lived this kind of compassion. People with problems constantly barraged Jesus. It's easy to become desensitized, building up a thick layer of apathy over hearts of mercy. But Jesus has not treated us like this, nor did He harden His heart towards people in His day.

In Luke 7:11–17, there's a widow whose one son is all she has left. But her son dies, and now she has nothing but her throbbing grief. When Jesus sees her, He has compassion on her. He's moved by her. As if merely out of His tenderness for the woman in her pain, He brings the boy back to life. The text

---

[95] Moo, *Colossians*, 276–77.

says, "and Jesus gave him to his mother" (17:15). Jesus gives the boy back to the mother like a gift just for her, all stirred by compassion.

To be Christ-like we replace calloused hearts with compassionate hearts.

Do you live your day with eyes open to see the hurts and needs of others? Do you put up walls around your heart to keep you from experiencing any tender mercy or concern for others? Do you remember how Jesus had compassion on you in all your sinfulness, pain, grief, rebellion, and waywardness? While compassion might not be your natural instinct, it can become a gospel instinct. Recalling Christ's compassion *to us* cultivates compassion *in us*.

Kindness

What comes to mind when you think of kindness? A kind person does good to others. Kindness treats others with love, concern, and gentleness for the sake of their well-being. The Bible regularly speaks about God's "loving kindness" when referring to His gracious ways toward us. For example, Paul writes, "But when the goodness and loving kindness of God our Savior appeared, ₅ he saved us, not because of works done by us in righteousness, but according to his own mercy," (Titus 3:4–5). Kindness is goodness poured out on another.

You see this epitomized in the life of Jesus throughout the gospels. Whether it's the story we considered where Jesus gives a widow her only son back (Luke 17:11–17) or Jesus healing and restoring a man with leprosy (Matthew 8:1–4), or even the way Jesus talks to and treats a shamed Samaritan woman (John 4:1–45), Jesus spreads kindness in every interaction. Jesus acts kind because He is kind. We can be kind because we've experienced the goodness and kindness of Jesus firsthand.

Who could you be kind to today, even in the smallest of interactions? An encouraging word, a thoughtful act, or a conversation where we listen and are present, these are little things that go a long way. Can you imagine how different your day could look if you acted kind to every person you talked to for one whole day? Just how God treats us kind when we don't deserve it, this way of pouring good out on others isn't done because they've earned it. It's given freely. There's nothing more Christ-like than loving the undeserving. Put on kindness.

In the next section, we'll pick up the final three virtues: humility, meekness, and patience. But assuming you're somewhat like me, and the calling to put on compassion and kindness is daunting enough, start today with small steps.

Meditate on the compassion and kindness of Jesus to those in His day or to you. Then, out of the overflow of the beauty of who Jesus is, put on compassion and kindness in your own life. Remember people aren't an intermediary inconvenience but God intentionally put them in your path. Be more concerned about showing them compassion and kindness than how you can move on to the next thing.

Applying Colossians

Questions
1) What are some examples from the New Testament of the compassion of Jesus?
2) How can you demonstrate compassion to others this week? Where in your life might God be calling you to put off callousness and put on compassion?
3) What are examples from the New Testament of the kindness of Jesus?
4) How can you demonstrate kindness to others this week?

- According to how you answered questions 2 and 4, look for specific ways you can put on and practice compassion and kindness this week. Ask a friend or spouse to pray with you about this and to follow up by asking how you lived these virtues out this week.
- Spend time reading through the verses in the "For Further Study" section and meditate on Jesus our example.

For Further Study

- **Compassion of Jesus**: Matthew 9:36; 11:28–30; 14:14; 15:32; 18:27; 20:34; Mark 1:41; 6:34; 8:2; 9:22; Luke 7:13 10:33; 15:20; Philippians 2:1–3; Hebrews 2:17.
- **Kindness of Jesus**: Titus 3:4; Matthew 8:1–4; 9:27–31.

PUT ON CHRIST (PART 2)

"Put on then, as God's chosen ones, holy and beloved, compassionate hearts, kindness, humility, meekness, and patience, 13 bearing with one another and, if one has a complaint against another, forgiving each other; as the Lord has forgiven you, so you also must forgive. 14 And above all these put on love, which binds everything together in perfect harmony" (Colossians 3:12–14).

As we continue contemplating Christ's virtues, we'll now consider humility, meekness, and patience. Strap on your seatbelt.

Humility

Put on humility. It's the virtue we want in everyone else but don't want for ourselves. We misunderstand humility by thinking a humble person lacks confidence, hangs their head, and is careful not to stand out. But at heart, humility is putting others first. A humble person is less concerned with themselves, including what others might think of them, and they're more concerned with others. Humility requires caring more about doing what's right and what's good than about appearance.

This is not the false humility of the rabble rousers in Colossae promoting self-abasement, self-punishment, or denying the goodness of creation. These activities puff a person up (2:18) because they boast in the acts they've performed.

If we're honest, we're prone to this kind of false humility. We serve others in part because of what we might get. We put others first and become demanding when the favor isn't returned. We employ social-media for our own humble brags. A false humility, humility with an agenda, opens the door for other vices to slip in.

Not so with true humility. The incarnation of Jesus, the infinite God who took on flesh, was the pinnacle expression of such a virtue (Philippians 2:4–9). For Him to take on humanity was to take on humility. He exchanges the glories of heaven for the agonies of earth. And He does so because He looked not to His own interests but He looked out for our interests (Philippians 2:4). As the Son, He always submits Himself to the Father's will. As the Mediator, He lived and died and rose for the good of His people.

Jesus embodied humility throughout His life, but one clear example was the washing of the disciples' feet (John 13:1–20). This was servant's work. It was lowly, dirty, awkward and embarrassing. Would you want to wash someone's feet? I didn't think so. But Jesus gets down on the ground in a posture of humility and serves His disciples.

The God-Man serves His followers. Jesus gets dirty to make the disciples clean. The scene is so counterintuitive that Peter objects. Peter knows they should be washing his feet, not vice versa. But Jesus displayed to them what humility looks like, all while giving a visual that He is the one who makes them clean. When we see humility, we instinctively are drawn to it in others. And yet, our fleshly impulses gravitate to pride, selfishness, and exerting our own agenda. We need to see the humility of Jesus. We need to put it on.

Meekness

Put on meekness. Biblical authors often pair humility and meekness together (Ephesians 3:2; Matthew 11:29). They're related but not the same. While humility is exchanging self-concern and self-promotion for putting others first, meekness has more to do with gentleness. Both humility and meekness involve a cost to our pride, prestige, and appearance.

A meek person doesn't respond by blowing up in anger. They aren't defensive, always claiming their rights, or proving they're the top-dog. A meek person isn't impressed with themselves but has a right view of themselves. They're gracious and gentle.

One example from Paul's writing is Galatians 6:1. "Brothers, if anyone is caught in any transgression, you who are spiritual should restore him in a spirit of gentleness." The "gentleness" in that passage is the same word as meekness.

What does meekness look like in the life of Jesus?

Jesus calls the weak and weary to Himself. "Come to me, all who labor and are heavy laden, and I will give you rest. Take my yoke upon you, and learn from me, for I am gentle and lowly in heart, and you will find rest for your souls. For my yoke is easy, and my burden is light" (Matthew 11:28–30). He assures us of His gentleness. He gives rest. He is not harsh. He will not disparage us in our weaknesses. He comforts and restores. He doesn't lay into us because we're still struggling.

Don't confuse gentle with wimpy. Jesus is tough and tender. He's the Lion and the Lamb. He knows when to flex His muscles in strength (usually towards the self-righteous religious leaders in His day). But He also knows when and with whom to be gentle. Haven't you experienced the meekness and gentleness of Jesus in your own life? When you deserved His wrath, He gave you mercy and patience? When He could have dealt with you harshly, He showed you the kindest and most tender love. Experiencing Christ's meekness helps us express Christ-like meekness.

Patience

Put on patience. Last, but not least, we have the virtue characterized by long-suffering, forbearance, and tolerance. A patient person doesn't respond in the moment to how they feel but lives with a long view in mind. They hold out, treating others with love and putting up with offenses.

Patience isn't easy. We're slow to give people the benefit of the doubt (or "the B.O.D." as we say in our home). We want immediate change and progress. We live in a fast-paced, microwavable, google-reliant society where the world is at our fingertips. This makes being patient in situations we'd like to control and change all the more difficult. Whether it's slowed traffic, an enduring trial, a delayed answer, waiting for something on our calendar, or a person who gets on our nerves, patience is not our first response. This is why we actively and purposefully put it on. Because patience is not instinctual it must be intentional. We choose it.

Just as God was long-suffering with a stubborn people in the Old Testament, Jesus acts patiently towards His disciples. He teaches them about humility and they debate who's the greatest. But He's patient. He performs miracle after miracle and they doubt Him. But He's patient. They misunderstand His teachings and parables, but He's patient. They deny His resurrection until they can see and touch Him. Jesus is still patient.

Paul testifies to Christ's patience (1 Timothy 1:16). Paul did horrible things deserving of a death-sentence. But Jesus was patient and gave grace instead of immediate judgment.

Isn't this your story? Jesus was patient with us, not giving us what we deserved (judgment). Like the disciples, we stray, sin, and stumble, but Jesus is patient. Even as believers, we continue to wander, resist, doubt, and pursue idols. All the while Jesus is patient, loving us despite our unloveliness. We put on patience toward one another because we've tasted the patience of Jesus toward us.

We put on Christ by putting on compassion, kindness, humility, meekness, and patience. This happens in the daily opportunities to bear with one another and forgive one another (3:14). It happens as we love God and love one another. Love helps us put on all other Christ-like virtues. Year-by-year, day-by-day, and moment-by-moment, we put on Christ. Some days we give in and resort to putting on the old me. But we don't give up. We keep seeking after Jesus and putting Jesus on.

Meditate on the humility, meekness, and patience of Jesus. Then ask for His help to reflect these attitudes and actions to others.

Applying Colossians

Questions
1) What are some examples from the Bible of the humility and meekness of Jesus?
2) How can you demonstrate humility and meekness to others this week?
3) What are some examples from the Bible of the patience of Jesus?
4) How can you demonstrate patience to others this week?
5) Of the five virtues listed (compassion, kindness, humility, meekness, and patience), which are hardest for you?

Next Steps
- According to how you answered the questions above, look for specific ways you can put on and practice humility, meekness, and patience this week. Ask a friend or spouse to pray with you about this and to follow up by asking how you lived these virtues out this week.
- Spend time reading through the verses in the "For Further Study…" section and meditate on Jesus our example.

For Further Study
- **Humility of Jesus**: Philippians 2:1–8; 2 Corinthians 8:9; Luke 22:27; John 13:5
- **Meekness Jesus**: 2 Corinthians 10:1; Matthew 11:29; 21:5; Isaiah 53:7; 1 Peter 2:23
- **Patience of Jesus**: 1 Timothy 1:16; Mark 10:35–45; Luke 22:32–24; cf. Romans 2:4; 3:25; 9:22.

PEACE, LOVE, AND THANKFULNESS

"And above all these put on love, which binds everything together in perfect harmony. 15 And let the peace of Christ rule in your hearts, to which indeed you were called in one body. And be thankful" (Colossians 3:14–15).

Whether you live with a spouse, a roommate, or parents, you've likely run into conflict a time or two…or a thousand. Sometimes my wife and I disagree, or one person hurts the other, or I've said or done something I shouldn't have. This creates a thick tension that fills our house. Conflict divides. It escalates hard feelings and hostility. It lays little land mines we tip-toe around to avoid another explosion. This isn't what either of us want. Our heart's desire, as much as other emotions might get in the way, is peace.

But what is peace during conflict? Are we simply hoping tension leaves the air? Do we need to agree to disagree, walk in a state of neutrality where we get along but aren't united? Is peace the absence of hostility? The world often talks about "peace" along these lines. Two enemy nations might sign a peace treaty, which means they'll do their best to stay out of each other's way and minimize the discord.

Biblical Peace

When the Bible talks about peace, it always means much more. Peace is oneness and intimacy. Parties not only put down their weapons, but they embrace one another as friends. Peace means wholeness, unity, and togetherness.

The word "peace" showed up in Colossians 1:20–21 where we're told that reconciliation creates peace. This peace doesn't come to us out of the blue. We don't decide to be at peace and magically it appears. Peace must be fought for and won. Through the "blood of his cross" (1:20) Jesus purchased peace. "In his body of flesh by his death" Jesus reconciles sinners to God, and sinners to other sinners. Robert Peterson writes, "Reconciliation is peacemaking. It involves God's taking the initiative to make friends out of his enemies."[96] Peace then comes through Jesus and in Jesus.

When Paul tells us to let peace rule in our hearts, he's not asking us to create peace where it doesn't exist. He's not emphasizing a fuzzy feeling of peace in our hearts. At the tail-end of this section about putting on Christ in the church (3:12–17), he's voicing the importance of letting the peace Jesus purchased for us have its way among us. To put on Christ is to put on peace. To put on the flesh is to allow division, conflict, hostility, anger, and disunity to rule.

For peace to "rule" (3:15) means that peace has the final word. Peace is the arbiter calling the shots; the controlling factor dictating our responses. It isn't a dreamy notion we talk about but ignore. It's not pushed aside until it's convenient and easy. Peace must rule. It's what God calls us to as one body in Christ (3:15). Whatever feelings and words might surge with all their might within us, we give peace the mic and silence those other voices within us.

This means peace must rule within the church, in all relationships and in every situation (Colossians 1:20; Ephesians 2:11–22; Romans 5:1, 10–11). Since sin first reared its ugly head, division and hostility have always existed among those who are different. Different ethnicities, religious groups, nations, genders, political parties, and socio-economic classes have often butted heads, creating severe and deep-rooted conflict. The world has never figured out how to promote true peace between warring parties.

Only the gospel makes friends out of enemies. Only the gospel unites those who otherwise would keep their distance. It's not a surface-level peace but a deep, eternal oneness. The church must let peace rule if Jesus rules her.

---

96 Robert A. Peterson, *Salvation Accomplished by the Son* (Wheaton: Crossway, 2012), 306.

As peace rules within our churches and among Christians, we become that "alternative city" displaying to the world a better way. Our unity and oneness proves the power of the gospel. "The social distinctions that usually separate and divide us form others must not be allowed to trump our fundamental unity in Christ. We tune ourselves to the peace of Christ—a peace that transcends race, age, gender, class, and personality type. We are 'called' to this peace 'in one body.'"[97]

Putting on Peace

Jesus endured the pains of a bloody cross to win such peace for His people. We need to know Christ's work for us and Paul's admonition to pursue peace as much as any other virtue. We then put it on. It won't be easy. We'll have countless opportunities to let peace fade and disunity surface with those we disagree with or don't understand.

Here's a sampling of scenarios in the church where peace must rule.

You prefer one style of music, a sound level, a particular version of the Bible, or a style of dress for Sunday attire. Peace, not preferences, is to rule.

When a program or ministry you're a part of in the church doesn't get as much attention as you think it deserves, peace is to rule.

Even as a family in the church, maybe discord or distance has wedged its way between you as a couple, or between parents and kids. We can't settle for just getting along or putting up with one another. Lean into peace and fight to put it on.

When miscommunication offends, hurts, annoys, or confuses you, peace must rule. Your posture should not be one of coming with guns blazing so

---

[97] Brian Hedges, *Christ All Sufficient* (Wapwallopen: Shepherd Press, 2016), 203.

you can say what's on your mind. Give the benefit of the doubt, let love cover a multitude of offenses, and let peace rule in the situation.

Pursue unity by practicing humility (Philippians 2:1–11). Bring people together through words of gratitude instead of sowing seeds of division through grumbling (Colossians 3:15).

When you're in a church and not everyone looks like you and you're tempted to focus on differences, peace is to rule. Black and white, male and female, blue collar and white collar, rich and poor, old and young, single and married, and republicans and democrats are at peace if they're in the same body. Peace unites us.

Christ purchased peace through the payment of His blood. It's already accomplished. God's not asking you to create peace, but to put on the peace He purchased and provided. Don't stir the pot of disunity or allowing differences to divide. Be a peace-maker and peace-keeper.

Applying Colossians

Questions
1. How did Christ's death and resurrection create peace for believers?
2. What are ways we might think, act, or speak that don't promote peace?
3. Why is racism so antithetical to the gospel? How can you grow in putting on peace among people of different ethnicities?
4. Are there any relationships right now where genuine peace isn't "ruling"? How can you work towards peace this week?

Next Steps
- One way to put on peace in your church is to simply start with one person or family. Have a meal with someone who is different from you (ethnicity, age, background, socio-economic status, etc.) and try to build a relationship.

- If there are any ways you've let conflict, division, and hostility exist in your relationships or be part of your church, confess and repent of those things. Seek out those with whom you're not putting on peace and do what you can to make things right.

For Further Study

- **Peace**: Colossians 1:2, 20; Ephesians 2:11–22; Philippians 2:1–11; 4:2; Romans 5:1–11.
- For more on thankfulness, see devotionals on 1:3 ("Thank God When You Think of Us") and 1:11–12 ("Give Thanks, and Mean It").
- **Giving thanks**: Colossians 2:7; 3:15, 17; 4:2; Ephesians 1:16; 5:20; 2 Thessalonians 2:13–14.

LORD OF EVERYTHING (3:16–4:1)

Colossians makes one thing clear: Jesus is the Supreme Lord over all things. In the hymn or creed found in chapter 1, we saw Jesus was Lord of creation (1:15–17), Lord of the church (1:18–21), and Lord of the Christian (1:21–23). He rules, reigns, and governs. In this section, Paul applies the lordship of Jesus to the church, the home, and the workplace. How many times do you see "Lord" or "Master" in 3:16–4:1?

If Jesus claims every square inch of the universe, then he certainly claims every aspect of our lives. We know Jesus is king, but we often try to climb up on the throne with Him and rule our own world. Repentance is, in part, giving up command and asking Jesus to forgive our attempts at self-rule. Repentance is surrender. It's stepping away from the wheel, taking the passenger's seat, and letting Christ take over.

This isn't easy, but it's always good. We at times act like Jesus being Lord means we're asked to sacrifice "the good things" to do what's right. But in fact, Jesus's lordship actually brings joy and fulfillment back into our lives as we discover the good things. Everything Jesus rules as Lord he restores and renews. Jesus always makes things better, not worse.

Paul referenced how Jesus's reign over His people should change the way we relate to one another (3:10–15). Continuing the thought, in 3:16–17 Jesus brings peace, unity, and mutual encouragement to the church.

In 3:18–4:1 Paul unpacks how Jesus's lordship should affect relationships, including relationships between spouses, parents and children, and masters and servants. Wherever we say yes to Christ's rule and ways—and no to ourselves or anything else—we let Jesus lead us in righteousness.

Jesus as Lord *of our life* changes everything *in our life*. The sooner we turn over any territory we're holding out on the sooner He can restore it.

SOAKING UP THE WORD

"Let the word of Christ dwell in you richly, teaching and admonishing one another in all wisdom, singing psalms and hymns and spiritual songs, with thankfulness in your hearts to God" (Colossians 3:16).

Whether you drink coffee, tea, wine, or soda (or pop or coke, depending on where you're from), the last thing you want is a weak, watered-down beverage barely resembling the richness of what it's meant to be. Good wine must age so the flavors mellow out and build depth. Tea takes time. Steep the leaves in the water. Don't drop in a tea-bag and then serve it two minutes later; leave it for a while. And coffee—that great gift to humanity—should never be weak. Don't skimp on the beans and don't pour the water through whatever coffee system you're using too quickly. The roasted beans need to have the water pass through them slowly, picking up all the flavors you want in your cup. A well-poured cup of coffee is a beautiful thing. Coffee tasting like brown-water is a cruel punishment.

When the Bible talks about our relationship with God's Word, it encourages us to abide in it. We're to saturate ourselves in the Word, not sprinkle it in or skim over it. The word of Christ, meaning the word about Christ or the Bible, is to dwell in us. It's to take up permanent residence.[98] We're to immerse ourselves in God's Word not dabble with it one toe-test at a time.

Steeped in Scripture

This surfaces a gap between *what we believe* and *how we live*. We often talk about the importance of God's Word. We esteem it. We value it. We even try to commit ourselves to regularly reading it. But the reality for many of us is our

---

[98] See Romans 8:11; 2 Corinthians 6:16; and 2 Timothy 1:14 where Paul uses "dwell" for something—the Spirit—to make His home or take up permanent residence at a place.

time in the Word is infrequent, quick, shallow, and not nearly as powerful as we'd like. We read the Bible and move on to the next thing.

Because we don't read the Bible and stay put, meditating on it, it doesn't dwell in us in power. Like a newspaper, we move from one sentence to the next as if the goal is finishing a section. But the goal isn't to cover ground by finishing chapters and books. The goal is to soak up and savor God's Word so it gets into us and changes us from the inside-out.

The great Puritan John Owen wrote, "If the Word does not dwell with power in us, it will not pass with power from us."[99] Does the Word of God dwell in you? Are you able to encourage, teach, and build up others because you've stored up God's Word in your heart? Do you notice that your Bible reading has little effect on your heart? Does it feel like a religious activity you do but not a means of knowing and growing in Christ?

Don Whitney writes, "If we settle for a poor quality intake of hearing, reading, and studying God's Word, we severely restrict the main flow of God's sanctifying grace toward us."[100] Our relationship with the Word must change if we're to change. One change I'd suggest for Christians today is we must seek to meditate on God's Word, not just read it.

Our quick and casual reading has led to the word of Christ passing through us like thin air instead of it dwelling with us with power. The encouragement throughout the Bible is not to read the Bible but to consider it, study, delight, abide, and to roll it over in our minds and hearts. Here are a few examples.

- And these words that I command you today shall be on your heart. 7 You shall teach them diligently to your children, and shall talk

---

[99] John Owen, *Works,* XVI:76, quoted by J. I. Packer, *A Quest for Godliness* (Wheaton: Crossway, 1990), 286.

[100] Donald Whitney, *Spiritual Disciplines for the Christian Life* (Colorado Springs: Nav Press, 1991), 33

of them when you sit in your house, and when you walk by the way, and when you lie down, and when you rise. (Deuteronomy 6:6–7)

- This Book of the Law shall not depart from your mouth, but you shall meditate on it day and night, so that you may be careful to do according to all that is written in it. For then you will make your way prosperous, and then you will have good success. (Joshua 1:8)

- But his delight is in the law of the Lord, and on his law he meditates day and night. 3 He is like a tree planted by streams of water that yields its fruit in its season, and its leaf does not wither. In all that he does, he prospers. (Psalm 1:2–3)

- I meditate on all that you have done; I ponder the work of your hands. (Psalm 143:5)

- I have stored up your word in my heart, that I might not sin against you…Oh how I love your law! It is my meditation all the day. 98 Your commandment makes me wiser than my enemies, for it is ever with me. (Psalm 119:11, 97–98)

As God's Word dwells in us, especially its focal message of the gospel of Christ (Colossians 1:5), we'll speak truth in love to one another that builds up the body of Christ (Ephesians 4:12–16). We'll sing Jesus-exalting songs to one another that teach and admonish (Colossians 3:16). We'll preach sermons and pray prayers rooted in God's Word. God's Word is alive and powerful. God's Spirit works through the Word, bearing fruit in us and maturing us through it (Colossians 1:5, 28). But to speak and sing God's Word we have to store it up.

Among the many things we might take away from this verse is how essential it is that our personal life, our family life, and our church life are centered on God's Word. And not in a way where the Word is a seasoning sprinkled in, but in such a way it's the meat and potatoes. It's the power at work. We're not just saying we value it but we're meditating on it so it can dwell with us in power. God's Word must first get in us if it's ever going to change us or come out of us.

Take some to evaluate what your Bible reading looks like. Do your rhythms and habits of Bible reading lead you to soak up the Word or sprinkle in the Word? How might extended time for study, reflection, meditation, and prayer enrich your reading? There's no one-size-fits-all method for abiding in God's Word, but there is the same command. Take the Word of God and plant it deeply within your heart.

Applying Colossians

Questions
1. What are differences between reading the Bible and meditating on it?
2. Looking back at your Christian life, are there times you can identify how being in the Word led to change? Are there times you can clearly see how not being in the Word hurt your walk with God?
3. How can you incorporate more Bible meditation into your devotional life?
4. Is the Word at the center of your church's life and ministry? How might you know if this is the case or not?

Next Steps
- Commit to a regular time of reading and meditating on the Bible. Cultivate this spiritual discipline, along with prayer and biblical community, as the foundational ways we grow in Christ. If it helps, start a Bible reading plan or ask a friend to encourage you in this.
- For ideas on how to meditate on the Bible, read Don Whitney's blog "17 Ways to Meditate on Scripture" at thegospelcoalition.org.

For Further Study
- **Meditation**: See Genesis 24:63; 1 Samuel 12:24; Job 22:22; Psalm 4:4; 19:14: 104:34; 107:43; Romans 6:11; 12:1–2.
- Read David Mathis' article "Warm Yourself at the Fires of Meditation" at desiringgod.org.
  http://www.desiringgod.org/articles/warm-yourself-at-the-fires-of-meditation

THE JOY OF SINGING

"Let the word of Christ dwell in you richly, teaching and admonishing one another in all wisdom, singing psalms and hymns and spiritual songs, with thankfulness in your hearts to God" (Colossians 3:16).

In your mind, go back to a recent Sunday morning where you gathered with God's people in your local church. One thing you did (I hope) was sing. When you sing, who do you sing to? Do you sing to God, to other people, or to your own heart? You could ask, who do you sing for? Are you singing to glorify God, to rehearse truth to yourself or give voice to your beliefs, or do you sing to build up others?

Like many multiple-choice questions, the correct answer is "D: All of the Above." We sing with all three audiences in mind. We might not always be conscious of it, but when we sing we voice and affirm our beliefs, we worship God, and we encourage one another.

If we only think about ourselves, we'll see congregational worship as karaoke time where we get to express ourselves and showcase our voices. If we ignore those around us and think about congregational worship only as God-and-me time, we make worship a vertical experience that cuts us off from the people we worship with. A source of unity becomes another opportunity for individuality. But if we sing only to encourage each other, we miss out on worshipping the living God. A divine moment turns into another shared human experience. All are important and each should be considered and included.

In Colossians 3:16 (one of many Bible verses on singing), Paul highlight two of those three audiences. Our singing is to "one another" as we teach and admonish each other through the Word, and our singing is done "in your hearts to God." It's upward (to God) and outward (to one another).

Singing to God

Singing allows us to glorify God in a unique way. It not only allows us to give voice to our faith, but it does so in an artistic, rhythmic, and poetic form that touches our hearts. Through the music and the lyrics our affections are powerfully engaged. Songs also offer a memory-tool to remember what we sing (which is why we have an alphabet song). Throughout Scripture we see God's people worship Him through song.

- Sing to the Lord, all the earth! Tell of his salvation from day to day. (1 Chronicles 16:23)
- Sing praises to the Lord, who sits enthroned in Zion! (Psalm 9:11)
- Sing praises to the Lord, for he has done gloriously; let this be made known in all the earth. Shout, and sing for joy, O inhabitant of Zion, for great in your midst is the Holy One of Israel. (Isaiah 12:5–6)
- About midnight Paul and Silas were praying and singing hymns to God, and the prisoners were listening to them. (Acts 16:25)
- Addressing one another in psalms and hymns and spiritual songs, singing and making melody to the Lord with your heart. (Ephesians 5:19)

Like prayer, singing takes place in every season and scenario. There are joyful songs of praise for deliverance as well as sorrowful songs of confession. The Psalms, the songbook of God's people, connect song with the full range of human emotions.

Singing involves our heart, mind, and body as we express faith in God, ascribe glory to His name, thank Him for His deeds, and remember His words and works. The truths we've seen and the realities we've lived in all week can come out in unique ways through singing to God. As we express our thoughts and emotions in song, we are reminded of God, His works, and His ways.

This isn't restricted to Sundays. Throughout the week we can find ways to sing God's praise. Grab a hymnal, find Christian songs to sing online, or use your church's Spotify list. Explore the many ways to exalt God in your heart by lifting your voice.

Sing to Others

As our text reminds us, we don't only sing to God. We also sing together as a means by which we "teach and admonish" one another. We instruct and warn. We encourage and exhort. "Music is a vehicle through which a message is delivered."[101] In Colossians 3:16, Paul doesn't say there's teaching of the Word and there's also (separately) singing. Teaching and admonishing happen both in our preaching and as we sing "psalms and hymns and spiritual songs."

This is why it's important that we sing and what we sing. It's not enough that songs sound good, that it moves us emotionally, are catchy, or have a pretty melody. We must also have doctrinally sound and God-centered lyrics. We must remind one another of God's promises, provision, works, blessings, and words. It doesn't matter how many hands are lifted or hearts are moved if it's not according to truth. We encourage and build one another up through songs drenched in the Word (3:16).

Think about this the next time you gather with believers to worship God. If you don't sing, you're not only robbing God of worship but you're failing to encourage those around you. As you sing, people are encouraged by how your voice—however pretty or terribly sounding—testifies you believe these things and have experienced these things.

Your song of worship isn't simply a fun musical act, but it's a testimony to the truth of God's Word and the faithfulness of God's ways. We sing because we are banking on these truths. How might that affect the way you sing as you

---

[101] Richard Melick Jr., *Colossians*, 305.

gather for worship? How might that affect the way you listen to others while singing?

Often, on a Sunday morning as our church sings together, I'm strengthened by those around me. When I see a person praising God and I know they've been through the valley, it fortifies my faith. When a family in the midst of loss, confusion, pain, or doubts continues to trust God and worship God in our singing, my faith is fed through them. Or, as I'm singing and see those around me and I know the circumstances they're in, I'm reminded to sing with even more passion, faith, and honesty. Singing isn't going through the motions in that moment but it's a tangible way to love on people around me. We sing for God's glory but we also sing for our neighbor's good.

Applying Colossians

Questions
1. Are there times during the week you sing to God? Why or why not?
2. What are ways you might better worship God through singing?
3. How can you sing with the gathered church more aware of both the vertical (to God) and horizontal (to one another) dimensions?

Next Steps
- Either grab a hymnal or search online for some hymns or worship songs. Find one you can sing right now or that you'd like to sing this week at various times (in the car, shower, etc.).

- How can you prepare your heart for corporate worship? Try to do at least one thing the night before or the morning of your church service to better set your heart on God.

For Further Study
- **Singing**: 1 Chronicles 16:23–29; Psalm 9:11; 89:1; 96; 107:22; Isaiah 12:1–6; Colossians 3:16–17.

WHOSE NAME YOU CARRY

"And whatever you do, in word or deed, do everything in the name of the Lord Jesus, giving thanks to God the Father through him" (Colossians 3:17).

I recently watched the film, *In the Heart of the Sea*. It's a story based on the 1820 sinking of an American whaling boat (*Essex*) which inspired Herman Melville's *Moby-Dick*. An important aspect of the storyline arises early in the film—a theme not uncommon in other films. It's the idea our lives, opportunities, successes and shame, and legacy are connected with the name we represent. More often than not, it's a family name, but at other times it might be a company, organization, team, church, or group that's represented. Names stand for something bigger than ourselves. Our life tells a story that affects the name we carry.

The lead character from *In the Heart of the Sea*, Owen Chase, is hired on as first mate. It's not a welcome position, since Owen has proven himself more than capable of a captain's commission. What's haunting him is his last name: Chase. His father's failures and lack of prestige isn't easily shaken. His name not only identified his family, but it was believed to say something about who he was.

While his father left one legacy with the name, Owen sets out to do everything he can to redeem the family name for himself and his unborn child. The young, inexperienced and ill-suited captain appointed (Captain Pollard) reaped the benefits of a prestigious name in the whaling industry. His family name spoke for itself. It opened doors. It came with benefits. It created trust in his inherent abilities to lead people and captain a ship. Both Captain Pollard and Owen Chase lived under the banner of the family name. The name made all the difference.

Our Family Name

In Colossians 3:17, Paul finishes up the immediate section about putting on Christ in the context of the church. He's told us ways to put on Christ-like love and how to encourage one another in Word-saturated speech. Almost as if to give a bigger, all-encompassing guideline for how we live, he sums it up by saying, "Whatever you do, in word or deed, do everything in the name of the Lord Jesus" (3:17). Words and deeds encompass pretty much all of life, but just in case they don't get it, he makes it inescapably clear by adding "everything."

Paul can't give them an exhaustive list of do's and don'ts. The Bible isn't a Dictionary of Morality where we look up each gray area and find a spelled-out answer as to what to do. Instead, the Bible teaches us to live all of life under the lordship of Jesus by walking in the Spirit. This means in any given situation we use wisdom to apply the Word rather than always creating a rule.

Lordship asks who is Lord of my life? Who do I live for? Who's in charge? Who do I represent? When Jesus is our Lord in our daily living, we recognize both that we should live to please Him and that our life represents Him. Being "in Christ" comes with countless family benefits, but it also comes with family responsibilities. Like kids whose behavior reflects on the parents—and the family name and history well beyond them—our words and deeds say something about Jesus. They can show His beauty, holiness, grace, and love as we bear His image. If we walk in the flesh, we can hide Jesus from people or display a false picture of what He's like. For Christ-following image-bearers, every thought, word, deed, desire, and decision reflect Jesus— positively or negatively.

Lord of All

It's easy to imagine Jesus as Lord over *some* things, but we often want to cling to being our own lord over other things. Is there a part of your speech, thoughts, desires, finances, relationships, habits, entertainment, or decision-making you keep to yourself? Do you bargain with God by saying you'll let Jesus be Lord in other areas if you can keep this sin? Or, maybe you think of Jesus as the Lord of spiritual things but the more tangible things (wealth, use of time, media intake) aren't a concern to Him.

When Jesus is Lord, every detail of our life is a concern to Him. Jesus cares about every sorrow and joy in any area of our life. But He also sees every word and deed—everything—under His jurisdiction as Lord. Not because He wants to be a tyrant holding us back or keeping us from happiness, but because He wants to set us free from enslavement to other idols.

When Jesus is King he leads us only into what's best. The more we resist this rule and submit to other kings—including ourselves—the more we are led into deceptive and destructive ways of living. Jesus is all-in when it comes to lordship. Thankfully, the Spirit is constantly working to help us yield every area of our lives over to Jesus.

Think about your own life for a moment and where you might cooperate with the Spirit's work. Your life consists of a thousand buckets or spheres. Is Jesus Lord in every arena or are you pushing Him out? Think about things like your marriage, singleness, vacations, finances, sexuality, parenting, friendships, gifts, vocation, use of social media, entertainment, thought life, speech, actions, church, and on and on. Ask God to make it clear if there are any places you've set up your own throne instead of letting Jesus rule. Only God can give eyes to see when this is the case. And only God can loosen you from the grips of the idols ruling you.

This principle also helps us with temptation or how we think about gray issues. Since we live all of life in the name of Jesus, ask, can I do this in the name of Jesus? Does it reflect His purposes? Can I do this as His representative? Will this show Jesus to others or keep others from seeing Him?

We're also reminded with the last phrase of verse seventeen that gratitude is part of how we live under Jesus's lordship. Thankfulness is part of how we fight off idols trying to take His place. We do everything in the name of Jesus, "giving thanks to God the Father through him" (3:17).

Thanksgiving helps us do all things in the name of Christ. If ingratitude (Romans 1) and grumbling (Philippians 2) are at the heart of idolatry, then gratitude is at the heart of worship. The more we can give thanks to God in all circumstances (see Colossians 3:15–17; 4:2), the more we can live under, for, and with the lordship of Jesus in those areas.

Submission to Jesus isn't a gritted-teeth, eyes-rolling, head-shaking experience where we do what he says even though we'd like to be in control. Instead, submission to Jesus is a joyful, trusting, worshipful posture that believes Jesus always knows what's right and best for us. Living in the name of Jesus means He rules us in a way that leads to our good. But living in the name of Jesus also means we reflect Him in a way that should lead to His glory.

Carry Christ's name with you today. Or more accurately, live aware that you do carry Christ's name with you. We bear the name of Jesus, including the responsibilities and the privileges. Whatever you think, say, or do today, do it all in the name of Jesus.

Applying Colossians

Questions
1. Why do you think Paul might have included verse 17 where he did?
2. Why is Jesus's lordship a good thing in our lives and not a restrictive thing?
3. What are some areas you're tempted to hide from Jesus or that you try to be lord over? How can you submit these areas to Jesus?

4. Why do you think Paul includes the last phrase about giving thanks? How do gratitude and grumbling come into play when it comes to what we worship and follow?

Next Steps

- Spend some time with a spouse, mentor, or trusted friend talking about what it means for Jesus to be Lord in everything. Allow them to speak honestly but graciously into your life about anything they think you might not be submitting to or following Jesus in.

For Further Study

- **Christ's Lordship**: Luke 6:46; Romans 10:9; 2 Corinthians 5:15–21; Galatians 2:20; James 4:7.
- Read through Colossians 2:6–4:6. Note where you see the lordship of Jesus showing up. Lordship has to do with us living life under, with, and for Christ.

LORD OF THE HOME

"Wives, submit to your husbands, as is fitting in the Lord. 19 Husbands, love your wives, and do not be harsh with them" (Colossians 3:18–21).

When I was single, I envisioned married life with many of the romantic scenes of a Hollywood rom-com. With music softly playing in the background, my wife and I would live daily in a dreamy, peaceful, and adventurous romance. While marriage should include healthy romance and companionship (things I need to cultivate more), at times it looks less like two lovers staring into one another's eyes and more like two entrenched war combatants.

Conflict is inevitable. Pride and selfishness pop up with weed-like frenzy and determination. While a Christian marriage should involve two people working together to advance Christ's kingdom, husbands and wives fight to protect their own kingdom. Paul calls us to surrender and blow up the kingdom of "Me" so Jesus can be King of the home.102

Discipleship isn't done exclusively in the church; it's also lived out in the home. We honor Christ by loving those in our family and living out God's good design.

Unlike other parts of Paul's letter, not everything in these verses about the household will apply to us. You might not be a spouse or a parent, and you're not both a husband and a wife. Here are three suggestions for reading this passage.

Read to understand God's design for the family, whether or not it directly applies to you. What responsibilities does Paul attach to differing roles? You are part of a local church (hopefully) with others walking in these various

---

102 Most good commentaries will provide an extended treatment on "household codes" in the New Testament. See Pao, Colossians, 263– 66 as one example.

roles, so learn how to better pray for and encourage them to be faithful in them.

Second, if you are married, prayerfully consider how you need to apply this before thinking about how your spouse should change. And third, Paul isn't fully expounding what the Bible has to say on marriage from this text. He gives one phrase, something we still can obey and apply, but the Bible says a lot more. Keep in mind that whatever role God has put you in, the Bible has much more to say to you than Colossians 3. But start here.

Wives

Everyone submits to someone. Children submit to parents. Employees submit to employers. Citizens submit to the authority of government (Romans 13). Husbands submit to Christ. Jesus submits to the Father.

Our culture sees submission as a dirty word. Submission sounds like becoming a doormat with no voice, no opinion, and being walked all over. Submission flies in the face of the god of our day: autonomy. While the Bible does picture submission as putting yourself under the direction, leadership, and even authority of another, it never calls for a loss of personhood or a door-mat mentality. Submission is not silence, just as leading is not dominance. Submission should never signal diminished worth or inequality, only differing roles among those equally valuable and equally necessary.

Douglas Moo writes, "Submission…suggests a voluntary willingness to recognize and put oneself under the leadership of another."[103] Notice it's a voluntary willingness. Submission is not to be demanded and enforced by the one in authority, though their good and caring leadership might compel it.

It's also not a blind obedience of whatever is asked. No believer should follow another person into sin, abuse, or harm. Third, wives are called to

---

[103] Moo, *Colossians*, 301.

submit to their husbands—not all husbands and not all men—as is fitting in the Lord. It's debated whether this phrase means to submit "as to the Lord" or in the sense of "which is appropriate for one in the Lord." It seems best—considering the context—to take this phrase as referring to behavior fitting because Christ is Lord.

God set up marriage so husbands lovingly lead their wives in a way that reflects how Jesus leads His church (see Ephesians 5:22–33). God designed this leading and submitting pattern for husband and wives to reflect God's design of Christ and the church. It's a beautiful picture of the gospel. Because sin fractures the most intimate of relationships and seeks to uproot God's good design (cf. Genesis 3:16), both husbands and wives will struggle to live out their God-given roles faithfully. But, as a wife, ask yourself the following questions.

- How can I better submit to my husband?
- How do I resist submission or take over my husband's leadership in inappropriate ways?
- How can I support, encourage, and follow my husband's leadership this week?
- How might submitting to my husband honor Christ? How might it help my own heart?

Husbands

Both submitting and leading create unique challenges and neither is easy. Leaders exist not for their own sake but for the good of those they lead. Leaders have power, authority, and influence, but it's to be wielded with love and care to serve others. Leadership should not only be servant-leadership but sacrificial-leadership. It means laying down your life and desires for the overall good of those being led.

Paul's word to husbands involves a positive (do) and a negative (don't): Love your wives and don't be harsh with them. The Bible says a lot about how we love one another. If as a husband, you're not sure where to start with loving your wife, ask her. But also, read Paul's exposition of love in 1 Corinthians 13. Then read Ephesians 5:25 where husbands are told to love their wives like Christ loves the church.

Jesus loves His church in an infinite number of ways so a husband will never reach the finish line when it comes to loving his wife well. But, in Ephesians 5 it at least means husbands should lay down their life for their wife. Husbands should love their wives by providing for them, protecting them, and pointing them to the truth of God's Word. Prioritize her well-being.

Second, don't be harsh with them. Paul protects wives by teaching that leadership is not selfish but selfless, and it should never lead to harshness, including abuse. Their leadership should not create bitterness toward them but garner respect. Husbands, ask yourself these questions.

- Am I loving my wife like Christ loves the church?
- What are ways I can put my wife before me and better sacrifice for her?
- Am I providing loving leadership in my home or have I cast aside this God-given role?
- Could any of my words, tone, or actions towards my wife be considered harsh?

Whether leading or following, we do so under Christ's lordship. Because of sin, both leading and submitting are difficult. Both require the Spirit's help to honor Christ in how we lead and how we submit. Both sanctify us. Both God as His design leads to our good and reflects the relationship of Christ and His church.

Applying Colossians

Questions

1. Reflect on the questions for a husband or wife again, depending on which applies.
2. What is one thing I might need to confess to God, and to my spouse, because I've been resisting His design and will for the role He's given me?
3. What is one way this week I can better honor Christ and love my spouse?

Next Steps

- If you don't feel like your understanding of the roles of husband and wife are rooted in Scripture, read up on God's design for the home. Recommended books on marriage would include *Marriage and the Mystery of the Gospel* by Ray Ortlund; *The Meaning of Marriage* by Tim and Kathy Keller; *What Did You Expect?* by Paul Tripp; *This Momentary Marriage* by John Piper; *Strengthening Your Marriage* by Wayne Mack.
- Talking about today's passage with your spouse. Confess ways you've fallen short, to receive honest but hard words, and to seek God's help for moving forward. Husbands, ask your wife for ways you come across as harsh, or for ways you lead that make submission a joy rather than a trial. Wives, ask your husband how you can better encourage, support, and follow alongside of him in his leadership.

For Further Study

- **Domestic Relationships**: Ephesians 5:22–6:9; 1 Timothy 2:8–15; 6:1, 2; Titus 2:10; 1 Peter 2:12–3:7.
- **Husband and Wife**: Ephesians 5:22ff; 1 Corinthians 7; 11:2–16; Genesis 1–2; Matthew 19:5; Hebrews 13:4.
- **Husbands**: 1 Peter 3:7; Ephesians 5:25–33; Proverbs 18:22; 1 Corinthians 11:3; 1 Timothy 5:8.
- **Wives**: Titus 2:3–4; 1 Peter 3:1–6; Ephesians 5:22–24; Proverbs 31:10–31.

CHILDREN AND PARENTS

"Children, obey your parents in everything, for this pleases the Lord. 21 Fathers, do not provoke your children, lest they become discouraged" (Colossians 3:20–21).

As I write this, my daughter is two. This means I'm sleeping much better than those first few months. I have some parenting experience under my belt and yet I know almost nothing about parenting. So far parenting has been a lot of dirty diapers, messy meals, exhausting days, and stressful close calls. Thankfully, they're balanced by laughs and giggles, milestones and first moments, hugs and kisses, slow chases around the house, funny words and sentences she comes up with, and precious playtime.

This is a big part of parenting. But it's easy to get caught up in the routine and focus on keeping your child fed, clean, entertained, and learning. As kids grow, parents are still tempted to prioritize school, sports, activities, getting from place to place, preparing for college, and setting them up for a well-paying career. None of these things are bad, but parents must remember their primary role is to "bring them up in the discipline and instruction of the Lord" (Ephesians 6:4).

Parents are commissioned to point children to Christ, fill their heart with God's Word, help them see the beauty in God's ways, and model God. Yeah, that's a big task, but also a noble and worthy one.

In this short text, Paul prompts children and parents to not lose sight of what matters. How they honor their parents or raise their kids is a spiritual issue. It will either honor or dishonor the Lord. How a child responds to their parent's authority and how a parent shepherds their children is part of their obedience to God. Lordship extends not just to marriage, but to the parent-child relationship.

Children

Paul first addresses children. These are most likely young children. Paul chose not to use words for young men or young women, but he also is speaking to children old enough to understand his words. The parallel passage of Ephesians 6:4 reinforces this as fathers are told to "bring them up," meaning they are still in the home and being raised.

Paul assumes these children will be with the adults when the church gathers to read this letter. They probably sang a rowdy round of "Father Abraham" to kick things off in those days. Paul wants these children to hear his words and obey. While it's important to have age-appropriate learning environments for children at church, they should also at times be part of the larger church gathering. It is a shame that in some churches, children will go from diapers to diploma and their entire church experience consists of age-specific classes. There must be times when children and teens gather with the larger church body to sing, pray, serve, and hear the Word.

The command is simple: "obey your parents." This command has a long history, stretching back to the Ten Commandments. "Honor your father and your mother, that your days may be long in the land that the Lord your God is giving you" (Exodus 20:12).

Children are a blessing to parents, but parents are a blessing to children. Parents love, provide for, and protect them—or at least they should. God gives parents as an authority for a child's safety, security, and overall well-being. Parents usually know more and have wisdom so they can guide children into what is right. God's design in commanding children to obey their parents is meant for their good. Like all authorities, the heart behind it isn't oppression but care and direction. As children obey their parents, it pleases the Lord.

Adult children at this point might wonder how they can still honor their parents. While the command to honor your parents doesn't go away in adulthood, it looks different. In his blog post on how adult children can honor their parents, Tim Challies gives six suggestions.[104]

1. Forgive them
2. Speak well of them
3. Esteem them publicly and privately
4. Seek their wisdom
5. Support them
6. Provide for them

Each of us who have living parents—even grandparents—might ask if we are pleasing the Lord in how we honor our parents. This list of six provides a great starting place.

Parents

Of all the things Paul could have told parents, he narrows his counsel here to one admonition: don't provoke your children. Other versions translate this as don't exasperate, embitter, or aggravate your kids. Paul addresses fathers, though both mothers and fathers play essential roles. Richard Melick Jr. writes, "The term may easily encompass both father and mother, as it does here, but it also served to remind them that the fathers bore the primary responsibility for the children in the home."[105]

In Ephesians 6:4, Paul flipped the command around and stated the positive: "bring them up in the discipline and instruction of the Lord." Here he tells them what not to do. Don't provoke them so they lose heart. Don't nag at them. Don't constantly push them and ask more of them. Don't discourage them by persistently pointing out weaknesses and failures.

---

[104] Tim Challies, "6 Practical Ways to Honor Your Parents" *Challies.com*, December 21, 2016. Accessed August 2, 2018.

[105] Melick Jr., *Colossians*, 315.

Encourage them. Affirm them.[106] Celebrate them. Teach them what is good and right with patience and a long-view rather blowing up or getting frustrated when they don't learn at your desired pace. Parenting is difficult. A home should be structured and teach God's good rules and designs, raising children with instruction and discipline. But this should always be done with great grace, love, patience, and gentleness.

Parents have a great opportunity to help their kids see the goodness of God. We can teach our children God's truth, model Christ before their eyes, practice humility and confession when we fail, give them grace upon grace (just like how God treats us), and encourage them in their pursuit of Christ. But, if we're honest, we resort to nagging and prodding over encouraging and modeling when things move slow. Our intentions are good, but Paul assures us this will discourage our children. They'll lose heart. And rather than following Jesus, they'll think they can never make Him happy and they'll run from Him.

Our Father God showers us with free grace time after time. When we fail, He offers grace again. Show your kids the Father's love by giving them grace piled on top of more grace.

Applying Colossians

Questions

1. What are practical ways you can honor your parents, whatever age or stage you're in?
2. What are ways you're trying to teach your kids about the role of parents, including why they should obey, honor, and respect you?
3. How are you or might you be tempted to discourage, nag, pick at, or exasperate your children? What might this lead to in them?

---

[106] Every parent would be helped by reading *Practicing Affirmation* by Sam Crabtree.

4. How can you encourage, affirm, and celebrate with your children this week?

Next Steps

- Be intentional with your children about their spiritual growth. What are some easy ways you can engage your kids about their relationship with Jesus? How can you pray with them, read the Bible together, practice disciplines as a family, celebrate moments and milestones, and talk about who God is and how He's at work? Talk with your spouse about ways you might be provoking, exasperating, or discouraging your children and ways to reverse that trend. Ask your kids when they feel discouraged and what you can do to better encourage them.

- Thank your parents for ways they loved you. This doesn't mean they were perfect or even that they didn't fail in significant ways. But how can you tell them thank you for ways they sacrificed for you, provided, protected, taught you, or loved you? Maybe a card, a text, a phone call, or a dinner would be a great way to express your thankfulness.

For Further Study

- **Honor your parents**: Exodus 20:12; Ephesians 6:1–3; Proverbs 1:8–9; 20:20; 23:22; 30:17.

- **Parents**: Deuteronomy 6:6–9; 11:19 Psalm 103:13; 127:3–5; Proverbs 13:24; 22:6; 29:17; 1 Timothy 5:8.

- Recommended books: *Shepherding a Child's Heart* by Tedd Tripp; *Parenting* by Paul David Tripp; *The Gospel-Centered Parent* by Rose Marie Miller and Deborah Harrell; *Gospel– Powered Parenting* by William P. Farley; *Give Them Grace* by Elyse Fitzpatrick; *Family Worship* by Don Whitney *The Life We Never Expected: Hopeful Reflections on the Challenges of Parenting Children with Special Needs* by Andrew and Rachel Wilson.

STOP WORKING FOR "THE MAN"

"Bondservants, obey in everything those who are your earthly masters, not by way of eye-service, as people-pleasers, but with sincerity of heart, fearing the Lord. 23 Whatever you do, work heartily, as for the Lord and not for men, 24 knowing that from the Lord you will receive the inheritance as your reward. You are serving the Lord Christ. 25 For the wrongdoer will be paid back for the wrong he has done, and there is no partiality. Masters, treat your bondservants justly and fairly, knowing that you also have a Master in heaven" (Colossians 3:22–4:1).

Slavery's shadow still looms out of America's past into the present day. It's a shameful part of our history and an ongoing wound that has never fully healed. It's a word loaded with emotion, pain, and complexity. Adding to the confusion, the Bible was used both to argue for and against slavery during the Civil War era.[107] The ripple effect of the Bible's misuse continues today. A popular line of contemporary reasoning says just as the Bible supported slavery—and was on "the wrong side of history"—the Bible can't be trusted with other modern ethical issues.

When we open our Bibles to Colossians 3–4 and we see God speaking to masters and slaves or servants, what do we do with this? Was Paul writing in a context similar to what we think of in America with racial and chattel slavery? Is this verse advocating slavery?

Those two questions must be answered with a resounding no. The master-servant relationship here isn't "pro-slavery" nor is it the same slavery most of us imagine with our American history lens. While this topic demands a lengthier response, I want to quickly explain why Paul is not advocating for

---

107 See Mark Noll's book *The Civil War as a Theological Crisis*.

slavery and then move to how we might apply this text in our modern world.[108]

Slavery in Paul's Day

The slavery or servanthood in Paul's day was not race-based, nor was it chattel slavery where a slave had no rights at all or any way of ever getting out. Slavery was a political or economic issue. People became slaves either through war or because of debt. It could affect any class, ethnicity, and profession.

This doesn't make it right or acceptable in either case. It still attacked the dignity of God's image-bearers, but as Tim Keller states, "It was more like what we would call indentured servitude."[109]

Paul does not advocate for slavery, but he does write to believers who live within the system. As we see in Ephesians 6:5–9 and Colossians 3:22–4:1, Paul addresses both masters and servants because there must have been Christians from both groups within the same church at Colossae. Paul wants them to treat one another like brothers in Christ (Philemon 17).[110] He wants those who are masters to not abuse, harm, degrade, or be harsh with their servants but to "treat them justly and fairly" (4:1). And he wants those who are servants to respond to their earthly authorities with hard work and sincerity.

Paul wants masters to treat servants with the mindset they have a Master in heaven. This provides them with a model of a Master who treats those under Him well. It also gives motivation to give the kind of treatment they've received as those under the Master. And Paul wants servants to not work for man but "as for the Lord" (3:23). They should fear the Lord (3:22) in their work and serve the Lord in it (3:24).

---

108 Consult the "For Further Study" section for recommended resources on slavery and the Bible.

109 Timothy Keller, *Every Good Endeavor* (New York: Dutton, 2012), 213.

110 See Paul's letter to Philemon on how the gospel should change master– slave relationships within the church.

Paul sees all relationships as being transformed by the gospel. We get our cues not from culture but from Christ. Paul speaks to the major relationships in his day—husband and wife, parent and child, master and servant—and tells them to not put any relationship or role outside their Christian walk. They don't follow Jesus at church but not at home or work. The home and the workplace are to look different for the believer.

Honoring Christ at Work

How might we apply this today? Acknowledging 21st century American workplaces look very different from servanthood in the 1st century, I think we can apply this passage to our employee-employer relationships. Paul is dealing with how Christians rightly act when they are in authority and when they are under authority. What's binding isn't the cultural understanding of either master-slave or boss-employee relationships, but how Christians work with others viewing Jesus as Lord. Our work matters to God; not just what we do but *how* we do it and for *who* we do it.

Many people work somewhere that's not their "dream job," and they work under harsh bosses. This passage asks us to look to and trust in the Lord in these hard circumstances, knowing He cares about our response. This can also alter the way employees work for supervisors, bosses, and employers. Like government, they are authorities to treat with respect.

Anyone who is an employer, boss, or supervisor should care for those under them and oversee them in with fairness and justice. Lead out of love, even at work.

We also learn in this text we don't work for "the man" nor do we work begrudgingly only for the paycheck. We work for Jesus. We work "as for the Lord and not for man" (3:23). The theme here has echoed throughout Colossians. Jesus is Lord of everything. This extends beyond the church walls and into our home, our relationships, our neighborhood and community, where we go for recreation and entertainment, and into our workplace. That's true whether we work inside or outside the home, whether we're self-employed or employed by another, and whether we like our job or hate it.

When we work for Jesus, we become better workers. We view work as a good thing instituted by God from Creation (Genesis 2:15). We aren't lazy but work hard. We work not only when the boss is looking but with the awareness that Jesus sees it all (3:22). To quote Tim Keller's excellent book on work again: "If *slave owners* are told they must not manage workers in pride and through fear, how much more should this be true of employers today? And if *slaves* are told it is possible to find satisfaction and meaning in their work, how much more should this be true of workers today?" When Jesus is our Master, even the most mundane or meaningless work matters.

Many of us wake up early and set our minds on God through our time in the Bible and prayer. Then we head to work, often wrongly thinking we now put God on the shelf for the next eight to twelve hours as we focus on our jobs. Paul says your work might be "secular" but it's still "spiritual." Though you work for someone else, you work for Jesus. How you honor Christ at work is just as important as how you honor Christ in the church (3:14–17) or how you honor Christ in the home (3:18–21). Work matters; what you do, how you do it, and for who you do it. Honor Jesus in all your work today.

Applying Colossians

Questions
1. How would you explain to someone why the Bible is not pro-slavery?
2. What are some of your temptations at work this text might speak into?
3. How can you better serve the Lord in how you work?

Next Steps

- This passage dips its toe into two big issues that the Bible talks about in greater detail, slavery and vocation. Pick up a book(s) on one of those topics to inform your thinking from Scripture.

For Further Study
- **Vocation**: *Every Good Endeavor* by Tim Keller; *The Gospel at Work* by Sebastian Traeger and Greg Gilbert; *Work Matters* by Tom Nelson; *Kingdom Calling* by Amy Sherman.
- **Slavery and the Bible**: "Why It's Wrong to Say the Bible is Pro-Slavery" by Gavin Ortlund at thegospelcoalition.org.; D. A. Carson, "The SBJT Forum: Racism, Scripture, and History" *The Southern Baptist Journal of Theology* 8, no. 2 (2004): 74–78; Andrew T. Lincoln, *Word Biblical Commentary: Ephesians* (Waco: Word, 1990), 415–20; *One New Man* by Jarvis Williams; *Bloodlines* by John Piper.

JESUS GIVES US A MISSION AND A COMMUNITY (4:2–18)

We've come to the end. We can imagine Paul struggling with how to close. There's so much he said in other letters that doesn't get mentioned in Colossians. No doubt the church in Colossae had other looming issues Paul could have spoken into. As he writes from prison (4:18), he must have felt the squeeze of "what else should I say?" So, what does he include? What can't he leave out? He closes by reminding us God gave us a mission (4:2–6) and a community (4:7–17).

Paul models the Christian life so well. He started with prayer (1:3–14) and finishes with prayer (4:2–3). His concerns aren't selfish ones. His heart beats to the drum of Christ's mission. Jesus gave a disciple-making mission to the church (Matthew 28:18–20; Acts 1:8). This motivates Paul's concern for the church's health (1:3–5; 4:7–17) and the gospel's spread (1:5–6; 4:2–5). The gospel reconciles us to God, but the gospel also unites us in a community and sends out on a mission.

These bookends to Colossians keep our priorities in line with the apostle. Our days are short and they're numbered. It's easy to get stuck in the mundane tasks and trials of day-to-day life. We could live as if eternity wasn't real and spiritual realities were of no significance. Many people do, and daily we're tempted to follow suit. Paul urges us to seize the day and to make the most use of the time (4:5).

For Paul, that didn't mean building his bank account, gaining power, maximizing fun while he can, seeking adventures, or following the mantra "you only live once." It led him to pour out his life to serve Christ's church and spread Christ's message. Even as the chains of prison cut into his weakened body, Paul's prayer isn't for himself but for open doors for the Word. The things on his mind are not the things of this world but the mission (4:2–6) and the people (4:7–17).

He expresses thanks to all those who are part of the inter-connected mission of the church. Some open their homes and others labor in ministry. Some are there to stay and some are there for a short period to encourage and update. But all participate. Every person is part of this one Body. And every person has a part to play in the body's ministry and mission.

In this final chapter of Colossians, we'll be nudged to step out. What is our ministry in the church? How are we a part of Christ's global mission? Jesus saves us and Jesus sends us. That sending might be global or local, but each of us have a "ministry to fulfill" (4:17). Jesus makes everything new. We get a new identity, a new way of living, a new eternal destiny, a new community, and a new mission.

PERSISTENT PRAYING

"Continue steadfastly in prayer, being watchful in it with thanksgiving. At the same time, pray also for us, that God may open to us a door for the word, to declare the mystery of Christ, on account of which I am in prison—4 that I may make it clear, which is how I ought to speak" (Colossians 4:2–4).

Describe your prayer life in three words.

What did you come up with? Are you happy with these descriptions? Most of us aren't thrilled about our prayer lives. We know we should pray more often, less selfishly, and with greater consistency. But thinking about changing can be overwhelming. Even if you wanted things to look different, where would you start? Colossians 4:2 maps out a simple place to start. Be persistent, watchful, and thankful.

Persistent

"Continue steadfastly in prayer." Other translations might say, "Be devoted to prayer." The verb gets at being persistent in prayer, persevering or not giving up, and it being a regular practice. In Luke 18:1, Jesus tells a parable teaching his disciples "they ought always to pray and not lose heart." Paul writes, "Be constant in prayer" (Romans 12:12) and "pray without ceasing" (1 Thessalonians 5:17).

This first phrase encourages us both in the frequency of prayer and in the manner of prayer. Prayer is not to be an irregular activity done when we need something. It's to be the normal, ongoing practice of the believer as they talk to God about anything and everything. We can bathe each part of our day in prayer. Every interaction and circumstance provide a platform for praise, thanksgiving, lament, confession, interceding, or supplication.

The manner of our praying should be persistent and persevering. We easily slip into discouragement when prayers aren't immediately or clearly answered. Continue turning to God in prayer and trusting God through prayer. Don't give up. Don't succumb to discouragement or doubt. Persist in praying to God even while you patiently submit those prayers to His will, timing, and plan.

Watchful

Paul says to be watchful or alert as we pray. This language of watchfulness conveys being awake, alert, on guard, and on the lookout. It could be both defensive (be on guard) and offensive (be expectant). We should pray with an awareness of our times, the surrounding needs, and in view of our enemy (1 Peter 5:18).

We should not be caught off guard because of neglect, apathy, or laziness. You might call to mind here any one of countless movies and books where some fortress, castle, or building is lost because those on the lookout were negligent. They were either sleeping, distracted, lost in conversation, or they didn't know what to look for. Don't be that guy or gal. Stay alert.

The language could also tell us to expect God to work and to be on the lookout for answers to prayer. Don't lob up prayers and never have eyes open to see if and how God works in response.

One simple and practical way we might better watch in our praying is recording things we pray about. Whether it's keeping a journal, saving requests on your phone, or having a place to write out prayers, this can be a way to better pray expectantly.

Writing down specific things to pray about can keep important things in front of us. While most of our prayers tend to be self-centered (we often sound like Veruca Salt with our "I want it now" demands), or to only focus on the physical needs of those closest to us, a prayer list can help us pray strategically. It also can promote looking for God to answer as we see what we've prayed about and we're more cognizant of how, when, and where God answered our prayers.

Thankful

Paul tells us to pray with thanksgiving. This last phrase is joined to "being watchful." We're not told here to pray by giving thanks to God, though that's true. Paul says in all of our praying we should be thankful. Thankfulness then isn't one kind of praying but the aroma that permeates all our praying. It's the Christian's attitude and posture in every prayer. "Thankfulness is the environment for good praying, and it provides a safeguard for informed praying."[111] What might that look like?

The Bible gives us plenty of examples where the focus is giving thanks (such as 1 Chronicles 16:34–35; Psalm 9:1; 18:45–50; 118:28–29; 12:1–4; Matthew 15:36; Luke 2:36–38; 22:17–19). Besides confession of sin, lamenting the brokenness and injustices in our world, praising God for who He is, and making requests to God, we should also pray prayers of thanksgiving. Intentionally include gratitude in your conversation with God by thanking Him for specific gifts, blessings, provision, works, His plan, promises, or what He shows you in the Bible. We all need this reminder because from the time we can muster half-spoken sentences as a kid we gravitate towards saying "Give me" instead of "Thank you."

But this verse suggests we not only pray specific prayers of thanksgiving, but that it characterizes all our prayers. As we lament, confess, intercede, or petition God, we do so in a humble, trusting, grateful spirit that allows us to give thanks in all circumstances (1 Thessalonians 5:18). Tell God you trust

---

[111] Melick, *Colossians*, 322

Him in the situation He's allowed you to be in that's led to prayer and thank Him in advance for His wise and good answer.

Give thanks believing God will hear you and for the very fact you can pray to Him. Give thanks trusting God acts as you pray. Thank God as you submit to God's will. And give thanks knowing God answers your prayers in His timing and way.

As we pray, we're on the lookout for how God works and we thank Him when He does. But we also give thanks when things are hard or we don't see an answer because we know everything that happens to us is filtered through the loving hands of our Father. This circumstance might not be what I want but there is something in it I can give thanks for. This trial might be painful or even tragic. It might be cause for me to pour out my complaints to God in lament. But even in this, I can by faith give thanks because I believe God will work this out for my good, for the good of others, and for His glory. We then not only pray at all times and in all circumstances, but we give thanks in all our praying.

Be persistent. Be watchful. Be thankful. How can you take a step in this direction? Is there anything you've stopped praying for you need to bring to God again? Is prayer something that characterizes your day or something you relegate to one part of your day? Be persistent. How can you pray intentionally and expectantly for God's glory and the growth of others around you? Be watchful. What can you thank God for in this season or from this week? Or, in whatever sin you confess, thank God for His grace. In whatever request you make, thank God for listening and His promise to hear and to do what's best for us and His kingdom. Be thankful.

Pray persistently, watchfully, and thankfully.

Applying Colossians

Questions

1. What were the three words you used to describe your prayer life (see first sentence)?
2. Which of the three (persistence, watchfulness, thankfulness) do you think you do the best right now? Which do you struggle with most?
3. What are a couple things you might do differently this week to be persistent, watchful, and thankful in praying?
4. While our prayers tend to be surface-level and self-centered, how can you grow in praying kingdom-minded, heart-focused, God-centered, and others-oriented prayers?

Next Steps

- Come up with a plan for how to grow in prayer this week. Maybe that's committing to praying for five minutes each day after you read the Bible, praying at specific times throughout your day, praying with a model like the ACTS (Adoration-Confession-Thanksgiving-Supplication) model, praying with someone, starting a prayer journal, or some other specific way to lean into prayer this week. Have a plan and then ask someone to encourage you and hold you accountable for that plan.

For Further Study

- **Continue steadfastly**: Luke 18:1; Ephesians 6:18; Romans 12:12; Acts 1:14; 1 Thessalonians 5:17.
- **Being watchful**: Mark 13:33; 14:38; Ephesians 6:18; 1 Thessalonians 5:10; 1 Peter 5:18.
- **With thanksgiving**: Colossians 2:7; Ephesians 5:15; 1 Thessalonians 1:2; 2 Thessalonians 1:3.

WALK WISELY

"Walk in wisdom toward outsiders, making the best use of the time. 6 Let your speech always be gracious, seasoned with salt, so that you may know how you ought to answer each person" (Colossians 4:5–6).

Have you ever had a meal that was missing something or just didn't taste right? It's one thing if this happens at a restaurant where you can send it back, but what if it happens in someone's home? (Not your home, of course, but someone's home.) You could have a meal where the food is cooked right, but if there's no seasoning, it can ruin a meal. You'll be slipping vegetables under the table to the dog or gulping water like a marathon runner all because they forgot the salt.

Paul wants believers to not be flavorless or distasteful people. He wants our words and our speech to be seasoned rightly. He wants us to be palatable and pleasing, not off–putting and pungent.

Paul gives two commands in verses five and six, each of which is supported with a reason. We should walk in wisdom before unbelievers to make the best use of our time. And we should speak graciously so our response is fitting and able to be received. Both have in mind our testimony and witness as Christians.

Walk in Wisdom

Earlier in Colossians, Paul prayed they would have wisdom (1:9). Then he located wisdom's source in Jesus (2:2–3) and warned against a worldly wisdom that looks good on the outside but is hollow (2:23). As his letter winds down, Paul returns to wisdom and tells them to walk in it (4:5).

It's a natural transition from the prior verse on praying for an open door to share the gospel (4:3–4). Pray for open doors to share the word, but also live in wisdom so your walk doesn't close the door. Does your life—your attitude, words, choices, and actions—invite people in so they want to know more, or does it push people away so they'd want nothing to do with Christ?

Walking wisely involves being informed by the truth of God's Word. It means following Jesus so that as we walk in God's good designs for us it leads to His glory and our joy. Walking in wisdom means not being foolish by either embracing evil or acting as if we're promised to live forever (see Ephesians 5:15–17). Walk in wisdom before the world by walking in the wisdom of the Lord.

We need wisdom to know how to seize the day by not only living our life to honor God but also having intentional and meaningful conversation with the people around us. Talking about the weather or sports isn't bad, and all conversations and friendships start somewhere, but is small talk with a lost person making the best use of the time? Ask God for wisdom and He promises to give it (James 1:5).

Suitable Speech

Not only should we walk in wisdom but our speech should be salty. Not "bad salty" like when you accidentally put salt instead of sugar in your coffee, but "good salty" like a well-seasoned entrée. Salt elevates a dish. No salt makes a meal forgettable, but just the right amount and you'll be talking about that dish for weeks.

Grace, or graciousness, should season our speech. In Ephesians 4:29, Paul writes: "Let no corrupting talk come out of your mouths, but only such as is good for building up, as fits the occasion, that it may give grace to those who hear." Our words matter. They can either build up or tear down. Douglas Moo summarizes the speech Paul has in mind.

Paul is calling on Christians to speak with their unbelieving neighbors and friends with warm gracious, warm, and winsome words—all with the purpose of being able to 'answer' unbelievers. By putting it this way, Paul assumes that unbelievers will be raising questions about the faith of the Colossian Christians, questions that may be neutral or even, perhaps, hostile. An appropriate Christian response will, of course, communicate the content of the gospel, but it will also be done in a manner that will make the gospel attractive.[112]

Not that we never speak hard words, since Paul earlier said we must teach and warn (1:28), but is the content and tone of our words delivered with grace? Is it fitting to the person we are talking to? Are we like Christ in being full of grace and truth (John 1:14)?

Tact and tone play a big part of this discernment in how to respond. Jesus answered the hardened Pharisees very differently than how He answered broken sinners. In wisdom and with grace, we should speak to individuals in light of their own questions, stories, experiences, and understanding. Paul doesn't say this is easy, but it is right.

We need more wisdom in our steps and we need more grace on our tongues. Both make Christ attractive and appealing to an on-looking world.

This might be a good time to reflect on some questions to help us seize the day.

- Do I walk wisely around unbelievers? Do my actions and words reflect the wisdom and life Christ offers or do they convey foolishness and folly from the world?

---

112 Moo, *Letters to the Colossians*, 331.

- Do I live aware that the days are evil and time is short? Am I intentional in my relationships and conversations?

- Is my speech full of grace? Does it bubble over in gratitude to God and kindness to others or grumbling to God and criticism towards others?

- Do I see people as people, listening to their questions and responding based on where they are rather than giving a canned speech or impersonal response?

- Am I reflecting Jesus to those around me? Do my words and my walk help draw others to Christ or push them away from him?

If we walk in Christ (2:6) we will walk in wisdom. If the Word of Christ dwells in us richly (3:16) then gracious, Christ-like speech will flow out of us. To walk and talk like Jesus, we have to know and abide in Him. "And whatever you do, in word or deed, do everything in the name of the Lord Jesus, giving thanks to God the Father through him" (Colossians 3:17).

Don't minimize the power of your words. Your tongue can point others to Jesus or get in the way. It can honor Christ or dishonor Him. The tongue is a bucking bronco, unruly and hard to tame. But with God's Spirit in the saddle instead of our flesh we can control our words. Walk in wisdom with grace seasoning your speech. Start today.

Applying Colossians

Questions
1. What are ways you might not make the best use of the time? How specifically does this relate to your witness to unbelievers?
2. What are ways we might not walk wise before others?
3. What does it look like to have speech that's salty and full of grace? What are ways your words might not look this way?
4. What does speech look like in your home? If your family pattern of talking to one another is full of sarcasm, criticism, discouragement,

nit-picking, or anger then it will probably be how you talk to others outside of the home. How can your family build gracious, encouraging, truthful, and joy-giving words into conversation?

Next Steps

- Write down three to five people you think might not be Christians who you interact with on occasion. Pray for them. Ask God to give you an open door (Colossians 4:4). Take one step this week in building these relationships so as to maximize the time.

For Further Study

- **Words**: Ephesians 4:29; 5:4; Matthew 15:11; Proverbs 10:31–32; 15:1–2; Psalm 141:3; James 3:1–2.
- **Evangelism**: Matthew 28:18–20; 1 Peter 3:15; 2 Corinthians 5:20; Mark 16:15; 1 Thessalonians 2:8.
- Read *War of Words* by Paul Tripp or *Practicing Affirmation* by Sam Crabtree.

WHAT PART DO YOU PLAY?

"Tychicus will tell you all about my activities. He is a beloved brother and faithful minister and fellow servant in the Lord. 8 I have sent him to you for this very purpose, that you may know how we are and that he may encourage your hearts, 9 and with him Onesimus, our faithful and beloved brother, who is one of you. They will tell you of everything that has taken place here. 10 Aristarchus my fellow prisoner greets you, and Mark the cousin of Barnabas (concerning whom you have received instructions—if he comes to you, welcome him), 11 and Jesus who is called Justus. These are the only men of the circumcision among my fellow workers for the kingdom of God, and they have been a comfort to me. 12 Epaphras, who is one of you, a servant of Christ Jesus, greets you, always struggling on your behalf in his prayers, that you may stand mature and fully assured in all the will of God. 13 For I bear him witness that he has worked hard for you and for those in Laodicea and in Hierapolis. 14 Luke the beloved physician greets you, as does Demas. 15 Give my greetings to the brothers at Laodicea, and to Nympha and the church in her house. 16 And when this letter has been read among you, have it also read in the church of the Laodiceans; and see that you also read the letter from Laodicea. 17 And say to Archippus, 'See that you fulfill the ministry that you have received in the Lord.' 18 I, Paul, write this greeting with my own hand. Remember my chains. Grace be with you" (Col 4:7–18).

What is your role or ministry in the local church? If the church is a body and its members are essential joints and ligaments helping it function, how are you part of the body's growth and health?

With the close of this beautiful, Christ-exalting book, we're reminded it's a personal letter written to the Colossians and surrounding churches (4:15–16). It's a warm, pastoral letter to people Paul loves.

These people with names—though we might not know how to pronounce them—are very similar to us. They were Christians with real struggles, temptations, and challenges trying to follow Jesus. Paul rebuked anything "not according to Christ" (2:8) and repeatedly magnified Jesus to see them mature in Him (1:28). Here he mentions other faithful ones in the Colossian church who labored like this among them (see 4:12). Their maturity takes place through personal ministry.

In this final section (4:7–18), we read the names of ordinary brothers and sisters living the Christian life *together*. Each member was necessary. Each member was part of the greater whole. They didn't "show up to church" as consumers but they were part of the church community. They received ministry from others and they ministered to others. They were interdependent, not independent.

While genealogies and letter closings might not be our favorite part of a book, the names and the descriptions teach us a few things we must see.

The Church is the Place We Grow

The church, Christ's messy but glorious bride, is the place where believers belong to one another and build one another up. "A call to discipleship and spiritual maturity is a call to biblical community."[113] The goal of gathering together and living life together outside the gathering was to see one another mature in Christ. There is nothing more beautiful than making disciples as we share the gospel and help mature disciples. We do this by walking with them in their journey of growing in Christ.

Paul knows the Christian life is lived in community. They are now a family. The church is not a Sunday morning destination where we get what we

---

[113] Ed Stetzer and Eric Geiger, *Transformational Groups* (Nashville: Broadman & Holman Publishers, 2014), 21.

need and leave, but a tight-knit people caring for and encouraging each other into maturity.

> It is hard for us to grasp the significance of this community identity, because we live in a radically individualistic culture. We bring this worldview with us into the church so that it shapes our understanding of the gospel. So we have a loose connection with Christians on Sunday, but then largely we go back to living our everyday lives on our own. No wonder we struggle to thrive. Our faith is animated on Sunday mornings as we sing God's praise and hear his Word. But it limps along during the week when we live apart from the body of Christ.[114]

Churches are United to Christ

A wonderful unity exists both within the church of Colossae and among the different churches in the region. Christian love produced such unity (3:14; 1:4, 8). Notice how believers from one church and city greet believers in other cities. They love Christ and they love to hear the exciting news about how the gospel is spreading and bearing fruit in many places.

Richard Melick Jr. explains the different groups in Paul's closing. "The list may be divided into three categories: those who journeyed to the church from Paul (4:6–9), those who sent greetings to the church (4:10–14), and those to whom Paul sent greetings through church members at Colosse (4:15–17)."[115] Three groups partner to see the gospel spread globally, local churches growing, and Christ's name glorified.

Every Christian is Critical

---

[114] Steve Timmis and Tim Chester, *Everyday Church* (Wheaton: Crossway, 2012), 53–54.

[115] Melick Jr., *Colossians*, 326.

Everyone has a role. Each person serves a purpose but they work together as one body for the good of the whole. There were many believers not mentioned, but in this section we get a glimpse of the body taking ownership for one another's spiritual health. This might cause us to ask, "What role do I play in my church?" How can I "Fulfill the ministry that you have received in the Lord" (4:17).

Imagine your pastor or elders were writing a letter to your local church. What would they say after your name in that letter? How would they describe you as a church member? Are you actively participating in the life of the church enough to be known? What ministry would they say you were fulfilling as one part of the body humbly serving the rest? How would you want to be known when it comes to your character, ministry, and relationships?

God gives each of us specific gifts (Ephesians 4:11–16) and walks us through experiences in life (2 Corinthians 1:3–7) so we can build up Christ's body. When we disengage from Christ's church or we approach the local church as consumers rather than servants and family, we weaken the body. It's a loss for us personally and a loss for the local church God sovereignly placed us in. You need others and others need you. This is what it means to be a body.

Paul struggled with all his energy—that Christ was producing in him—out of love and for the good of these people (1:29). But he's not the only one. This personal close to the letter tells us about others doing the same. Are you loving others in the church well? How are you engaged in Christ's local and global mission to make disciples? How are you allowing God to pour into you His energy as you pour out your energy to point others to Jesus (1:29; 4:12)?

Christ's plan is to put you into a local people to spread a global gospel. Love Christ by loving His church.

Applying Colossians

Questions

1. Who are people in the church who have shaped you spiritually?
2. Who are people in the church you are trying to shape spiritually?
3. In what ways are you actively participating in the life of your local church to help others grow and to see the church fulfill its mission?
4. What stands out to you from your time in Colossians? What are a couple of personal takeaways?

Next Steps

- Evaluate whether you are actively participating in your local church, and take whatever next step is fitting.
- Different churches in various cities and countries partner together for the global spread of Christ's gospel. Spend time praying for other local, regional, or global ministries and missionaries. Write an email or personal letter to encourage some of them in their work.
- Paul affirms those who are involved in the gospel ministry for how they labor to see others grow. Spend a few moments to write short thank you notes to leaders in your church or members (present or past) who have influenced you in how they served.

For Further Study

- **Tychichus**: Colossians 4:7; Ephesians 6:21–22; Acts 20:4; 1 Corinthians 16:1–4; 2 Timothy 4:12; Titus 3:12; **Epaphras**: Colossians 1:7–8; 4:12–13; **Aristarchus**: Colossians 4:10; Acts 19:29; 27:2ff; **Luke**: Colossians 4:14; 2 Timothy 4:11; Luke & Acts; **Mark**: Colossians 4:10; Acts 13:13; 15:39; 2 Timothy 4:11; **Onesimus**: 4:9; Philemon; **Demas**: Colossians 4:14; 2 Timothy 4:9–10; **Archippus**: Colossians 4:17; Philemon 2.
- **Other closings in Paul's letters**: Romans 1:17–27; 1 Corinthians 16:12–24; 2 Corinthians 13:11–14; Ephesians 6:21–24; Philippians 4:21–23.

Closing Colossians

If you're like me, goodbyes are never easy. At a party or event, I'm that guy who doesn't know how to just say my final farewells and close the door behind me. I linger. I struggle to know what the last words should be and if I'm leaving too early or too late.

Sadly, it's time to say a temporary goodbye to the book of Colossians—though I hope you'll return to it often. There's so much more I'd like to say; so many things we didn't get to talk about.

As we finish our study of Colossians, I want to retrace our steps and remind us of three lessons. Colossians is full of stunning truths about Jesus, gospel– promises to grab onto, admonitions and counsel to heed, and encouragements for endurance together as Christ's church. Before proceeding, take a couple minutes to answer these questions. What stands out to you about Colossians? What do you remember most? How would you summarize the book in one to two sentences?

Jesus is Supreme

If we're summarizing Paul's message in Colossians, we have to start with the Supremacy of Jesus in all things and over all things. Some in the church of that city were tempting believers to add to Jesus or move past Jesus to arrive at a more complete or "higher" form of Christianity. Whether in rules, ascetic practices, experiences, or a hidden wisdom, they offered something "more." You can't add to Jesus without diminishing His supremacy.

Paul's theme laced throughout Colossians is Jesus alone is supreme and sufficient. We need nothing besides Him. He is enough. Out of the fullness of who Jesus is, we find fulfillment.

Paul pens paragraph after paragraph exalting (lifting up) and exulting (delighting in) over Jesus. The pinnacle of this Christ–centered letter might be 1:15–20. Paul can't help Himself. He holds up before us Jesus like a precious jewel. He tells us to behold Him as the one who made everything and whom everything exists for.

In an equally powerful passage (2:11–15), Paul unpacks the work of Jesus on the cross. In Him we move from death to life. In Him the old us is put to death and we are made new. We have forgiveness as our debt is paid through Christ's precious blood. And in Him we are freed because Jesus has defeated our enemies and conquered all foes. We rest in His reign.

Paul wants us to see who Jesus really is, because if we know Him, we will rest in and delight in Him above all things and in all things. He sanctifies us by being the One who satisfies us.

Colossians puts a real, living, powerful, tender, wonderful, trustworthy Savior on display. It's easy to settle for thin and vague notions of Jesus. But just like how impersonal and general impressions of people in our life cause us to assume they're bland, settling for a shallow view of Jesus leads to people thinking He's not that impressive. Paul paints a clear and compelling picture of the person and work of Jesus. If we look and listen, it will awe us. We will want more. We will see how everything Jesus is perfectly answers everything we need. Jesus is supreme and sufficient, but Jesus also satisfies.

Jesus is Sovereign

Out of this amazing theology of who Christ is develops a second significant theme. The two relate. The Supremacy of Jesus above all leads to the Sovereignty over all. Jesus is King and Lord over Creation, over the church, and over the Christian. Colossians opens our eyes to how widespread Christ's kingdom spreads and how pervasive His lordship must be in our life.

The application here for us is we must surrender every aspect of our life to Jesus our Lord. He doesn't come to only rule over our salvation, Sundays, and devotional life. Jesus is Lord over our deeds and our words (3:17). Jesus is Lord over our thoughts, actions, decisions, and relationships (3:5–12). Jesus is Lord in our churches, families, homes, and workplaces (3:18–4:17). Jesus is Lord over everything, so in every part of our life we follow His lead and let Him call the shots.

Behold to Become

Paul connects our worship of Jesus to our walk with Jesus. Seeing the supremacy of Jesus transforms us into His likeness (3:10). As we behold Him, we become like Him. Revering leads to reflection. Knowing Jesus compels us to follow in His steps so we image Him.

Paul sees the end goal of Christian maturity not as being a better me but being a new me. It's a version of me where the flesh gradually disappears and the Spirit shapes us into the likeness of Jesus (2 Corinthians 3:18). Recall Colossians 1:28 where Paul condenses his message into a single verse: "[Jesus] we proclaim, warning everyone and teaching everyone with all wisdom, that we may present everyone mature in Christ." Paul proclaims Jesus to them as the way he forms Jesus in them. Paul magnifies Christ in order to mature us in Christ.

As we set our hearts and minds on Jesus, He gets ahold of our affections and our thinking. We put off who we used to be (3:5–9) and put on who we actually are in Him (3:10–17). Our identity is firmly established in Jesus. This is laid out from verse two onward as we're called "saints and faithful brothers [and sisters] *in Christ.*" The more we understand who Jesus is (chapters 1–2 generally) the more we understand what it means to walk in Him (chapters 3–4 generally). As individuals, and together as the church, we walk *in Him.* We live for Christ and with Christ because we are in Christ.

Who we are is now determined by whose we are. Our identity is in Christ. Our life is so uniquely and intimately connected to Christ that Paul summarizes it by saying "Christ is our life" (3:4).

Our life and identity in Christ directs everything we do. We think of ourselves as God does: in Christ. We put on behaviors fitting with this identity in Jesus and shed anything inconsistent with Jesus. As individuals and the church, we reflect Jesus to the world (imperfectly). We image Him or show Him to others.

Paul's letter tells us almost nothing about the controversial "Colossian heresy." It reveals a few details about Paul himself, but not much. Paul aims the spotlight on Jesus. He puts Jesus front and central, and never moves on. George Whitefield once preached words that echo this letter: "Nothing but Christ! Nothing but Christ! Give me Christ, O God, and I am satisfied! My soul shall praise thee forever."[116] Paul's words point us to Jesus. There is no one like Him, and there is nothing we need besides Him.

Jesus is sufficient. We need no one else and nothing else.

Jesus is supreme. All things exist for Him and should lead us to Him.

Jesus is sovereign. Every inch of the universe and every part of my life is under His authority.

Jesus is satisfying. All the joy and fullness I desire is found by worshipping and delighting in Him.

Jesus is Savior. Forgiveness of sins and acceptance before God is final, full, and forever.

---

[116] George Whitefield, "The Lord our Righteousness." Accessed August 6, 2018 http://www.biblebb.com/files/whitefield/gw014.htm.

Applying Colossians

Questions
1. What stands out to you from Colossians?
2. What did you learn that was new or a needed reminder?
3. How can you move forward with a heart and mind set on Jesus?

Next Steps
- Read through Colossians again and any notes you've taken. Capture key lessons, applications, truths, promises, and takeaways you want to hold onto.

APPENDIX 1: KEY CHARACTERS IN COLOSSIANS

Paul (1:1; 4:18)

The primary author of Colossians and the man responsible for 13 of the 27 books in our New Testament is the apostle Paul. He was invaluable for the early missionary activity of the church, writing the New Testament, and the establishment of the Christian faith.

Paul was born in Tarsus, into a family of wealth, from the tribe of Benjamin, inheriting Roman citizenship (which was not common for Jews).[117] Our first glimpse of Paul isn't a good picture. In Acts 7:58 Saul (Paul) enters the story not as a hero but as the enemy and villain. He oversees the death of Stephen, giving the thumbs up as heavy–stone after heavy–stone rains down on Stephen's body. It goes on to say that Saul was "ravaging the church, and entering house after house, he dragged off men and women and committed them to prison" (8:3). Saul made a living imprisoning, persecuting, and even killing Christians. He did all of this as a zealous Jew, thinking he was promoting the righteousness that belonged to Israel.

God had other plans for Saul and wanted his glory to shine brighter by redeeming a man committing the darkest of evils (1 Timothy 1:16). As Saul approached Damascus to do more harm to the church, the risen and exalted Jesus appears to him and forever changes him. He reveals Himself as Jesus, Paul's Lord whom he has been persecuting. For the rest of his life "to live was Christ" (Philippians 1:21). Everything he did was in response to the grace he'd received and was to push further and further into knowing and serving Jesus. The second half of the book of Acts recounts the stories, ministry, and missionary journeys of Paul. He becomes the apostle to the Gentiles and is used to take the gospel to the ends of the earth even as he's imprisoned by

---

[117] The best sources for putting together Paul's story are Acts 7:58–8:3; 9:1–31; 11:25–26; 13–28; Galatians 1:11–2:21; Phil. 3:4–11.

Rome. Paul's letters provide some of the richest and deepest explanations of the work of Christ. His personal letters remind us he was a theologian, missionary, church planter, and a pastor.

Timothy (1:1)

Paul identifies himself and Timothy as the writers of Colossians. However, 4:18 lists Paul as the primary author, which fits with the Pauline language of the book and the singular nouns throughout. Timothy worked alongside of Paul and two of the New Testament books are letters to him. Besides 1 and 2 Timothy, he appears throughout Acts (Acts 16:1–5; 17:14–15; 18:5; 19:22; 20:4) and in other New Testament letters as an important part of Paul's ministry (Romans 16:21; 1 Corinthians 4:17; 16:10; 2 Corinthians 1:1, 19; Philippians 1:1; 2:19; Colossians 1:1; 1 Thessalonians 1:1; 3:2, 6; 2 Thessalonians 1:1; Philemon 1:1; Hebrews 13:23).

Timothy's importance can also be seen by the fact Paul strategically places him as the pastor in Ephesus (1 Timothy 1:3). We learn much about his upbringing and call to ministry in 1 Timothy 1:18; 4:14–16; 2 Timothy 1:4–6. He was the son of a Greek father and a Jewish mother (Acts 16:1), and it seems at least his mother Eunice and grandmother Lois were followers of Christ (2 Timothy 1:5). "Perhaps Paul included Timothy [in Colossians 1:1] because he was from the general area of the church and because he was the 'heir apparent' of Paul's ministry."[118]

Epaphras (1:7–8; 4:12–13)

Epaphras probably heard the gospel when Paul preached in Ephesus (Acts 19:10, 20:31). It seems likely that Epaphras would have returned to his native Colossae to share the message about Jesus the Messiah. Through the

---

[118] Richard R. Melick Jr., *Philippians, Colossians, Philemon* (Nashville: Broadman & Holman, 1991), 188.

proclamation of the gospel others were converted and the church in Colossae was born (Colossians 1:7–8). We don't have much insight into his ministry at Colossae but it's clear he was a faithful minister of Christ (Colossians 1:7) who labored for them in prayer (4:12) and hard work (4:13). Like many of Paul's companions, Epaphras served an important function of updating Paul on the well-being of the church and reporting to the church the ministry and teachings of Paul. From Colossians 4:13, it seems Epaphras had become a co-laborer with Paul for the region covering Colossae, Laodicea, and Hierapolis. He's later imprisoned with Paul, sending his greetings to his fellow Colossian: Philemon (Philemon 23).[119]

Tychicus (4:7)

Tychichus was a follower of Christ and companion of Paul. He was from Asia Minor (Acts 20:4) and we see references to him scattered throughout Paul's letters (Ephesians 6:21–22; Colossians 4:7; 2 Timothy 4:12; Titus 3:12). Paul relied upon him to safely deliver his letters, help with the collection for the Jerusalem church, and visit Ephesus and Crete. He also provided reports to the churches on Paul and his ministry, as well as informing Paul on the health of the churches (Ephesians 6:22). He's an example of a name in the New Testament we don't know much about. What we do know speaks to his courageous gospel-ministry on behalf of Paul and their great Lord Jesus Christ.[120]

Onesimus (4:9; see also book of Philemon)

Onesimus was a runaway servant of Philemon who became a Christian through Paul's ministry (Philemon 10). Some have suggested he fled to Ephesus or Rome after having stolen property (Philemon 18), while others believe he tried to escape. Onesimus became a servant of Jesus as he

---

119 For more on Epaphras, see Melick Jr., *Colossians,* 198–99, 328–29.
120 For more on Tychicus, see Melick Jr., *Colossians*, 327.

supported Paul in his ministry (Philemon 11–13) and he delivered Paul's letters with Tychicus (Colossians 4:7).

Paul's appeal to Philemon demonstrates how much Paul loved Onesimus. He says he became his father during his imprisonment (Philemon 10). Paul says for him to send Onesimus back to Philemon is to send his very heart (Philemon 12). He calls him "our faithful and beloved brother" (Colossians 4:9). Furthermore, we see Paul's Christ-like example when he tells Philemon to receive Onesimus back just as if Paul were coming to him. If Onesimus had wronged Philemon or owed him anything then Paul would take the charges upon himself and pay for the debt.

We see in Paul a Christ-like example of being a peacemaker and working for the full restoration of Onesimus. We might even look into Paul's words deeper and see a parallel between Onesimus' spiritual redemption and the physical redemption Paul is putting forward. Maybe it's to make clear the reality of gospel-redemption clear to Onesimus and Philemon, but I think Paul wants to fully pay Onesimus' debt so as to restore their relationship and thereby embody what Christ has already done in redemption.

Onesimus was of great use to Paul's ministry and could be a support of Philemon as well (Philemon 11, 13). Paul seems to appeal to Philemon to receive him back not as a slave but as a brother (Philemon 16). Paul takes the right treatment and reconciliation of Onesimus so seriously that he's willing to give Philemon the gentle reminder that he owes him. I think Paul's flexing some of his apostolic muscle here to guarantee Onesimus isn't mistreated when he returns. He knows legally a wrong needs to be addressed. He seeks justice for both men, wanting Philemon to be restored and Onesimus to be cared for, but wanting this to happen in a beautiful way beyond the bounds of the law (Philemon 8–16). We see in this Paul's love for Onesimus, his concern for Philemon's holiness in how he treats Onesimus, and his zeal for the ministry of the gospel.[121]

---

[121] For more on Onesimus, see Melick Jr., *Colossians*, 327–328, 337.

Philemon

Philemon, whom the New Testament Pauline letter is named after, was a wealthy Christian who faithfully supported Paul's ministry (Philemon 2, 7). He seems to have been converted under Paul's ministry (Philemon 19) and Paul says the church in Colossae actually met in Philemon's house (Philemon 2). The letter to Philemon demonstrates how much Paul esteemed him for his faith and love (Philemon 2–7). Paul expects to come to Colossae and he asks Philemon to prepare a room for him (Philemon 22).

Philemon is also known for being the slave/servant owner of Onesimus. There's nothing in this letter to suggest Philemon had ever mistreated Onesimus in any way and the letter carries a warm and friendly tone. We're unsure of the timing related to Philemon's conversion and Onesimus' departure, but what is clear is that Philemon has been wronged in some way by Onesimus (Philemon 18). Paul sends Onesimus back to Philemon, but he says to fully receive Onesimus back, not as a bondservant but as a brother. If anything had been stolen or there was any financial loss to Philemon, Paul wanted that debt credited to his account so he could pay it. His concern is that both are restored in fellowship, that the wrongs are made right, and that both would see themselves and each other in light of how they can further the ministry of the gospel (Philemon 11–16).

APPENDIX 2: IDENTITY IN CHRIST STATEMENTS

- We are saints (1:2, 4)
- We are forgiven and redeemed (1:14; 2:14; 3:13)
- We are holy, blameless, and above reproach before God (1:21)
- Christ is in us (1:27)
- We are united to one another (1:2; 2:2; 2:19)
- God is our Father (1:2; 3:17)
- The Spirit is in us (1:8)
- There is a hope laid up in heaven for us (1:5)
- We are bearing fruit and growing (1:6)
- We have understood the grace of God and the truth of God (1:5–6)
- We get the knowledge of His will (1:9; 2:2)
- We get wisdom, knowledge, and understanding (1:9, 10; 2:2)
- We walk in a way that pleases Him (1:10)
- We image or reflect God (1:10)
- We receive God's strength and empowerment (1:11)
- We have an inheritance (1:23)
- We're delivered from the domain of darkness into Christ's kingdom (1:13)
- We're forgiven of sins and redeemed to Christ (1:14; 2:13, 14)
- We're reconciled back to God and made at peace with Him (1:20, 22)
- We have the hope of glory because Christ is in us (1:27)
- We are maturing in Him (1:28; 4:12)
- We are filled in Him (2:10)
- We are circumcised in our hearts (2:11)
- We are dead to the old man/flesh and the things of the world in Christ (2:11, 12, 13, 19; 3:3, 9)
- We are raised with Him as a new man (2:12; 3:1)
- We have victory over spiritual rulers and authorities (2:15)

- We are nourished and grown by Christ our Head (2:19)
- We are seated with Christ at the right hand of God (3:1)
- Our life is hidden with Christ in God (3:3)
- Christ is our life (3:4)
- We will appear with Christ when he appears in glory (3:4)
- We have put off the old self with its practices and put on the new self with its practices (3:9, 10, 12)
- We are being renewed in knowledge after the image of our Creator (3:10; 17)
- We are in Christ, and Christ is all and in all (3:11)
- We have the peace of Christ ruling our hearts and the word of Christ dwelling in our hearts (3:15–16)